# Masking and Unmasking
the Female Mind

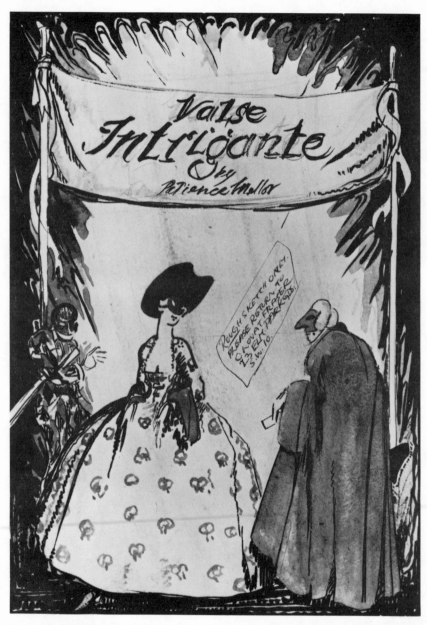

**Design by Claud Lovat Fraser, from the Adelman Collection.** *(By permission of Bryn Mawr College Library.)*

# Masking and Unmasking the Female Mind

Disguising Romances in Feminine Fiction, 1713–1799

Mary Anne Schofield

**DELAWARE**
Newark: University of Delaware Press
London and Toronto: Associated University Presses

Associated University Presses
440 Forsgate Drive
Cranbury, NJ 08512

Associated University Presses
25 Sicilian Avenue
London WC1A 2QH, England

Associated University Presses
P.O. Box 488, Port Credit
Mississauga, Ontario
Canada L5G 4M2

The paper used in this publication meets the requirements of the American National Standard for Permanence of Paper for Printed Library Materials Z39.48-1984.

**Library of Congress Cataloging-in-Publication Data**

Schofield, Mary Anne.
  Masking and unmasking the female mind : disguising romances in feminine fiction, 1713–1799 / Mary Anne Schofield.
    p.   cm.
  Includes bibliographical references.
  ISBN 0-87413-365-3 (alk. paper)
  1. English fiction—18th century—History and criticism.
  2. English fiction—Women authors—History and criticism.   3. Women and literature—Great Britain—History—18th century.
  4. Romanticism—Great Britain—History—18th century.
  5. Masquerades in literature.   6. Disguise in literature.   7. Sex role in literature.   8. Women in literature.   9. Masks in literature.   I. Title.
  PR858.W6S36   1990
  823'.5099287—dc20                                      89-40006
                                                          CIP

PRINTED IN THE UNITED STATES OF AMERICA

*For my parents*
*with love always*

Oh! what romantic stuff! is a common exclamation, if any one ventures to feel or to express themselves out of the style of common and every day life. But why is it romantic? I should be sorry, it is true, that a daughter of mine, suffering her imagination to outrun her reason, should so bewilder herself among ideal beings as to become either useless or ridiculous; but if affection for merit, if admiration of talents, if the attachments of friendship are romantic; if it be romantic to dare to have an opinion of one's own, and not to follow one formal tract, wrong or right, pleasant or irksome, because our grandmothers and aunts have followed it before; if not to be romantic one must go through the world with prudery, carefully settling our blinkers at every step, as a cautious coachman hoodwinks his horses heads; if a woman, because she is a woman, must resign all pretensions to being a reasoning being, and dares neither look to the right nor to the left, oh! may my Medora still be the child of nature and simplicity, still venture to express all she feels even at the risk of being called a strange romantic girl.

—Charlotte Smith, *The Young Philosopher* 2 : 14—15

# Contents

# Preface

There is such a pretty Air of Romance, as you relate them, in *your Plots,* and *my Plots,* that I shall be better directed in what manner to wind up the Catastrophe of the Pretty Novel.

— Richardson, *Pamela* 2 : 17 (emphasis added)

Quite unintentionally, yet importantly, Samuel Richardson un-covers the key to understanding the feminine fictions of the eighteenth century. The "Air of Romance" accurately describes the writing that predominates in the age, a writing that increasingly becomes the "woman's work" of the period. Reading any of the currently pub-lished histories of the novel does not support this statement, however; these tomes written by male scholars focus on male novelists, those accepted in the eighteenth-century "canon" and, therefore, those who present an inaccurate view of the true eighteenth-century reading and publishing world. Unlike Richardson, who is aware of the two plots of these novels, contemporary critical surveys consider only the male text.

Nancy K. Miller in her essay, "Emphasis Added: Plots and Plau-sibilities in Women's Fiction," succinctly draws attention to the per-vasive problem: there are two plots, two stories in fiction: the mas-culine and the feminine. As sophisticated critics of the novel and students of Sandra Gilbert and Susan Gubar *(The Madwoman in the Attic),* Carol Christ *(Diving Deep and Surfacing),* and Annis Pratt *(Archetypal Patterns in Women's Fiction),* for example, we have been taught to look for "two stories" in nineteenth- and twentieth-century fiction. The same critical apparatus and sensibility can and must be applied to eighteenth-century fiction as well, for the eighteenth-century novel also participates in this two-level rhetorical structure. Feminine stories and masculine plots do, indeed, exist. Contrary to Richardson's observation, the sex of the narrator-creator does not necessarily determine the ending; however, I can conclude that male writers tend to favor "happy," whitewashed, patriarchally approved endings, whereas female writers subvert happy, satisfying closures and instead present unfulfilling, nagging, worrisome, tragic endings that underscore the sense of separateness in which women exist and write.

It is my purpose here to uncover the "two plots" of the minor fiction of the eighteenth century by examining the disguises the female romancers-novelists employ in an effort to present a more truthful and accurate picture of the eighteenth-century novel and world. These disguises include not only the actual physical masquerades their characters put on within the plots of their fictions, but the masks the novelists themselves adopt by disguising their serious statements under the cloak of the romance.

This study naturally falls into two parts, for the midcentury appearance of Samuel Richardson's *Pamela* together with the somewhat later publication of Sarah Fielding's *The Cry* provide a natural demarcation in the feminine literature of the period. The early work, 1713 to 1749, offers unsophisticated yet startlingly accurate contemporary attempts to anatomize the romance. The early works of Aubin, Haywood, Barker, and Davys indicate the dissatisfaction the popular female writer (and reader) had with the male-imposed romance genre. Their novels corrupt the approved romance form and offer scandalous, incriminating details of the far-from-utopic life most women lived at that time. The midcentury publication of *Pamela* followed by Fielding's codification of this archetypal seduction tale in her novel allows the next generation of female novelists (the later Haywood, Fielding, Lennox, Smith, Inchbald, and West) to explore the romance form not only through plot manipulation and disguises, but through a more thorough critique of the genre itself. Gone are the omnipresent masks necessary for plot manipulation; in their place we find prefaces, novel-writing characters, and prose redactions of the romance story—all elements of the critical, unmasking apparatus.

Investigating the use of the ubiquitous disguise and the romance topoi in popular feminine fiction, 1713–99, this study discovers, then, that although women have always been masked, never able to speak without the language of the romance or without being hidden behind the mask of the disguised romance heroine, women have, indeed, always spoken. It attempts to reveal the power that lies beneath the disguise of feminine submission and marital compliance, romantic love and female powerlessness, the controlling ideologies of the eighteenth century. *Masking and Unmasking the Female Mind* provides a lesson on how to read the popular romance and the predominant masquerade set piece. It examines the eighteenth-century voice of feminist writers as they explore and anatomize women's issues through the language of the popular "diversions": the romance and the masquerade.

Much recent scholarship has considered this critical issue of the subplots and subversions of nineteenth- and twentieth-century British and American female novelists. Nancy K. Miller, Patricia Meyer Spacks, Elaine Showalter, Carolyn Heilbrun, Catherine Stimpson, Sandra Gilbert, and Susan Gubar, to name just a few, each, in her own way, has taught valuable skills necessary for uncovering and reading the female text. Eighteenth-century texts are just beginning to come under investigation. The seminal work of Dale Spender, Jane Spencer, and Katherine Rogers is invaluable. This study attempts to contribute to this growing body of eighteenth-century feminine criticism.

Because of the nature of this study—the discovery of the eighteenth-century female romance voice—little critical attention is devoted to male novelists such as the popular triumvirate of Richardson, Fielding, and Smollett. It is assumed that the reader is familiar with these men and their accepted, canon works. Instead, this work concentrates on the lesser known but clearly no less important female novelists of the period.

Because of paucity of available female texts (although Garland and *Scholar's Facsimiles* have done much to remedy this situation), a fair amount of quotation from primary sources occurs in this study. In a few more years when more texts are readily available, such extensive detail will not be necessary.

I would like to acknowledge the following staffs, colleagues, and friends who have helped with the preparation of this book. My sincere thanks to Mary Leahy and James Tanis of the Rare Book Collection of Bryn Mawr College Library, to Gertrude Reed and Anne Denlinger of Bryn Mawr College Library, to Dan Traister and Georgianna Ziegler and their staff at the Rare Book Collection of the University of Pennsylvania, and to Theresa Covley of the Friedsam Library of St. Bonaventure University. Special thanks go to Jerry C. Beasley, who read an early version of the book; to Cecilia Macheski and Doreen Saar who read a later version; and to my many eighteenth-century colleagues who listened to numerous papers and read many articles during the years about these eighteenth-century female writers. The kind words of Barbara and Dwight Beucler, Diana Wheeler, and Liz Madden Boucher, and all my friends at Martin's Dam are also appreciated. A very special word of thanks to Karen King Haskins, who so ably helped with the preparation of the manuscript. Last, but most important, I thank my parents, who never lost sight of my goal.

* * *

The illustration, a drawing by C. Lovat Fraser from the collection of Major Haldane Mactall, appears by permission of Bryn Mawr College Library, Adelman Collection.

Masking and Unmasking
the Female Mind

# Chapter 1
# The Masquerading Romance

In 1970 William Park illuminated the "new species of writing" introduced in the 1740s by Richardson and Fielding in his seminal essay.[1] Subsequent histories of the novel following Park's lead continued to trace and elucidate the new patterns and rhetorical strategies introduced by Richardson and Fielding in the works of the other canon-accepted novelists such as Sterne and Smollett. Park suggests that this new fictional tradition is one that first displaces and then replaces romance elements with novelistic ones, thus simultaneously heightening the presence of the author in the text while introducing dramatic, realistic elements as well. This new novelistic, realistic tradition, so the theory goes, runs counter to the other tradition of the modern romance, with its emphasis on morality and the familiar. The theory continues explaining that works like Richardson's *Pamela* belong to the latter category; Richardson masks his presence in the work as an attempt at verisimilitude, whereas Fielding's novels are included in the first class because of his essential presence in the text. (Both are credited with introducing familiar scenes, nature, and moral instruction, which is what was "new" about the "new species of writing.") I suggest that in the female/feminist writing of the period the two original strands of romance and novel are woven together even more closely and importantly; the new creation of the "disguising romance" combines with the psychological realism of the old romance and with the dramatic elements of the new novel, thus producing the distinct brand of eighteenth-century feminine fiction. Under the careful artisanship of these minor women writers, the romance genre is transformed into a document of female assertion, woman, and writer. In this feminine fiction of 1713–99, the creation of the woman as conscious literary artist with a voice distinct and separate from the male voice occurs, so that the "new species of writing" is not so much the new, realistic life breathed into the old romance forms touted by Richardson, Fielding, and their critics, but is, instead, the vibrantly aggressive and assertive work of most new writers of the period: the women.

neglected things."[12] Defoe, in his *Essay on the Education of Ladies* (1720)[13] had advocated a similar position. Addison and Steele,[14] with their essays in *The Tatler, The Guardian,* and *The Spectator,* reached a larger audience than either Astell or Defoe. Writing in *The Spectator,* Steele observes that "the general mistake among us in the educating our children is, that in our daughters we take care of their persons and neglect their minds. To make her an agreeable Person is the main Purpose of her Parents . . . and from this general Folly of Parents we owe our present numerous Race of Coquets." He concludes that "the True Art in this Case is to make the Mind and Body improve together; and if possible, to make Gesture follow thought, and not let Thought be employed upon Gesture."[15]

This "gesture" is translated by female writers as the take-over of male-controlled literary forms, most especially that of the romance, to articulate female concerns and concepts. Unlike Astell and colleagues, the novelists conducted their educational campaigns within the confines of their romances.

The romantic quest is subverted by the female novelists who redirect this power in an effort to return to their own authentic identity. Reading the romance in the eighteenth century means learning to hear the feminine voice inscribed in the masculine, romance narrative, and thus reading the female text of the feminine quest in place of the male story.

Thus, the feminine, masquerading romances of 1713–99, present two voices, two plots, two levels of rhetorical structures, two opposing ideologies of the feminine definition, and two distinct types of female characters presented and championed.

*    *    *

In an effort, then, to understand these mixed, contrary ideologies and decode them for their readership, the female novelists approached their arduous task cautiously. Unwilling and, frankly, unable to alienate their readers, these writers employ the popular form—the romance—together with its attendant romantic love and disguise in an effort to examine the true state of being a woman. They explore the romance by writing romances and subverting the plot; they study the pervasive ideology of female powerlessness by allowing the "other side" of women, their aggressive natures to be displayed in the disguise.[16] Thus, both the romance and the masquerade provide a way to determine and define the female self. They redirect the power of the romance in an effort to rediscover the female self.

The age presented what Judith Newton has labeled, on the one hand, the ideology of romantic love—the assumption that female life gains value through romantically conceived marriage; yet, the nonfiction literature of the age, conversely, presents a diametrically opposed vision of what Newton asserts in an ideology of female powerlessness, a vision of female life that presents the reader with a very low ceiling of female expectations and aspirations. Novel texts explore female experience as distinct and separable from male stories and exploits, while still deferring to patriarchal authority: romance is valorized, but the woman herself, individually, is not. Romantic love gives a raison d'être for female powerlessness. The prevailing ideologies required circumscription of feminine power as vigorously as they insisted on marriage (with more loss of power). Value in the female life, then, did and did not exist. Contradictions not only abound about the value of women's lives, but they are explicitly presented in such ideologies, and it is just these ambivalences that are delineated in the feminine romances of the eighteenth century.

From its inception in the seventeenth-century works of de Scudery, the romance had a psychological basis. She outlines this view in *Le Grand Cyrus*, through her character of Sappho, by remarking:

> She even expresses so delicately those sentiments which are the most difficult to express, and she knows so well how to anatomize the amorous heart . . . that she can describe exactly all the jealousies, all the anxieties, all the impatience, joys, chagrins, all the complaints, despairs, hopes, rebellions, all the tumultuous sentiments which none has ever understood save those who feel or have experienced them.[17]

It is important to note here that a woman is speaking to other suffering women, and she is describing emotions that are understood by that sex; she is discursively describing a nondiscursive, nonrational level. The romantic story exists on two levels: male rationality and female emotionality. It is my contention that historically with the works of de Scudery, we are still dealing with two layers: female passion and male reason. Baker tells us that the history of the heroic romance is one in which "the cult of love and gallantry was carried to extravagant lengths . . . the mania for sentimental analysis went to the same extremes of oversubtlety and deviation from nature."[18] It is this "oversubtlety" that is the product and goal of the minor female writers, for it is through the subtle projection and obsession with the nonrational "romance" that they are able to speak to each other of their fate. (The romance with its emphasis on lack of restraint, frivolity, irrationality, and silliness allows women to become an "other" and speak through this disguise of feeling about the real issues of being female). The romance speaks to what Radway labels the asymmetric nature of male-female relationships and presents a "mythic

Not only do the masquerade and romance topoi allow the woman-heroine to experience a self antithetical to her real self, thus providing a psychologically necessary outlet for female frustration, but the actual creation of the romance and the mask functions as a disguise for the novelist as well. As her heroines put on a different self and reveal other selves heretofore hidden from public view, so the novelist herself can express her own anger and frustration at the female condition through her adoption of the disguising romance. Barker, Davys, Haywood, Fielding, Smith, Inchbald, and the others engage in a process of double writing. Not content merely to adopt a masquerade technique in terms of their female protagonists, these novelists use the cover story of their romance plots to mask their own feminist, aggressive intentions and to unmask the facile and fatuous fictions they are supposed to be writing as members of the weaker sex. Thus, the novelist appears to be telling a fashionable tale of love and romance but is actually presenting a vivid picture of the exploitation and frustration of her sex in the eighteenth century. The novelist uses the ubiquitous masquerade to reveal feminine aggression; she takes on the accepted romance pattern, deconstructs it, reinterprets it, and reconstructs it, thereby telling a tale far different from the surface romance. She decodes and reinterprets both the use of disguise and the closure of the romance. Both are reencoded to reflect the feminine perspective.[24]

Second, this double writing technique of both the disguise and the romance's closure is reflected in the female protagonist: the divided heroine. Using the angelic, virtuous heroine mask, the novelist tells the male-approved romance story of love, female acquiescence and submission, the happily-ever-after feminine fate. The novelist overtly disguises her own feelings of anger and frustration in this character but covertly displays her emotions by creating the virgin's double, the avatar of her own pent-up emotions, the virago, who oftentimes appears as the villain in the tale. The virago is the virgin unmasked. Both virgin and virago provide the masquerade for the novelist herself, and thus, the entire novel, read in these terms, becomes a "masquerade" for the writer.

Specifically most romances of the 1720s, 1730s, and 1740s do not present a falsified, happy ending; more often than not, the virgin's unmasking leads to her demise. It is the virago who survives temporarily (at the end, she, too, must die,), and it is the virago who is closest to the real self of the novelist. In most of the tales, the happily-ever-after, boy-gets-girl ending of the popular story is eschewed. Instead, the piece that begins with all the romance trapping ends in a debacle of these very conventions: heroines commit suicide, die, or are exiled; they leave the world and form female communities. The romance world cannot be the same again, its inner workings have been exposed, and it has been stripped of its mask; the characters, plot, and author lie exposed.

*   *   *

In the novels of the 1750s, 1760s, 1770s, and 1780s, the happy ending reasserts itself, but the presence of the truth-telling, "authorial" character mitigates this rosy view and blunts the facile edges of the male romance. In a word, a hegemony is created that addresses the female condition.

It is small wonder, then, with this ever-increasing desire to discover the female being that had been hidden for so long that the writers would use any means to uncover this essential self. Because the masquerade was *the* form of entertainment during the early years of the century, it is understandable why it became the predominant topos in the fiction. It had been introduced into England from Italy (where it evolved from the carnival), and with the arrival of the Swiss "Count" Heidigger in 1708, it was well on its way to becoming the quintessential English frolic,[25] with between seven hundred and one thousand attending weekly in the 1720s and 1730s;[26] it regained its popularity again in the 1760s and 1770s.

The masquerade is the celebration of topsy turveydom as Bakhtin reminds us, and a special kind of freedom is permitted by its very nature. As he notes:

> We find here a characteristic logic, the peculiar logic of the inside out, of the "turnabout," of a continual shifting from top to bottom, from front to rear, of numerous parodies and travesties, humiliations, profanations, comic crownings and uncrownings. A second life, a second world of folk culture is thus constructed.[27]

For Pope, Hogarth, and many restrained others, the masquerade became the archetypal scene of excess and corruption. An "Essay on Masquerade" (attributed to Boswell) published in the *London Magazine* (1774) notices that when a disguise was assumed, "those whom modesty restrained, being by means of it set loose from check of sensation, which in some degree applies the place of principle," felt a freedom to follow their passions.[28] The masquerade provides the opportunity for "organized disorder"; Castle notes that it serves "both as a voluptuous release from the ordinary cultural prescriptions and as a stylized comment upon them."[29] She continues: "the masquerade projected an anti-nature, an intoxicating reversal of normal sexual, social, and metaphysical hierarchies."[30]

ing ideologies of the age, for it is the "failed romances," those that see
the heroine maimed or dead at the end, that should be classified as
negative, which become the positive disguise for the female writer and
that allow the feminine voice to be heard in protest.

Thus, the romance novel of the eighteenth century exposes the
ubiquitous romance form and all the ideologies that cling to it.
Looking at the eighteenth-century feminine novel, we find that the
period falls roughly into two halves. Before the 1740s "antiromances"
were being written; however, the texts were disjointed, little closure
occurred, and they seemed to be all facade. Barker, Davys, Aubin, and
the early Haywood individually attempt to destroy this romance
mask. But their approach is nonsystematic, if revolutionary. It is only
after Fielding anatomizes the approach they are taking, that the later
novelists react to this anatomization and simultaneously write romances while criticizing them.

Rabine has aptly defined the two voices that exist in the romance:

> The dominant masculine voice of traditional romance narrative imposes a
> totalizing structure on romantic narrative and represses an independent
> feminine other. Reducing the heroine to a reflection of himself, the hero
> makes her an "intermediary," as Simone de Beauvoir says, through whom
> he can realize his desire to return to a mythical union with himself. . . .
> The hero and/or narrator in each of these works posits the heroine at first
> as an autonomous other and then in the end absorbs her back into his own
> identity. . . . Yet an autonomous feminine voice remains in the romantic
> text, in the form of a fragmented excluded other. . . . Her silenced voice
> gives evidence of itself not in overt utterances, but in the conflicts between
> levels and elements of the text that disrupt the dominant narrative voice.[38]

It is this disruptive voice, this other that I examine in *Masking and
Unmasking the Female Mind*.

\* \* \*

This study explores the art of the feminine eighteenth-century
novelist, her power that is hidden beneath the seemingly facile and
fatuous forms of the romance, and the ubiquitous disguise topos. Just
as the romance-narrative structure tells the story of the heroine's
transformation from an "isolated, asexual, insecure adolescent who is
unsure of her own identity, into a mature, sensual and very married
woman who has realized her full potential and identity as the partner
of a man and the implied mother of a child"[39]—the ideology of
romantic love—so in the corpus of eighteenth-century fiction, we have
noted several romances that do, indeed, conform to this pattern. Here
the romance provides only temporary masquerading shelter; the reso-

lution of the story is the exploration of the initial reason for disguise. This text is euphoric because it uses the disguise topos and romance positively—that is, it uncovers portions of the female self that need not be hidden any longer; it is the display of these hidden tendencies that allows the integration of the heroine into society. The disguise or masquerade works positively here.

A second, and larger, group of novels use the romance and masquerade not to reveal happy endings but instead to explore the true feminine reality; the topsy-turvy world of the masquerade ably allows the masks of aggression and demonic anger to be uncovered as the true nature of the woman. No integration for his heroine occurs; the euphoric text becomes dysphoric, the mask slips to reveal the horror beneath. The romance becomes "unromantic," the mask a mere shell.

The 1780 anonymous novel, *Masquerades, or What You Will* (By the Author of *Eliza Warwick*) offers, I think, the most succinct summary of masquerading and romance reading. The main lover, Osmond, writing to his friend, Montague, observes:

> Under masks there was nothing extraordinary in the declaration I had made Lady Julia. It might pass as a masquarade conversation,—but the disguise once removed, I dared not continue to address her in the same style, though she must have plainly seen my heart wished to be allowed such happiness.[40]

Osgood does not dare to speak without the romance mask or the disguise of the lover. Conversely, *Masking and Unmasking the Female Mind* will attempt to do so.

lude in part 2 tells Luvania's story, another version or mask of the duped female story).[2] As the narrator questions halfway through the novel:

> But now's the Question? Who is Amanda? This Female-Page? This Fair Unfortunate? To satisfy the Curious, we'll relate as far as we have leave the real Truth. (116)

The "real" truth, however, is more fiction, as Florio/Amanda, the beseiged female, continues to be harassed and exploited. The wicked Carlo (Luvania's villain), the unscrupulous Beauville, and the dishonest though lovable Bellfond all want Amanda.

> Thus was the unthinking young Amanda circled with Dangers unforeseen, and trusted Foes her new made Sisters Conduct taught her Caution; but for Luvania, who could think her base? with all the Beauties that could charm the Soul. (223)

Amanda is even persecuted by women, and an especially upsetting subplot is Luvania's treachery to her. As Amanda writes to her onetime confidant, Luvania:

> I blush at my Soul's weakness, when I reflect I once confided in thee, and thought *Luvania* faithful as *Amanda:* What shall I say? I will not call thee base: The villain that undoes thee gets my Curse. . . . What can describe the agonies I felt when I resolv'd to part with false *Luvania.* . . . You have taught me Falsehood and Mistrust. (222)

Luvania, however, trapped by Carlo, must act the arch deceiver. Amanda can find no one who is not masked. Luvania finally breaks away from Carlo's tyranny, and unmasks and rescues Amanda by substituting a slave masquerading as Amanda for the assignation that Carlo demanded. When he discovers the deception, he stabs the slave, but the real Amanda has escaped.

The third part continues the chronicle of the deceived woman and begins by recounting how Count Beauville lied to Amelia and raped her, making her think that they were married; he had taken one of his gaming companions and dressed him in the habit of a priest, "who in a grave Manner perform'd the Ceremony, and deceiv'd the innocent Lady, who then made no Scruple of receiving the Imposture to her Arms, and so deluded, thought herself for some Months truly happy" (247). When Amelia learns of his deceit and miscarries, however, Beauville is also wracked with pains and wishes that he had, in truth, married her. Then he leaves. She has had two children plus twins with him, for he frequently would return, make up another story to wed her, and disappear. Her father dies. Amelia concludes:

> Oh! think false Beauville what you've made me suffer; I am now scarce six months past Twenty one, my Fortune's large, my Family is Noble, my Person hath been thought agreeable, yet you have ruin'd me as Traitors fell the Kings, they seem to serve; trepann'd me to your Arms, and there deceiv'd me, robb'd me of Ease, of Honour and of Health, and triumph in the Villainy you've acted. . . . kill me deceitful Murderer with your Sword, but do not torture me with gilded Falsehoods. (260)

Despite all of the pain and suffering, the final result is a positive one and the happy endings occur. The women find it is finally safe enough to unmask. The correct couples are married, the villains are punished, and the rightness of the world is reestablished at the conclusion; the topsy-turveydom of the masquerade is righted. The ending is precipitous, however; Boyd quickly loses interest in her story and is anxious to bring the narrating strands together.

The novel has become an exercise in masking, and one can take Boyd as the best spokesperson and *The Happy Unfortunate* as the clearest example of the early disguise romance. Here, at last, all identities are recovered. One may question, however, has anything been gained? Has the female position been improved? Boyd's one attempt did not change the direction of women's fate, and the more numerous efforts of Penelope Aubin did not effect a drastic new concept of femininity to counter the prevailing ideologies. The problem with the masquerade romance is that the early attempts were unable to make a large impact. The literary scene had to wait for the prolific and versatile novelist, Eliza Haywood, with her sixty-odd romances and novels to explore fully this theory of the mask and identity in an effort to stimulate new ideologies about the eighteenth-century woman. Yet Aubin's disguises, like Boyd's, are not to be dismissed, for in them she is able to present a true, horrific portrait of a woman's life during that time.

protagonist, Ardelisa (de Vinevil) must mask her qualities. As Aubin writes in *The Strange Adventures:*

> Her Mind well suited for the fair Cabinet that contained it; she was humble, generous, unaffected, yet learned, wise, modest, and prudent above her years or sex: gay in Conversation, but by Nature thoughtful; had all the Softness of a Woman, with the Constancy and Courage of a hero. (2)

*The Strange Adventure* is a tale like its heroine, deliberately covered in mystery. When the Count decides to uproot himself and his daughter, Ardelisa, and move to Turkey, the pattern of necessary disguise begins. She is told by her beloved Count of Longueville, her betrothed and quasi ward of her father, that she should hide herself in the Turkish house so that she would be safe, "but so many Bashaws, and Persons of Quality, came to her Father's to traffick for European Goods, that she could not avoid being sometimes seen" (21). Once the young Mahomet sees her, he is instantly enthralled with her, but "knowing that her Father (being a Christian) would never consent to her being his, he conceal'd his Affection, resolving to wait for an Opportunity to steal her away, or take her by force" (21). Mahomet will not reveal himself, but instead continues to send veiled threats to Ardelisa. Longueville becomes more and more upset and finally suggests a plan that will enable them both to escape.

Fate intervenes, however; Longueville and Ardelisa are separated when a great storm severs the cables of his ship and carries it out to sea. When Mahomet comes to ravish and carry her off, he finds that Ardelisa is gone. In his fury he stays long enough to murder her father. Meanwhile, Ardelisa, realizing that she is not safe, disguises herself as a man and retreats to the Consul's (a supposed ally) country house at Domezdure. Even this place proves unsafe, however, and she finally hides herself in a hut buried deep within the forest; she lives there undisturbed with her maid for three months. (She does not know what has happened to Longueville.) When she at last makes a move back to Constantinople to get a ship for France, Ardelisa and her maid are still disguised; even so, she is apprehended by a great Turkish general named Osmin. Staging a fire, she escapes back to the Consul's house and then to a ship, the *St. Francis,* and finally arrives safely in France after three years. Other adventures happen, but, at last, all the good characters are united in France. Only one last disguise is practiced; Longueville is told that Ardelisa perished in the voyage from Venice, but it was just a test of his constancy. When he appears to be dying, the truth is told, and he is lovingly reunited with Ardelisa and life.

Aubin describes the fearful and fateful state of the early eighteenth century in this tale of adventure, disguise, and intrigue. Masking is important in this early novel for the protection that it affords the wearer. It also acts paradoxically, for the disguise is a teaser: women are more enticing and enchanting when covered with men's clothes; therefore, they subconsciously provoke the attacks made on them. Aubin herself practices this paradoxical art of necessary deception by masking her moral tale in the deceptive guise of an adventure story and a romance.

Aubin's *The Noble Slaves: or, The Lives and Adventure of Two Lords and Two Ladies* (1722)[3] continues her disguised art; now she writes to rival the popularity of masquerading and gaming. She still hopes, under the cover of the fiction, "to encourage Virtue, and expose Vice, imprint noble Principles on the docile Souls of our Youth" (preface, viii).

Again Aubin presents the reader with a complicated, masked tale of intrigue, mistaken identity, exploitation, harassment, and tyranny. The female protagonists, Teresa and Emilia, are both kidnapped by powerful men; Emilia's plight is, perhaps, the worst because she is drugged and shipped off by her beloved's father who does not approve of her. She ends up, after a shipwreck, on the same island that Teresa has been stranded on. They are both cared for by the indians, but this retreat is not blissful. No such haven exists in *The Noble Slaves*.

The tone of *The Noble Slaves* is more strident than Aubin's usual work. More harassment and suffering occur. Although women seem to be more in control, the amount is negligible, for it is a control that only allows them to harm themselves. For example, in one of the first stories, we learn of Tanganor's love for Maria; however, when the Emperor demands her, and Tanganor must yield, he runs away and disguises himself, unable to do anything else. Maria, conversely, rather than adopting the passive disguise designed for her by the Emperor, actively works for her freedom. She gouges out her eyes to avoid losing her virtue to the Emperor. Only then is she free to return to Tanganor, the man she loves.

Maria is not the only one to take action. After Emilia and Teresa are captured·and taken from the rescue ship, they are sold into slavery in Algiers. Emilia will not stand for further inhumane treatment, and she kills Selim, the tyrant. She assumes his habit and his power. "She had Selim's Habit on, and in her hand a Woman Slave. 'Disguise yourself in this, said she, my dear Teresa, and follow me, with this I will free us both or die.' Here she drew forth a bloody dagger Selim wore" (39). Ultimately, they do escape, only to have to disguise themselves again—this time in habits supplied by the widow Saraja; they appear romance. Like Boyd, most of her tales end euphorically, that is happily with the union of hero and heroine, thus solidifying the romance pattern of movement from isolation to union, from unknown to known. With Aubin, however, the movement is treacherous, the final outcome tenuous at best. She is unsatisfied with the romance pattern, and her entire oeuvre demonstrates her desire to challenge the romance form. *The Life of Charlotta Du Pont* (1723),[6] though not a polished work, demonstrates her desire to reconsider the form. She writes in the preface:

> The story of Madam Charlotta Du Pont, I had from the Mouth of a Gentleman of integrity, who related it as from his own Knowledge, I have joined some other Histories to hers, to embellish, and render it more entertaining and useful, to encourage Virtue, and excite us to heroic Action, which is my principal Aim in all I write. (vi–vii)

Aubin makes several points here. First, Aubin indicates that she is decoding or perhaps encoding the male version given to her; she is embellishing his version together with including even more of her own versions to excite her readers to action. Aubin tells a romance story that exposes the very nature of the romance. Charlotte, as if to demonstrate the depth of Aubin's commitment to the romance genre, repeatedly throws off her disguise and pleads for mercy and her life as a woman. She is repeatedly put in positions in which she must bargain for her life. She and the other heroines frequently resort to force; much stabbing occurs with any object at hand (for example, a sharp bodkin, a penknife, a dagger). Yet the besieged women are incapable of totally returning the ill treatment they receive. The following passage is typical of the brutality of this novel and the Aubin world in general:

> Don Duarte having heard some little noise was started up, and sat upright in the Bed: This gave Alonzo a fair Opportunity for his Revenge, and he stabb'd him to the Heart with his Dagger: the poor Lady shrieking out, he tore her out of Bed by the Hair, cut out her Tongue, and discharging one of his Pistols in her Face, which he had loaded with small Bird-shot on purpose, left her on the Bed bleeding[;] her Eyes and Face . . . all torn to pieces. (3:172)

Such descriptions, such treatment is not the stuff of which romances are made.

Thus, Aubin, understandably given her front-runner position in the century, is extremely ambivalent in her criticism of the romance.

Although her prefaces harp on the realistic, moral vision she intends to inculcate in her readers, her pieces through 1723 and *The Life of Charlotta Du Pont* teach virtue and present reality through a simply scandalous, overwhelming presentation of the wrongs visited on women.

\*    \*    \*

In *The Life and Adventures of the Lady Lucy* (1726),[7] Aubin presents her quintessential examination of the necessary feminine disguise. She is unsure of the reception of her tale, however, and writes apologetically:

> I fear my own Sex will now be displeas'd with me, for Henrietta's Story; but I was oblig'd to follow Truth, and I hope that one ill Woman, amongst a great many others of singular Virtue, will be no injury to the good Opinion which I would fain persuade all my own Sex to deserve, and Mankind to have of us, who are the sole Authors of our being wicked, whenever we are so. (x)

She further cautions her readers "not to give credit to Appearances, but to examine well into the Truth of Things" (xi). Once again Aubin is writing an exposé of the romance.

The story begins with isolation and alienation. The Lady Lucy and her mother are forced from their home and into hiding when the revolution occurs; they live with an honest farmer and his wife, and "here they remain'd for some time in quiet, and had time to digest their Sorrows and change of Fortune" (12).

Lycidas, the nephew to Lady Lucy's mother, comes to the farmer's cottage, wounded and disguised as a coarse peasant to free his beloved Henrietta, who, in his absence, has been forced to marry a loutish and tyrannical man. He hides in Henrietta's castle, undetected, for a week, then, still disguised, moves to the town but pays nightly visits to her apartment and engineers her escape. Their disguises fail, however, and they are discovered by the old Knight: Lycidas is wounded and Henrietta taken away. Several plot disruptions occur, but the reader ultimately learns that Henrietta, disguised as a man, after her year of penance, is allowed to marry Lycidas. The narrative structure has not advanced much from her early pieces. Aubin still presents a series of tales that tell of feminine abuse and the necessity of masking.

Aubin returns after several of these interpolated stories to Lucy, who has married Albertus and moved to Heidelberg. His kinsman, Frederick, comes to stay with them and instantly falls in love with

Chapter 4

# Eliza Haywood

Eliza Haywood's (1693?–1756) career spanning the years from 1719 to 1756 together with her incredible number of novels and romances (sixty-odd, discounting her translations) certainly qualifies her as a representative figure for the eighteenth-century feminine novel. Not only was she the leader in sales and popularity, but, I think, she made the most magnificent use of the disguise romance in both the early and late fiction's history. She not only wrote a novel entitled *The Masqueraders* but also has the greatest number of disguising heroines in eighteenth-century fiction. It is my belief that Haywood's work is the best example of feminine masquerade in eighteenth-century fiction.

Disguise functions in two ways in Haywood's works. First, we find, as in Boyd and Aubin, heroines (such as nuns, shepherdesses, and courtesans) who adopt conventional masks that further emphasize the secondary, submissive nature of the female. The disguised women do nothing to counteract this exploitation. A second and larger (and certainly more impressive) group of masquerading women is represented by heroines whose disguises are chosen so that they can articulate the unspoken ideologies of the women themselves; their masks denote the desire for power that women have. They discard the typical, submissive shepherdess role and choose, instead, to mask themselves in disguises of aggression as the gypsy, demon, or prostitute. Unfortunately though, such disguises only lead to their further ostracization and frequently their death. Yet the sheer number of these masked heroines and their tragic plots shows that this form best articulates Haywood's concerns.

In essence, her heroines actually disguise themselves to display their hidden nature. Women attempt to take over and control. For Fantomina and Placentia, the disguise is a positive force working for the woman; they manage to reach the telos of marriage at the end of their romance journey; however, these are the minority figures in Haywood's fiction. In *The Unequal Conflict*, Haywood creates Antonia, another type of masked heroine, who is disguised and yet still able to control; however, the other protagonist of the novel, Philenia, is unable to be protected and saved by her disguise. Philenia and characters like her are the transitional ones between the Placentias and the Gigantillas, and they move us to the most numerous and popular type of Haywood heroine: the masked heroine whose aggressive disguise leads to an assertive behavior that results in her exile or death. In *The Injur'd Husband* (the Baroness de Tortillee) and *The Perplex'd Duchess* (Gigantilla), the heroines drop the mask forced on women by polite society and display what previously had been their hidden nature. But their attempt to assume male power and control is truncated, and they, too, must die at the end. They have had, however, the opportunity to try and take control of their lives, and Haywood has been able to unmask her own intentions through the intertextuality of disguise.

\*   \*   \*

Haywood provides the paradigmatic text for this entire disguise-romance genre with *The Masqueraders; or, Fatal Curiosity* (pt. 1: 1724; pt. 2: 1725).[1] Her opening remarks emphasize the ubiquitous nature of the masquerades owing in large part to Heydigger's efforts:

> Great Britain has no Assembly which affords such variety of Character as the Masquerade; there are scarce any Degrees of People, of what Religion or Principle soever, that some time or other are not willing to embrace an opportunity of Partaking of this Diversion. (pt. 1, p. 5)

In the ensuing tale, she chronicles the blatant use and misuse of the disguise by one Dorimenus, "a passionate Lover of Intrigue" (pt. 1, p. 5). He is a rake par excellence, and the novel details the life of the omnipresent eighteenth-century rogue. On the surface, *The Masqueraders* is a male story, with Dorimenus contented that he has never been refused an assignation, liaison, or love intrigue. He is blissfully unaware of the small influence he does exert. Almost the entire plot of *The Masqueraders* is engineered by women—that is, in part 1 Philecta plots how to take Dorimenus away from the naïve, easily manipulated Dalinda. She succeeds even beyond her own expectations, for "Never woman was pres'd to obey the Dictates of her own Inclinations with more subtility and Vigour" (pt. 1, p. 26).

But the strength of the woman is not enough, and part 2 opens with Dorimenus triumphantly wed to Lysimina. The attraction, however, is not of long duration. Dorimenus is impervious to the female mentality, and though he can physically penetrate their disguise, he is totally incapable of understanding the level of powerful femininity below the mask. He mouths the popular ideologies of feminine powerlessness and romantic love, thinking that he forces women to virgin and virago, as both male and female heroine. Through Fantomina, Haywood is able to engage in the necessary aggressive displacement that her fiction explores.

*Fantomina* is about illusion, disguise, and control. The novella opens in the playhouse appropriately enough. The protagonist is more interested in watching the unofficial "play" or game of men trying to win illicit favors from esteemed "ladies of the evening." Fantomina decides to indulge in her own version of control, fiction making, and play acting. For "the gratification of an innocent curiosity," she "dress[ed] herself as near as she could in the Fashion of those Women who make sale of their Favours, and set herself in the Way of being accosted as such a one. . . . She no sooner design'd this Frolick, than she put it in Execution [and soon] found her Disguise had answer'd the Ends she wore it for" (3:258). She is soon surrounded by "a Crowd of Purchasers" (3:258), chief among them the infamous Beauplaisir. Fantomina, Haywood writes, "Found a vast deal of Pleasure in conversing with him in this free and unrestrain'd Manner" (3:259) and is enchanted with the degree of freedom her disguise affords her.

Fantomina revels in her newly found freedom. Her disguise has freed her hidden, aggressive self, and she quickly adopts the virago role. But the disguise is not, emotionally, that easy, and Fantomina tearfully confesses "that she was a Virgin" (3:262). When Beauplaisir offers her money, the mask slips, and the real injured virgin speaks: " 'Is this a Reward (said she) for Condescensions such as I have yielded to?—Can all the Wealth you are possess'd of make a Reparation for my Loss of Honour?'" (3:263). Beauplaisir is aghast; he is totally unable, like Dorimenus, to read *her* text correctly (see 3:263), and Fantomina continues to control. She makes fiction, casting herself in the role of country heroine, "the Daughter of a Country Gentleman who was come to Town to buy Cloaths" (3:264). She continues the hoax, moving quickly from the "Slippers, and a NightGown loosely flowing" (pt. 3, p. 266), the habitual dress of the languishing Fantomina, to the "lac'd, and adorn'd with all the Blaze of Jewels" dress (3:267) that marks the "Awe inspiring Lady" of Quality, the Lady of Control.

Fantomina continues this fiction making and disguising as Celia, the Chamber maid of Bath, with "a round ear'd Cap, a short Red Petticoat, and a little Jacket of Grey Stuff . . . a broad Country Dialect, a rude unpolish'd Air . . . with her hair and Eye-brows black'd" (3:268).

Next Fantomina adopts a new personality, orders a dress "such as Widows wear in their first Mourning, which, together with the most afflicted and penitential Countenance that ever was seen, was no small

Alteration to her who us'd to seem all Gaiety" (3:270). Again, she is quick to supply a suitable fiction for the Widow Bloomer and, again, Beauplaisir is completely taken in.

Perhaps Fantomina is so successful because she is able not only to disguise herself so well, but, as Haywood writes, because "she was so admirably skill'd in the Art of feigning, that she had the Power of putting on almost what Face she pleas'd and knew so exactly how to form her Behaviour to the character she presented, that all the Comedians at both Playhouses are infinitely short of her Performances (3:274). In addition, Fantomina varies the fiction; she adjusts her writing and speaking skills to each character. Beauplaisir is totally "outwitted" (3:277).

Fantomina attributes her success at keeping Beauplaisir to her imaginative endeavors, and she challenges "all neglected Wives, and fond abandon'd Nymphs" (3:283) to heed and practice her method. "Men would be caught in there [*sic*] own Snare, and have no Cause to scorn our easy, weeping, wailing Sex!" (3:283).

Her disguise does succeed, and as the virago, she has been able to triumph over the male sex. Unfortunately, nature and her mother intervene. The mother returns, finds Fantomina to be pregnant, sends her to a convent in France, where Haywood's tale ends with the birth of a baby girl. Fantomina is not defeated, however, only temporarily set back. Although the end demonstrates a certain ambivalence in the ultimate success of the disguise, Haywood's (and Fantomina's) assessments of its viability are clear: the romance can be controlled; women can write the scripts and make them work.

\* \* \*

Haywood's best-known *Philidore and Placentia; or L'amour trop Delicat* (1727)[3] presents her most sophisticated (for the period 1719–49) exploration and use of the disguise and romance topoi. Placentia not only disguises herself as the aggressor in the relationship, whereas Philidore disguises himself as a faithful swain to serve her, but Placentia actively creates the tale, the fable of their adventures. Haywood herself with the repetition of the main story on two other levels, with less important characters, further identifies the importance of the fiction-masking process as she indulges in it to an almost unprecedented degree in one romance.

*Philidore and Placentia* is a story of interpolated, interlocking narratives. Each variation of the original story becomes a disguise or mirror for the central characters, Philidore and Placentia, and their actions. It is a story of love carried to extremes, William McBurney writes in his introduction (xxv) to the work; more to the point, it is a example, represent in their disguises the hidden portions of Philidore and Placentia; for example, Philidore with his self-effacement and self-deprecation has, in effect, castrated himself; hence, his disguise is like Bellamont, the Christain Eunuch. Likewise, Placentia by adopting the role of seducer, can be found in the character of Arithea, the femme fatale for whom the Eunuch hazards everything.

The eunuch masquerades as a painter; unable actually to have the real Arithea, "Pygmalion-like, I now doted on an image of my image of my own formation, and could kisses have inspired breath into the inanimate plate, mine must certainly have warmed it into life" (201). He continues: "My time was now wholly taken up between the shadow and the substance! . . . and I find myself no longer master of my reason" (201). Like Philidore, the Eunuch has fallen in love with the image, the angelic illusion he has created of Arithea. When the Eunuch is caught, robbed of his picture, imprisoned, "and slashed with iron whips a hundred strokes on my hated back" (202), Haywood is metaphorically beating all men who have tried to destroy women's true self through their illusion making. Not only is he whipped, but she has the Eunuch admitted to the seraglio—a journey into the interior of the male and female psyche where he confronts the real Arithea. His submission is matched only by her aggression, and in a scene reminiscent of the earlier confrontation between Philidore and Placentia, Haywood writes:

> she led me to an alcove, and making me sit down by her, by a thousand tender words and looks encouraged my submissive passion to proceed to the greatest liberties with her. I was just on the point of being as happy as the utmost qualification of my desires could make me when suddenly from behind the arras rushed out the bashaw attended by five or six armed slaves. (205)

The man is not allowed satisfaction, for that would mean condoning his romance-making power. Instead, Haywood orders the ultimate male punishment—castration. With the physical dismemberment comes a psychological maiming as well, and he no longer cares to fantasize, to "angelicize" women.

Arithea, too, is a mask for Placentia; Pygmalion-like, she rises from his canvas to life. So, too, Placentia recounts, after Philidore's rescue of her, that after his departure, "I was in effect no more than a piece of imagery wrought by some skillful hand which walks and seems to look, yet knows not its own notion" (214), a mere image arising from the male fiction.

A final interpolated tale, that of Tradewell's son who falls desperately in love with Emanthe, Placentia's servant, further emphasizes the masks that both sexes have assumed. Tradewell gave up an Oxford career to chase after Emanthe only to be kidnapped by his father and sent to Lisbon to be cured of his infatuation. His ship is captured by a Turkish galley, and he becomes a prisoner (of love). Emanthe, servant, is another manifestation of Placentia, slave to love.

Placentia still struggles with the imprisoning ideologies and tries one last time to cast off "love's slave" mask in the closing pages of the romance. Reduced to slavelike conditions by losing her fortune, she goes in search of Philidore and reaches the ultimate zenith of the female position—she creates Philidore—"I made such as [I] could wish to find you, and such you indeed now prove yourself—all gratitude, all constancy and love" (215). This is the point to which the entire novel has moved. Haywood underscores the importance of this mental state by juxtaposing this scene with another, one of the most brutal in the novel. On her way to find Philidore, Placentia has booked passage on a ship. There she is propositioned and then brutally attacked by the captain who sees her only as an object to gratify his sexual desire.

Placentia is rescued by pirates but then is imprisoned by them, sold into slavery, and, finally, rescued by Philidore. They return to England where further adventures still await them. Reunited with her brother, the Baron Bellamont, who is the Christian Eunuch, Placentia, it would appear, has brought the story full circle. The tale is not circular, however; Philidore and Placentia are not the same characters that we saw at the beginning. Their fictions have been replaced with a realistic vision; fictitious and angelic roles have been discarded and the real selves of Philidore and Placentia have been discovered.

The fictions of *Philidore and Placentia* present what Haywood would like, in fact, to occur; it is a novel of role reversal. In both cases, the disguise is therapeutic—it allows both sexes to explore "other selves" in an effort to achieve a proper stance, a proper understanding of self. But like Fantomina, Haywood will conclude that the masking, though necessary, does not free the woman; at the end, Placentia is forced back into acceptable female roles and masks. She has been able to assert herself for a small time, but to live in the eighteenth-century world, Placentia must return to accepted patterns and roles. Like *Fantomina, Philidore and Placentia* has investigated the ambivalence of the feminine ideologies of the age; yet Haywood is forced to conclude that such masking and unmasking can take place only in fiction.

*Fantomina* and *Philidore and Placentia* present positive views of the romance and the disguise, yet Haywood prevaricates and at the end makes the heroines reassume the masks they had initially so willingly discarded. Such works are the minority in the Haywood canon, and so much was he deluded by her Artifices that even her Vices appeared Virtues; the Profuseness of her Expences seem'd to proceed from a Generosity and noble Magnanimity of Soul, which, however destructive to his Fortune, he could not but applaud. In fine, every Thing she said, every Thing she did, was a new Charm to him; and neither the palpable Neglect which he found the whole World treated her with, nor the Remonstrances which some of his Friends, griev'd at his Infatuation, at last, grew free enough to make him, could oblige him to look with a jealous Eye on her Conduct, or in the least abate his Dotage. (2:128–29)

And should she ever see any inkling of suspicion in his eye, Haywood writes,

she knew how to bring herself off; she had Signs, Tears, Swooning, Languishments, at command: no Woman that ever liv'd was Mistress of more Artifice, nor had less the Appearance of being so. (2:129)

As the mistress of artifice, "the Baroness has never known true reality; her passion, her love, 'twas to them all, indeed, but feigned" (2:132), yet it is this feigning that will, ultimately, lead to her downfall. When the Baroness meets Beauclair, she feels the first pangs of real love. "I am resolv'd to triumph over this happy Rival, or die in the Attempt (2:136), she tells DuLache (an equally unprincipled accomplice, who acts as her pimp; he procures the Marquis de Sonville, the Chevalier de St. Aumar among others for her). He is a creature of cunning and brings disorder and disharmony wherever he goes. In a sense, DuLache is also the Baroness's creation, for she controls him; he does not act at all without her directions. Thus, when she is determined to have Beauclair, she first turns to DuLache to help her initiate her plans and her fictions. The poisonous tale created between them involved Montamour's supposed infidelities with a Monsieur Galliard. Because Beauclair is gullible and wary of indignities created and attributed to his own person, he is quick to believe the stories DuLache tells him; Beauclair will not tolerate "Artifice," "damn'd Deceit" (2:148). He is "sooth'd by the base arts of the most treacherous of all Villains" and his belief and naïve incredibility help him to "join in the Deceit against himself" (2:148), as he gladly permits DuLache to dictate, or create, a letter to send to his now scorned Montamour. DuLache continues his fictions, and soon Beauclair is interested in the Baroness.

The untrue fictions do not stop there, however. Not only does DuLache force Beauclair to accept false stories, thus using words for his own end, but the Baroness continues to shape words to suit her own purposes and disguise her entire personality as well. In an effort to secure Beauclair, having throughly [*sic*] inform'd herself by DuLache what best wou'd suit his Humour, she threw the vain Coquette entirely off, and wore the Appearance of the Woman of Honour. Her Carriage, tho' affable and complaisant, was all on the Reserve; nor did she (so exact was she in Dissimulation) in the least word or Action, all the time he stay'd with her, swerve from the most nice Punctilio of Modesty. (2 : 153–54).

The Baroness continues the masquerade and decides that she cannot yield too quickly to his desires if she is to win him. She faints, plays the extraordinarily sensitive woman in an effort to control; the masquerade has now become not merely the adoption of clothes and certain speech patterns, but, even more important, it includes thought patterns; the Baroness together with DuLache has been able to mold Beauclair's.

The Baroness's mind control of Beauclair has been so complete that in his own dealings with the once loved, then scorned Montamour, he transfers to the innocent Montamour, the hideous, deformed qualities that rightfully belong to the Baroness. For example, Montamour writes a letter declaring her dismay at the abrupt end of their relationship. His reaction to this letter is indicative of how much brainwashing he has been subject to:

The cold Disdain with which it seem'd to be writ, fir'd him, at first, with Indigation; He thought she gloried in her Falshood, and rejoic'd in an Opportunity to break with him; but when he consider'd it more carefully, he fancy'd he found a certain Stiffness in the Stile, which persuaded him her Indifference was but feigned.—One Moment she appear'd to his Imagination, as she really was, all heavenly Truth and Innocence languishing, dying with the cruel Alteration of her Fortune, and only counterfeiting to despise a Heart which had so ungenerously abandon'd her:—The next, he thought he saw her, as her Enemies had represented her, false, perjur'd and inconstant. (2 : 161)

Beauclair's vacillation about the true state of Montamour and her love is not allowed to move to a recognition of her real self, for the Baroness controls all minds, and she continues to ruin Montamour as she fabricates more stories about her.

Montamour does engage in a little disguise—she muffles herself up in a hood, and without telling even her maid, she goes to the Tuilleries to spy on the meeting between the Baroness and Beauclair. Yet it is the Baroness who actually engineers the scene that Montamour witnesses; her soul is so agitated by that scene that "her every Sense flew frighted at the Tempest, and left her body motionless on the Earth" (2 : 184). Her fainting is not a disguise, nor is it a bid for power;[8] it is only a natural reaction to stress. Montamour remains the only undisguised, nonpower-seeking character in the novel.

The latter portions of the novel shift to a use of disguise as a positive force—that is, Beauclair disguises as a common laborer to see her; Montamour continues to be truly angelic. The honesty of these disguises together with the advantages of a happy heart precipitate the reconciliation that occurs. Beauclair is able to recognize "the Delusion of DuLache, and the Artifices by which he had been brought to a Belief of her Inconstancy" (2:233), and Montamour continues to be herself.

Only in a closing incident does Haywood employ the use of disguise as she had done earlier. Here, Montamour masks herself as a chevalier with "darker Hair, a far less delicate Complexion, and a certain Boldness in his Look" (2:245). It is the "proper" aggressive female behavior, for unlike the Baroness, Montamour will get her man and not be punished. It is a disguise prompted by goodness of heart and a proper definition of the female self. The disguise offers feminine aggression only when and in the correct amounts that are necessary. The female must be true to herself. Not only does the disguise permit Montamour to voice her true feminist feelings, but when in the closing pages, Beauclair is brought to trial for the Baron's murder, Vrayment is able to speak in his defense and, because of this testimony, free Beauclair.

In *The Injur'd Husband* Haywood explores the nightmarish world of the aggressive woman. Because she has been so long suppressed, when she is at last able to control, she punishes all men. The Baroness's world is one gone mad; it is the romance gone awry; it is a topsy-turvey one that ends in punishment and death for all. Countering this masochistic, sadistic world is the romance world of Beauclair and Montamour. Montamour's disguise, unlike the demonic aggression of the Baroness, presents the proper amount of female aggression. She is able to maneuver and save her beloved Beauclair and is happy (almost embarrassingly so) to discard her male disguise and thus fit back into the romance patterns. Haywood has been able to voice her displeasure at the female scene and through this double disguise is able to explore the intertextuality of her tale and present the two stories of female aggression.

The extraordinary density and complexity of this text indicates the pervasiveness of the disguise and romance topoi. Here in *The Injur'd Husband,* it is possible to observe perhaps one of the most invidious, nasty kinds of masquerade. Unlike those of *Fantomina* (which were merely adopted to increase and prolong physical pleasure) or like those in *Philidore and Placentia* (which, at least on the surface, were adopted to create a happy ending for the love story even though the disguises did reveal some hideous interior states), here in *The Injur'd Husband,* the masquerade motif has taken on a negative, insidious tone. Now disguises are not only adopted to catch a mate but are prolonged after the supposed happy event to gratify unhealthy, selfish, lustful desires. The Baroness, not satisfied with merely using the disguise to trap her husband, continues to masquerade to supply men for her own voracious sexual appetite. The masquerade subtly shifts to a form of mind control, and the entire world presented in the fiction is suddenly inverted.

Haywood uses the disguise topos to characterize this state, thus rewriting the romance. But her examination of the female power cult, which is what she explores in most of her novels, leads, in the final analysis, to defeat. In the concluding pages, the reader watches as the Baroness grows "above the care of her Reputation, and thought it beneath her to regard any thing but the pleasing [of] herself" (2:174). She tries to poison her husband (2:196–97) and when that fails, she incarcerates him in a lunatic asylum (a place of all fictions and no truth). He is freed and returns home to discover Beauclair and his wife making love in his very own house; the Baroness's explanation that she is being raped almost convinces the Baron. She is the master of disguise. Succeeding in this, her greatest fiction, the Baroness becomes extremely careless with her behavior; she ceases to worry about the other tale she has created, and soon all her lovers know of her deception. When de Sonville exposes her, the Baroness discards the remains of her disguise; "no hope from Artifice, no relief from Dissimulation, she threw the mask of Softness off; unheard of Curses issued from her Mouth; her eyes shot fire; in all her Art the Fury stood confess'd" (2:203–4). "Never was Woman so exposed and ridicul'd— so despis'd and hated" (2:208). She is revealed in all her demonic colors. Such hateful aggression cannot be permitted to continue; both she and DuLache are exposed: "He was a known Deceiver; a Villain proclaim'd, as his Patroness was a jilt: and all that either of them could do, was to vent some part of their enervate Malice in Curses" (2:215). The Baron's return and his final realization of her baseness and deception together with the apprehension of Toncarr and LeSonge spell her doom:

> All her Policy forsook her; she no longer had the power of dissembling; not durst lift up her eyes to him she knew wrong'd beyond a possibility of Forgiveness. Streams of *unfeigned* Tears now trickled down her Cheeks; *real Sighs* heav'd her *disorder'd Breast;* and if she felt not a true Repentance for her Guilt, she did a *severe* Regret for the Condition it had reduc'd her to. (2:242; emphasis added)

*The Injur'd Husband* is important because of Haywood's experimentation with fictional strategies, romance, and rhetorical disguises. She examines her own writer's craft, as the maker of fictions and masks, and finds that, indeed, it is possible, through the topsy-turvy world of the mask, to discover the true and genuine reality of women.

\* \* \*

Haywood's *The Perplex'd Dutchess: or, Treachery Rewarded* (1728)[9] continues this masquerade of intertextuality as the story is presented in the guise of a letter written to an unidentified "Sir" by an equally unknown author. Apparently, the letter addressee has requested information about the duchess; the addressor-writer will supply what information he can, he writes, having "made it my Business to search into the most secret Part of her History" (1). He will, in effect, unmask her true self. He hints that such revelations will, perhaps, "render her Character less famous than that of *Fredigoud,* or *Brunehalt* for Cruelty [but] will equal either of them for Ambition, and Deceit" (1). The letter writer takes great pains to attest to the truth of his account, promising "that all the letters here transcrib'd are Genuine, and have neither been diminished nor anything added to them in the Copies taken from the Originals" (2). This tale is no romance, full of imaginative splendor. Instead, it is unvarnished realism. In fact later on in the tale, the narrative voice interrupts and, uncharacteristically for Haywood, announces that this is not a romance:

> 'Tis more the business of a *Romance,* than a *Narrative of true Facts,* to expatiate on the Despair of Lovers, when interrupted by any intervening Accident in the Progress of their Passion; I shall therefore omit any Description of those Anxieties with which the Minds of *Theanor* and *Amarantha* were agitated in this separation, and with as much brevity as possible go on with the History of Gigantilla. (52; emphasis added)

Oddly enough, the letter writer is ostensibly a man. Why, then, does he take such pains to portray the female side so evilly and fiendishly? The man is a supporter of the romance and the ideology of romantic love, yet Haywood undercuts this entire position with her ventriloquism act. Gigantilla is made larger than life in almost mythic proportions by the male voice on the story level perhaps to detract from her, but more important, on the secondary level to display how the woman is larger, more powerful than the man. Gigantilla, because of her obscure origins and larger-than-life size, seems to become a mythic figure, a representation of the female sex.

Her origins are unknown but blessed with an "ambitious and aspiring Soul" and "an uncommon Share of Cunning" (2); she soon wheedles her way into the favor of a great lady of the court as her companion. Gigantilla is a supreme actress knowing "how to embellish the Charm she had from Nature, with all the Aids of Art" (2). As was the case with Fantomina, so too with Gigantilla: the names used are already parts of the disguise; like Fantomina, she too, disguises herself to attract the Duke of Malfy and exercise her control.

First, amid a profligate and passionate court, she alone appears to remain untouched by this emotion. (In reality, she is touched but her mask of indifference attracts the Duke). Second, when he first approaches her to speak to him, she appears demure, then haughty by turns. Haywood writes that she "*assumes* an Air of haughtiness" (6; emphasis added). Examining her speech, one sees that she "assumes" several masks while talking to the Duke; her favorite:

> she assum'd the utmost Tenderness in her Voice, and Eyes, and without seeming to have lost any thing of her former Bashfulness; she affected to feel an innate Sensibility of the Passion he profess'd, and with the Air of endeavouring to conceal a Softness she was asham'd of, discover'd it in a thousand Words, and looks, which has the appearance of the most artless Innocence, but were in reality the produce of the deepest Deceit. She play'd her part with such admirable Artifice, that the Duke . . . felt an Increase of Admiration. (11–12)

Gigantilla is in control.

Not only does she disguise her true intentions from the Duke, but she also hides her aggression from Artemia, the Duke's fiancée. Gigantilla consciously lays a "plot" both to win the Duke and oust Artemia. This plotting is her fiction making; specifically, she discredits Artemia in the Duke's eyes, by forging letters from Artemia to her supposed lover, Philemont. The Duke is completely taken in by this fiction and follows Gigantilla's lead in the proposed plan that will catch the lovers in the very act.

Her scheme is so successful and the Duke so gullible that he does, indeed, believe Artemia is both false and fair, as Gigantilla has suggested, and Philemont his rival for Gigantilla's affections.

Artemia is ruined and no longer even cares for life in the court; she becomes a priestess of Vesta. Gigantilla's fiction has succeeded: Philemont is dead, and Artemia self-exiled.

> The wicked Gigantilla in the meantime triumph'd in her successful Wiles, and so strangely was the Duke infatuated with her Beauty, her dissembled Love, and well-feign'd Modesty and Virtue, that, contrary to the advice of his Council, the Entreaties of those who were most his Favourites, his own Interest, and Glory, and every Motive which ought to sway a Prince, he

married her, and from the meanest Rank of people rais'd her to the supremest Dignity in his power to bestow. (33–34)

Her triumph is short-lived, however; Gigantilla is hoisted by her own petard. She is ruined by her own fictitious lies, for "she knew all the homage she receiv'd, all the seeming regard with which she was flattered, was paid only to the Dutchess, and that Gigantilla of herself was the Object of Detestation to all the Virtuous and the Wise" (34). She can never rest; "her Brains were forever at work contriving Means to prevent her own undoing" (35); Gigantilla must forever create fictions and cover the truth. Haywood continues: "she was not one moment free from Apprehensions, that one day or other the Duke's Eyes might be open'd to see things as they in reality were" (40).

All Gigantilla's plans are foiled; her evilness is no match for Theanor, the Duke's brother, and the romance hero who was "more lov'd, more ador'd by the Populace, more revered by the Great and Good, and more dreaded by the Wicked" (36). Although she tries "to lessen this young Prince in the Opinion of his Brother" by making "his most disinterested Actions appear mean Designing, and his very Virtues, Vices" (36–37), Gigantilla is unsuccessful. Confronted with honesty and truth, her machinations and lies cannot succeed. She is exposed. Such demonic fiction making cannot go unpunished. When the Duke dies and the Duchess is exiled "At a small Village some thirty Leagues distant from the Confines of Malfy" (53), Theanor reclaims the throne, marries his beloved Amarantha, and reestablishes the romance order. Gigantilla is not publicly punished; "they . . . set no Price upon her Head, nor publish[ed] any Edicts in her prejudice" (60). Her punishment is an interior one; she is tormented daily with the fictions and the lies that she created, and "all her Riches [are not] able to procure her one Moment's ease from the Racks of a guilty Thought" (60).

The story ends with a return to the letter writer and his statement: "I [have] given you as faithful an Account as possible, of the Rise and Fall of this once haughty woman" (60). The speaker has anatomized the aggressive female, has unmasked the interior of the female self. Again, because the Duchess is punished at the end, the romance characters, Theanor and Amaranth, triumph, supporting the approved fictional world of masked, docile, submissive women. Yet the story is not Amaranth's; it is Gigantilla's. It is an antiromance that unmasks the ideologies of the day and defines the position of the aggressive woman.

*  *  *

*Idalia: or The Unfortunate Mistress* (1723)[10] provides an even more potent examination of the punishment and fate of the nonsubmissive, duped female. In fact, I find *Idalia* to be one of the most detailed examinations of the female psyche in Haywood's early fiction and, almost without doubt, of all minor fiction of this pre-1749 period. Here the exterior, acquiescent, docile mask, which most female characters put on, is disregarded by this protagonist. Although introduced in typical, sentimental, submissive heroine jargon, Idalia quickly declares her nontraditional attitude. She will not put on the "face" expected of her; "and had her Conduct been such as might have been expected from the Elegance of her Genius, and the Improvements of Education . . she had indeed been the Wonder of her Sex" (3:2), but such is not the case. Idalia is "unable to endure Controll, disdainfull of Advice, obstinate, and peremptory in following her own Will" (3:2). She is loathe to follow parental advice, yet she cannot always have her way; her father screens her suitors and attempts to order and control her future. Idalia, however, will have none of it. Although she wants the romantic outcome—a man to love and a happy life—she wants to arrange and control this end herself. But this aggressive desire will be her downfall. Idalia is representative of most heroines—unable to adjust to the necessary state of submission and docility, their aggression leads to their death.

Idalia flirts with Florez, a suitor not approved by her parents, and agrees to an assignation with him, convinced that she will be the controller; she is, however, the dupe. Don Ferdinand, Florez's patron, persuades Florez to let him go in his place; having seen the beautiful Idalia, he wants to enjoy her first. Ferdinand dictates the letter to Idalia, and arranges the rendezvous; "Idalia believed him now . . . entirely her Convert" (3:13–15). All was artifice he tells her, however, and she is raped (3:17). Having had her, Florez and Don Ferdinand soon bundle Idalia off to Henriquez de Valago, Ferdinand's intimate friend. Because of the violation, Idalia is bent on death, and Henriquez does all he can to prevent it. In the meantime, he falls in love with her, and Idalia is even more exploited.

The entire story of Idalia is built on a fiction: Florez masquerades as a lover; Don Ferdinand declares passionate love, which is a mere cover for lust; and Henriquez fabricates stories to "save" Idalia from Ferdinand for himself. Idalia becomes all mask, merely a desirable object to be possessed by whatever men get her.

She has been "solicited for a Prostitute" (3:53), has been turned into a possession, a mere sexual plaything by Florez, Ferdinand, and Myrtano. Her cry—"can e'er the Days of Innocence return . . . Can I again appear a Virgin?" (3:63)—is one echoed by all Haywood's women. The answer, however, appears to be a resounding no. The woman as represented by Idalia seems to be unable to cast off the fettering mask the man has foisted on her; she seems incapable of discovering and asserting a true self, and accepts instead the "selves" presented her by the men. She becomes an archetypal woman who is exploited, harassed, and used. Although she claims: "I still am Mistress of myself,—my own unconquerable Will!—*Idalia* can be nought but Inclination subdued" (3:64), the self revealed is still a self masked, a person defined by the opposite sex.

In her effort to escape the not unwanted but certainly not approved attentions of Myrtano, the third suitor, Idalia makes her way to Verona and a monastery under the protection of a "Servant," a man actually in the employ of Ardella, Myrtano's betrothed. He hides her in the country, but Idalia is convinced that he is not what he seems, that he, too, is disguised. Myrtano has been cast in the role of hero, but, Haywood writes, it is a role only when he is viewed from a distance; on closer inspection, he is all lover (see 3:46).

Idalia has been ill treated enough now to doubt any man. To escape this evil (as yet undefined), Idalia disguises herself as a plain country lass "counterfeit[s] a Chearfulness" (3:70), and decides to make her way to Naples where she will meet her friend who is in the Convent of Benedictines there. Procuring passage on a ship, she is attacked and almost raped by Captain Rickambull; she is rescued by the Barbary Corsair Abdomar, who is the only man she meets who does not try to exploit her. Taken on board his ship, she meets his beloved Bellraizia and soon listens to her story.

The interpolated tale functions as a mask by which means Idalia can view a reflection of her own fate. Bellraizia tells of her arranged marriage to Prince Mulyzeden, but her passion and love is for Abdomar. She is imprisoned by her father, and, we can assume, will be forced to wed the Prince when her narrative is interrupted and a great storm occurs. In the midst of the wreck, Idalia is cast off from the ship and saved by some people on shore. When she is well enough to travel, she "could not resolve in what Manner: Her Beauty had led her into so many Dangers, that she resolved for the future to disguise her Sex till she should arrive at a Place of Safety" (3:107), and she adopts man's clothes as protection.

Male clothes do not afford protection, however; she is attacked, robbed, and has her horse killed by bandetti (3:110–11); her recourse: she swoons. A lady of quality passing by rescues the "seeming Chevalier" (3:113). The lady lies to her servant and takes Idalia back to her house, where she fabricates quite a story about her "male" self. The ironies increase as first Donna Antonia falls in love with her, and then Idalia learns Donna Antonia's husband is none other than Myrtano, who, he says, continues to love Idalia. Idalia is literally hounded by men.

In *Idalia,* Haywood is able to probe the psychological reality behind this happily-ever-after mask that women are forced to put on. *Idalia* reveals the horror and sheer tragedy that lurks beneath the surface. Here the disguise only reveals the facileness, the utter vacuity of such frivolous fantasies. No romance exists for the woman. The reality, the true condition of women, is revealed in Idalia's plight. She cannot escape and leave as a princess aboard a marvelous ship bedecked with crimson satin and gold trappings. Her reality is not to be beloved; rather she is turned into officially what the men had tried to force her to become—a courtesan. Her distraught state and the use of disguise precipitate her final tragedy.

She sees Florez, "the Villain who had first betray'd her from her Father's House, and been the Cause of all her Woe" (3:160), and she determines to be revenged on him. Disguising her hand and self, she sends him a letter as the "enamour'd Incognita" (3:161); the letter unfortunately falls into Myrtano's hands, who "muffled himself up in his Cloak, and went himself at the appointed Time to the Place of Assignation" (3:161). Without waiting to discover the identity of the cloaked figure, assuming it to be Florez, Idalia plunges a dagger into his breast; when she discovers her mistake, "she tore her Hair and Face, rav'd stamp'd curs'd Fate, and scarce spar'd Heaven in the Extremity of her Anguish" (3:162) and plunges the dagger into her own heart. (Later, Florez is apprehended for a murder he committed and is executed.)

Death is the only road to freedom after such wholesale abuse and exploitation of the female self. The only control Idalia can have over her life is her own choice of whether or not to continue it. This position is the most extreme one that women can find themselves in, and *Idalia* is Haywood's most blatant revelation of the state and fate of the eighteenth-century woman. It is an account that the narrator has assembled "from the imperfect accounts I received from those who gave me the History of her Life" (3:47). The claim is for realism, not romance.

No lighter, romantic world is offered as an alternative to the bleak, dark, murderous one of *Idalia.* Haywood's insistence on the dark world aligns her with Aubin and certainly prepares the way for the severe criticism of the romance that would follow later in the century. Unlike her contemporaries, Barker and Davys, Haywood does not use preface material to explore and explain her romance theory. Instead, she directs her attention to the actual telling of the tale with the destruction of the romance form.

In pieces like *Fantomina, Philidore and Placentia, The Unequal Conflict* and *The Injur'd Husband,* Haywood presents both positive and negative heroines who actually create fictions—in the case of *Philidore and Placentia,* a positive one that ultimately does no one any harm; with Gigantilla and the Baroness, fictions that are destructive. Both types try to construct the romance, upset the ideologies of female helplessness and powerlessness. They attempt to control. Only in the case of Placentia does this control turn out positively—though, ironically, she gains control only by losing it. The Baroness and Gigantilla are punished by the male world they attempt to control. Both stories expose the romance world by subverting its rhetorical strategy.

In works like *The Unequal Conflict* and *The Injur'd Husband,* however, Haywood does portray the usual romance world. In the stories of Philenia and Montamour the reader encounters the seemingly placid world of love, female devotion, and submission that Haywood and other female novelists try to counteract. The tale of these heroines are sandwiched in between the torrid, devastating tales that attempt to corrupt the form. These heroines appear even more vulnerable when surrounded by the other stories Haywood relates.

# Chapter 5
# Jane Barker

Jane Barker (fl. 1688–1718) begins her fourth and last romance novel, *The Lining of the Patch-Work Screen* (1726), by having one of the female protagonists, Dorinda, confess to her male rescuer: "It was such Romantick Whimsies that brought upon me the Ruin and Distress in which you behold me. I had read Plays, Novels, and Romances, till I began to think myself a Heroine of the first rank; and all Men that flatter'd or ogled me, were Heroes" (106). Her vision has been corrupted, she explains, by her voracious romance reading. Dorinda is one of Barker's most vocal, rational heroines, and she truly echoes Barker's own opinions, for she, too, is aware of the narcotic, stupifying effect that the romances have had on their female readership. (Barker is cognizant of the French heroic romance tradition: her third novel, *Exilius,* is a direct imitation of the earlier works. She is also aware of the French salon and attempts to recreate such a scene with her own identification as Galesia.) She sets out, then, in her small corpus to anatomize *the* female form—the romance—to help her readers understand themselves. It is extraordinary that Barker attempts this scathing analysis so early in the century.

Jane Spencer argues that Barker is able to examine the romance form so intensely because she turned it into an autobiographical account. "In her Galesia narratives Barker not only provides herself with a romantic pseudonym, but wraps her life story in the conventions of romance."[2] Thus, she does not criticize the form so much as examines her own life. Spencer reasons that Barker used this "disguise of the romance" to appear as the "heroine" of her work, thus using the romance form as it was intended: to find self-identity. Rather than having her characters adopt an aggressive disguise and act out the part, she herself would play this role. "By making her autobiography into a romance about a version of herself called Galesia, Barker gained all the advantages of a heroine's identity" (167–68) without having to partake of the disadvantages. Further, her superimposition of her own life story on the literary conventions of the romance heroine's social and sexual initiation allows her to offer another alternative to the fate of the eighteenth-century woman—she can live alone as Barker successfully does. Barker's identification with the heroine also permits her an unreserved look and criticism of the romance form. Just as Galesia's intertextual story is one of success because she becomes a poet when Bosvil casts her off, so Barker herself can have the promise of a single, successful writing career rather than the imprisoning life of a married heroine.

Barker's criticism of the popular form is extraordinary. Her position as an exile, both nationally and religiously (she was Irish and Catholic in Protestant England), made her acutely aware of the powerlessness of women; yet she counters this frailty with her subversive romance writing. Unlike the typical Boyd novel or the final outcome of an Aubin piece, no happy endings occur for most of her heroines. Barker's women, at the end of their tales, find themselves abandoned and alone, and most oftentimes, not knowing why they are in such a state. Unlike the Aubin women, they are not so much physically tortured as they are victims of a mental rape far more insidious and deadly. Having decided that such is the accurate picture of the life and fate of the eighteenth-century woman, Barker still finds herself in an ambiguous situation. She cannot be false to herself, her conscience, and her readership, nor can she blatantly present these concerns outrightly and risk losing her means of support. Like most eighteenth-century female writers, she resorts to a hidden agenda and a rather obvious subtext that presents a true picture of the woman's life.

\* \* \*

*Love Intrigues: or, The History of the Amours of Bosvil and Galesia* (1713)[3] is Barker's first venture into this subliminal, confusing world of romance; it is shocking in its intensity and sophisticated examination of the feminine psyche. The dedicatory lines, "To the Author of the following Novel," by "S. G." (20 May 1713) immediately call attention to the quintessential problem of the novella, when the speaker remarks:

> Methought I scorn'd of Nymphs and Knights to dream,
> And all the Trifles of a Love-Tale Scheme;
> Poor dry Romances of a tortur'd Brain,
> Where we see none but the Composer's Pain.

The popular romances are tortured because they do not mirror the true state of the writer's pain, but instead gloss over the hurt and misery with the disguise of the "Trifles of a Love-Tale Scheme." The speaker concludes, however, that this very disguise can be uncovered if the piece is read correctly. Galesia's exposure of the romance is extremely sophisticated. Not until Fielding's *The Cry* (1754) will another early author attempt to anatomize and expose the romance as a stultifying narcotic offered by the male population. As Galesia concludes: "I thought the *Mumming* went too far when the Masqueraders murther'd those they pretended to divert" (39).

The story begins as Galesia recounts the happenings of her early years to her friend, Lucasia, telling her that "notwithstanding I had arm'd my Thoughts with a thousand Resolutions against Love, yet [the] first Moment I saw this Man [Bosvil] I lov'd him" (5–6). Her passion smothers her reason, and she soon "disguises" her feeling for him, while she acts out her role in the ensuing masquerades. Galesia continues her disguise when she returns to the country, followed by Bosvil, who pleads only "common Civility" in his pursuit. Galesia observes: "tho' in Bosvil's Presence I made a shift to keep up this Outside of a seeming Insensibility of Love . . . interiorly I was tormented with a thousand Anxieties, which made me seek Solitude where I might without Witness or Controul, disburthen my overcharg'd Heart of Sigh and Tears" (12–13). Because the scenario has not been the romantic one she has been taught to expect, Galesia adopts other "masks" in an effort to comfort herself, resolving first to be "a Goddess, as the Worlds Flatterers had made of me" (10), then deciding to espouse a Book, and spend my Days in Study . . . I imagined myself the Orinda, or Sappho of my Time" (15). Next she tries a physical disguise, dressing herself in "a plain kind of Habit" seeming "to scorn (what I really courted) popular Applause; and hid a proud Heart under an humble Habit" (17). She wears "an outside Indifferency, with a Heartfull of Passion. Thus a Mask is put on, sometimes to conceal an ill Face, and sometimes to preserve a good one: and the most part of Mankind are in reality different from what they seem" (19–20).

Bosvil continues his "game," one time declaring his love, the next not, and returns after a three-week absence extremely indifferent. During his absence, Galesia has begun to come to terms with the false note he is playing and her own subsequent counter to it: she becomes a poet. It is certainly a new position for the women to adopt, for the normal eighteenth-century story offered only two solutions: seduction leading to catastrophe or avoided seduction leading to marriage. Spencer argues that one must read the novella autobiographically to comprehend this alternative fully. She notes: "Galesia is not, like the typical heroine-narrator, recalling her pre-marital life or excusing a sexual lapse; instead, she is explaining the lack of sexual relationship in her life. She attributes to herself the characteristics of heroines whose destiny she does not share in order to make her single life seem equally valid as another kind of heroine's destiny" (170).

Even though Barker herself is comfortable with this fate, Galesia still continues to struggle. Galesia is unable to mask her extreme unhappiness and anger, and she imagines herself going "towards the Place of his Abode, supposing a Rapier in my hand, and saying to my self, The false *Bosvil* shou'd now disquiet me no more, nor any other of our Sex; in him I will end his Race, no more of them shall come to disturb or affront Womankind; this only son, shall dye by the hands of me an only Daughter" (43). This dream sequence is critical, for Barker is able to subvert the romance form completely with these thoughts of death and destruction. By this point in the *Love Intrigues,* Galesia/ Barker is far too sophisticated for a simple lover. Her dealings with Bosvil now figure only secondarily to the main intent of the tale: Barker's education of the reader. In a letter that Galesia sends to Bosvil, Barker outlines the double reading that is necessary for the woman to adopt. Galesia observes: "In the Simplicity of these Words were a great deal of Cunning, and under the shadow of Forwardness, lay cover'd much Kindness, which I knew he must discern, if he had any real Affection for me in his Heart" (47).

Her guile is too complex for him, however, and he reads words at only face value. With such an impass, the conclusion of the story is quickly and predictably told. Bosvil continues to misread her actions and marries his London mistress; Galesia is left to "perform the Farce of a well pleas'd Kinswoman" (69) and welcome Bosvil and his new bride to her father's home for dinner. At the end, Galesia is left alone with Lucasia in her father's house, ready to be summoned to prayers.

*Love Intrigues* is a disrupting and disturbing romantic piece of fiction, most especially because it is Barker's first work. In it, Barker carefully deviates from the typical romance plot; Galesia's tale has departed from the expected seduction and rape story that is at the center of the feminocentric text (that story that codes female sexual vulnerability as the prime motive in female and male behavior), for Bosvil never attempts a destruction. The entire tale involved the masquerading and misreading of the actions of both Bosvil and Galesia by the other. Spencer argues that this textual confusion is a result of Barker's imposition of her autobiographical story onto the heroine's text.

I argue that although an autobiographical tendency emerges in the work, Barker actually examines the romance tradition and the eighteenth-century ideologies that code feminity in this early work. She masquerades her story (albeit, portions of which are autobiographical) under the guise of the accepted and popular form, but the ambivalence of the period is reflected in the ambiguous ending of the tale. Although Barker through Galesia has been able to counter the typical heroine, she is unable to integrate this new species of woman into the complex structure of the accepted eighteenth-century ideology. She is left, in the end, with a highly unsatisfactory heroine and story— neither can provide the positive wish fulfillment that is the romance's stock-in-trade. Because Galesia has played the "game" of masking and hiding her true feelings too well, she is left at the conclusion with no sense of closure, no happy ending, and certainly no romance. Because Galesia did not act like the proper heroine, she cannot have a proper heroine's destiny: marriage. Her investigation of the romance form has found it to be hollow. For Galesia and the eighteenth-century woman, no alternative exists; Bosvil is allowed to go off and marry, but Galesia must learn to make do with her unromantic heroine life, and instead she becomes the heroine poet.

\* \* \*

After her blockbuster *Love Intrigues* (1713), Barker turned her attention to the standard romance, producing *Exilius* (1715).[4] Read with her other three iconoclastic pieces, it is extraordinary to believe that the same pen wrote them. Gone is the attempt to discredit the romance genre. Instead, *Exilius* becomes a "model" romance as she writes in the preface: "The study of these Books, helps to open the Understanding of young Readers, to distinguish between real Worth and superficial Appearance" (A4). She concludes by observing that "the young Readers may also reap many Handfulls of good Morality, and likewise gather some gleanings of History, and Acquaintance with the Ancient Poets. In short, I think I may say of Romances as Mr. Herbert says of Poetry, and hope, that a pleasant Story may find him, who flies a serious Lecture" (A5).

*Exilius* is so much a typical romance (the subtitle is *Written after the Manner of Telemachus*) that the entire tale exists merely to have the happy ending for all the right couples. No attempt occurs to deal with the ambiguities of the romance form, and instead Barker uses it to critique the contemporary marriage scene. Such open declarations place *Exilius* and Barker in the camp that celebrates and upholds the male-created female ideologies. *Exilius,* like the ideologies, renders the woman powerless and helpless. *Exilius* provides "love lectures"(preface); all of the tales hold to the romance pattern of movement toward integration and sexuality for the female, with most of the stories ending with a homecoming and reunion.

Barker begins her tale by placing her heroine, Clelia, in a grove, waiting to begin her adventures. When she is accosted by "a Youth in the Habit of a Page" (2), she is "both angry and astonish'd" but even more so, when the youth, "pulling off some little Disguise" (2), is revealed to be her cousin, Scipiana. Although Barker would have her story be morally right, "to open the understanding of young Readers" (preface), it is interesting to note that great ambivalence emerges in her presentation of the numerous female characters. Not only is Scipiana disguised at first, but Clelia indulges in a secret correspondence with Marcellus; she has been forbidden to see him because he is supposedly engaged to Jemella, though he has been flirting and courting Clelia. When Clelia is hidden away at her uncle's home, Marcellus accidentally finds her, and again, like the secret correspondence, dons a disguise—that of a young officer in the army (16)—to continue to see her. It is all a masquerade, however; when he is absent for a few days, Clelia learns that Marcellus, though claiming to be ill, has been secretly trying to seduce Libidinia, who confesses all to Clelia, unwilling "to disguise the truth" (20) any longer. Clelia is stricken with this confession, and even more dismayed when she sees how easily she was taken in by his disguise: "I perceived to my Sorrow how Passion had closed the Eyes of my Understanding, and rock'd my Reason into a lethargy" (21–22). Although awakened at the last, Clelia is left in a nonintegrated, excluded position at the end.

The second history to be recounted, Clarenthia's, is another example of disguised, misdirected love. When her father is unable to make her marry his bastard son, Valerius, he approaches her himself, and "contrary to all Morality" (228) disguises himself and abducts his daughter; however, she is rescued by a stranger who unwittingly kills her father. Then Clarenthia is carried off again, this time by Valerius, the bastard son, in disguise, who has not yet heard the true story about the father's seduction and rape. Clarenthia ponders the problems of disguise, appearance, and truth. She is carried off to Sicily and imprisoned by Valerius and his mother, Asbella, under the "mask of truth" that they are helping her till all is cleared with the Senate about her father's death, but Clarenthia questions, "whether it was a real Face or only a Mask I could not tell" (39). She escapes, ultimately meets and falls in love with Lysander, her unknown rescuer, only to be torn from him and washed up on the shore of Africa where she "conceal'd her Name and Quality" (56). Her story is left unfinished; her fate unresolved. We learn in a subsequent tale that she has become a servant to Emelia, is beloved by Hannibal, but remains true to the memory of Lysander.

And so proceeds the tale of *Exilius;* as each new character enters, many pages are spent detailing his or her story. Thus, it is that we learn of Scipiana's trials and tests, the actual history of Exilius, and several others. When the characters are allowed to interact, we read that Exilius saves Scipiana when she runs away (actually floats away) from Clodius; then he and his father arrange her transportation back to Alexandria where she disguises herself as Exilia until she can contact her own father. Exilia is placed as a servant to the queen, who several pages later relates her history and so on. The entire structure of *Exilius* is history buried within history; the characters are so similar that after awhile they tend to blur, and one is left without any one distinct impression, but instead forms a composite picture of the lords and ladies of the Egyptian landscape.

The mundaneness of the plot is also mirrored in the predictable use of the masquerade topos: first, as protective device (for example, Scipiana becomes Exilia to protect herself from the senate when she is banished and yet living in Egypt; and, second, disguise as confusion (for example, Exilius loves Scipiana/Exilia, but because of her seeming siding with the enemy, he retreats yet is unable not to love her). No major criticism of the romance structure exists in this text; only the standard use of the masquerade occurs. It is a strange work to appear after the innovations of *Love Intrigues* and preceding the avant garde *A Patch-Work Screen* and *The Lining of the Patch-Work Screen*. One can only assume that it is Barker's attempt to cater to the popular taste, demonstrating all the current, narrative, fictional modes that she was capable of using.

\* \* \*

After an excursion into the imitation of French heroic romances with *Exilius,* Barker returns in *A Patch-Work Screen for the Ladies* (1723)[5] to an examination of the feminine romance tradition as she explores "History reduc'd into Patches" (iv). By employing the popular needlework topos, and by analyzing the various parts that go into the making of a patchwork screen, she is able to catalog and examine the parts of a typical romance.

*A Patch-Work Screen* begins with an introduction that is a collection of stories told-on-the-road, so to speak, and is the usual conglomeration of wit—for example, "Whence bad Periwigs came to be called Caxtons"—and romance—for example, "The Heroick Cavalier; or the Resolute Nun." It is this last piece that introduces the disguise theme; in usual fashion, the reader encounters a cavalier, who, to get to the girl he loves (who has been placed in a nunnery), disguises his servant as the "Page-Damsel" so that he can gain access to the beloved. This disguised page carries a letter from the chevalier to the almost-nun, and she writes: "Your letter has so ruffled my whole Interior, that I know not how to write common Sense; Therefore, if my Answer be unintelligible, blame not me, for I am utterly lost in an Abyss of Confusion" (introduction, a). The confusion is also heightened by the double masquerading that is taking place, for the "Page-Damsel" reveals that she is really a triple masquerader: "For, indeed, said she, I am not a Boy, as I pretended to be, but a foolish Girl, that took that Disguise upon me to be near your Person" (introduction, a2). The Page-Damsel, after engineering the union between the chevalier and the beloved, joins the nunnery and "Things were brought to a happy Conclusion" (introduction, a2).

The main story of *A Patch-Work Screen for the Ladies* is a con- tinuation of the story of Bosvil and Galesia from the earlier *Love Intrigues*. Under the pretext of organizing a screen from "Pieces of *Romances, Poems, Love-Letters,* and the like" (introduction) with her Ladyship, Galesia further chronicles her own love exploits. Galesia continues her studies and forgets Bosvil. So engrossed does she be- come in her studies that she is courted by other men, but "Amongst this Train of Pretenders (some of which address'd to my Mother, and some privately to me), I think there is nothing worth Remark" (40). Galesia will not disguise herself either as "the formal Prude," or the "ever scorn'd . . . impertinent Coquet" (40). Galesia's disguise, if, indeed, she has one, is that of innocence. As she observes: "in all Places, and at all Times, my Country Innocence render'd me a kind of Solitary in the midst of Throngs and great Congregations" (55).

In general, *A Patch-Work Screen* appears to be a story of unmasking and of decoding the popular romance form. Most of the interpolated tales emphasize failed relationships, unsuccessful initiations, doomed marriages. Barker presents characters and facts as she sees them, with no coloring over. Thus, for example, when she meets "a Person in Quality of a Nurse" (59), "whose Words, Air, and Mien, appeared more like one entertaining Ladies in a Drawing Room, than a Person whose Thought were charg'd with the Care of her sick Patients" (50), Galesia/Barker is anxious to hear the unvarnished truth, and coaxes the nurse into telling her "Story, without the least Disguise" (60). Hers is the age-old story: she falls in love with a clerk of the Inns of Court and secretly carries on this amour. When her father learns of the attachment, he forbids further contact, because the young man had "little or no Foundation, but his own Natural Parts" (61). Her father arranges a marriage for her, and she is ultimately forced to see it through. Unfortunately, her husband turns out to be thoroughly unsuccessful, whereas her first love becomes a highly acclaimed law- yer. Disguising her true feelings has not led to any sort of reward for her, and she is not allowed a happily-ever-after romance.

"The Story of Belinda" is another example of the typical disguise that leads only to female dissolution. Allowing the insinuations of her lover (though he is a married gallant) to penetrate her heart, Belinda watches as "the Mask of *Platonick Love* was pull'd off" (76), and she is undone. Discovering her pregnancy, Belinda is taken to the country and abandoned. Finally, she comes under the care of Galesia and her ladyship, and admits to them that now, indeed, she knows how to read the male text (76). Again, it is important to note that Barker antici-pates Fielding and the critical theories she will develop in *The Cry*.

In the final analysis *A Patch-Work Screen for the Ladies* is not a sustained critique of the romance, but is instead a pastiche of verses, recipes, courtesy book etiquette, and the like. It contains segments of romance, and yet the tales are so fragmented and disguised that Barker is, in effect, anatomizing the very genre she writes. By placing the romance stories within such a female world, Galesia (and through her the reader) is able to explore the ambiguity of the mask of women's helplessness and aggressive control. It employs much female iconogra-phy—sewing and cooking—and explores the nonromantic side of life. Yet, it is a statement of the ambivalence that is built into the state of being female, for romance and recipes exist side by side.

I think that *A Patch-Work Screen* is troublesome. The woman's fate at the end is not resolved; one cannot make a finished screen of the ambiguous fragments presented in the tale. Because, according to this text, no way exists to have both a successful romance and a successful career, Galesia chooses the vocation.

\*   \*   \*

A similar lack of closure in terms of romance is found in Barker's final work, *The Lining of the Patch-Work Screen;* here Galecia's saga continues as she moves to London. This piece is composed of charac-ters' histories that enable Galecia (spelled this way in this work) to make general observations about humankind, and allow her to further explore the romance and her rewriting of it.

In Captain Manley's tale, for example, we meet with female inno-cence and male betrayal. He observes: "One Evening at the Play I saw a pretty young Creature, very well dress'd, without Company or Attendants, and without a Mask (for she had not yet learn'd so much Impudence, as to put on 'that Mark of Demonstration'" (7). Drug-ging him, she tells him in the morning of her ruined financial status and her powerlessness to aid herself—she will marry or live with any man who can support her. Manley quickly envisions setting her up in a house making her a "Heroine, or petty Goddess" (9), with him becoming "a Beau of the First Rate" (9). When he sees her the next night, however, she is in the process of soliciting yet another man.

Manley has been gulled, he thinks. When he meets a male friend in the mall, hears his story, and tells his own, it is yet another example of men who are taken in by feminine wiles. Chloris, however, is not to be blamed. Her disguised maneuvers are survival tactics she has had to adopt in order to cope with the male ideologies. Her mask, then, is one created by the man, for though Manley remarks: "I lov'd her as well as any Hero in a Romance" (19), he sees her in the role of submissive heroine so that he can come to the rescue. Manley's "woman" is totally controlled; he keeps several mistresses and yet persuades his wife to leave a substantial amount of her income to him when she dies. A deathbed repentance of sorts occurs, when his wife actually dies, but by and large Manley remains a typical example of the unrepentant rogue.

*The Lining of the Patch-Work Screen* presents many stories of the powerlessness of women; from Philanda's story of the nun who leaves the convent to marry the cavalier but who ends as his murderess (as well as the murderer of his best friend and her second husband) to the "Story of Mrs. Goodwife" who tries to find money to save her family and her self, each tale emphasizes the imprisonment of the woman. The plethora of romance tales with unhappy endings emphasizes Barker's dissatisfaction with the form, and her attempt to reinterpret the male closure. Nuns leave convents for lovers with whom they live and have children but do not legally marry; women defy parental orders and marry for love only to have the lover killed with themselves in destitution. Like Aubin, here Barker criticizes the form more through the plot lines of her stories rather than through the heroine's-author's acutal critique of the romance. Only once or twice does Barker permit a heroine to observe that surely she had been reading "some ridiculous *Romance*, or *Novel*, that inspired her with such a Vile Undertaking" (102).

"The History of Dorinda" is the best example of this merging of romance and romance criticism, and the use of masquerade. Barker is perceptive in linking the two traditions here. First, it is important to note that the storyteller is a man, and he recounts how he rescued Dorinda from a possible suicide. Once he has restored her to life, she tells him that, indeed, he had known her earlier. They had met at the playhouse. Her voracious reading of "Romantick Whimsies" causes her to think herself "a Heroine of the first rank; and all Men that Flatter'd or ogled me, were Heroes" (106); she thinks her rescuer one to be sure. But when she learns that he is married, she abandons him: "For Amongst all my Freaks and romantick Frolicks, I preserved my self from the great Offence" (107). Dorinda is one of Barker's most vocal, rational heroines; her analysis of her "Romantick Humour"

(108), which formed her thoughts for so long, is sophisticated. When she explains how her romantic vision clouds over her reason, she tells how she was enamoured of the footman:

> my Romantick Brain would make me imagine that he was of an Origin; (if known) above what he appeared: for he had been a Beggar-Boy, taken up at my Father's Grace, and was bred up in our House. . . . Then again, I would draw that Curtain from before the Eyes of my Reason, and behold him as the poor Beggar-boy *Jack*, whose business it had been to clean the Dog Kennels, and at last, for a reward of his well doing he was advanced to put on Livery. (111–12)

Her "Romantick Humour" wins, however, and she marries him. She is still disillusioned. Even when he invites her, after they are married, to attend him at his house in the country, she says:

> I was a little pleased, hoping my Romantick Notion was come true, and that I should find something suitable to his Person, which was truly handsome. But, good heavens! When we came to the Place, how was I amazed to find my self brought to a poor thatch'd Cottage! (115)

He leaves her there and goes off to London to visit her maid, where he thrives, gambling and whoring, nearly running through all her money. Dorinda's solution is the attempted suicide from which the narrator rescued her. Through him, she is reunited with her lost son.

Dorinda's tale is one of the few positive, happy-ending ones in *The Lining of the Patch-Work Screen*. Galecia compares these tales to "the Old *Romances*" (128) and remarks: "Amongst the Old Romances, said she to her self, we find strange and improbable Performances, very surprizing Turns and Rencounters; yet still all tended to vertuous Ends, and the Abhorrence of Vice" (128). It is just for such an educative purpose that Barker writes. As she remarks:

> Those honourable Romances of *Old Arcadia, Cleopatra, Cassandra* etc. discover a Genius of Vertue and Honour, and Heroines, as well as in the Authors that report them; but the Stories of our Times are so black, that the Authors, can hardly escape being smutted, or defil'd in touching such Pitch. (129)

Barker, however, is not stained by her contact with the romances and, in fact, tries to rescue their reputation through her own work. By and large, though, her greatest means of criticism is by rewriting their endings. She eschews the prevailing ideologies and does not find that romantic love justifies the powerlessness of women. Like much of the nonfictional literature, her heroines are caught in secondary, menial, subservient positions. As Jane Spencer concludes when considering the Galecia narratives in toto:

> While other writers were just beginning to experiment with the novel as the story of the heroine's journey to identity through marriage, Jane Barker was already offering an alternative pattern for the novel, with the creation of an unmarried heroine who achieves her identity through study, the practice of medicine, and writing.[6]

I argue further that Barker rewrites the romance by exploring the real fate of the seduced and harassed woman. Taken together, the women present a cavalcade of exploitation and disruption. Barker hopes to upset her readers from their complacent, romantic expectation with a view toward their new self-definition.

# Chapter 6
# Mary Davys

Mary Davys (1674–1732) more than any of the other pre-1740 novelists is concerned with examining the nature of fiction. Specifically, she is concerned with the viability of the romance genre, and she carefully scrutinizes its present state to ascertain how much she can subvert the form. She insists throughout her numerous prefaces that she is writing fact, not fantasy or romance. She provides a picture of the "truth," especially endeavoring "to restore the Purity and Empire of Love."[1] Although Aubin and Barker also study the romance form, it is Davys who takes the most critical view of the genre, realizing, indeed, the innovativeness of the form. "I had a Mind to make an Experiment whether it was not possible to divert the Town with real events just as they happen'd," she writes.[2]

Like her colleagues, Davys buries her radicalism in her scrupulous following of the established male tradition. In the preface to *The Reform'd Coquet,* she clarifies the men's position in her work by observing: "When I had written a Sheet or two of this Novel, I communicated my Design to a couple of young Gentlemen, whom I knew to be Men of Taste, and both my Friends; they approved of what I had done, advised me to proceed, then print it by Subscription."[3] According to this observation, male approval is necessary, if male patterns are followed. Yet, in the preface to *The Accomplish'd Rake,* echoing Defoe and Richardson, Davys argues for an independent use of the imagination: "Now this is to lose the only advantage of invention, which gives us room to order accidents better than Fortune will be at the pains to do, so to work upon the reader's passions, sometimes keep him in suspense between fear and hope, and at the last send him satisfied away."[4]

The prefaces also stress the importance of moral values (a prefigurement of Richardson), and it is as a moral instructor that the female novelist can succeed. Thus, to rescue the romance from the insipid state into which it has fallen and to justify the imagination is the author's goal. In her effort to reinterpret the male text, she concludes: "since Passions will ever have a place in the Actions of Men, and love a principal one, what cannot be removed or subdue'd, ought at least to be regulated."[5] Perceptively, Davys concludes that "if the Reformation would once begin from our Sex, the Men would follow it in spite of their Hearts."[6] In addition, she says: "My Pen is at the Service of the Publick, and yet it can but make some impression upon the young unthinking Minds of some of my own Sex, I shall bless my Labour, and reap an unspeakable Satisfaction."[7]

Thirty years ago William McBurney argued that Davys was a "forerunner" and "influence" on the accepted, canonical, eighteenth-century male novelist and his works with her rejection of the sensational, her support of the unconventional, and with love and marriage as the usual outcome of the romance. He concludes:

> Mrs. Davys is interesting as one of the few writers before 1740 to formulate a conscious theory of the novel, to show how realistic comedy might be adapted to the new genre, to place emphasis upon characterization and setting rather than upon simple variety of action, and to bring sturdy commonsense and humor to a literary form which had been dominated by the extravagant, the scandalous, and the sensational.[8]

McBurney presents the view of the female novelist that has been the accepted one until the last seven or eight years. Although his assessment of her literary endeavors is accurate, he is unaware of the extraordinary ambiguity that exists in the works themselves. Without a contemporary sensibility he is oblivious to her rebelliousness and hostility. Her prefaces speak to the controlling ideologies of the age; her novels offer rebellious alternatives to these ideologies.

\* \* \*

Davys's first venture, *The Lady's Tale* (1700),[9] is Abaliza's account of her love affair with Alcipus to her friend, Lucy. By recounting her amorous tale, she "unmasks" for her friend and displays her true self. Further, by having the beloved herself tell the tale, Davys is able to unmask the romance form, as she can be both participator and commentator on the action, for it is the oppressed-suppressed voice that speaks and reveals itself.

The story unfolds as Abaliza recounts her first meeting with the beloved stranger. Interestingly enough, their initial discussion concerns masks. Alcipus teases her:

> I see by that cruel Cloud, with which you have eclipsed your fine face, you thought me too happy when I gazed upon it bare. How many Advantages have you Ladies above our Sex, who can screen your beauties from Sun and Sight, whilst we are forced by Custom to expose ours to both, tho' sometimes, perhaps, we wou'd be glad to hide them? (2 : 354)

Abaliza is only superficially masked; her interchange with her father about his proposed lover clearly indicates that she is well aware of her heart—"for I shou'd think myself weak indeed, shou'd I give a Heart to one who never offer'd his" (2:356).

Abaliza forthrightly chooses not to disguise herself as the romantic heroine when she declares to Alcipus: "to let you see how industrious I am to secure you from broken Vows, I will never make you any, and then you will be sure that I at least shall never deceive you" (2:371). Rather, it is Alcipus who plays the disguised romance hero, for he has Adrastus initially pursue Abiliza and present his suit to her.

Alcipus continues his blind masquerade when he rushes off supposing Abaliza to be in love with the man on whose lap she is sitting. Unaware it is her uncle, he disguises himself as a wretched, scorned lover and "he [who] was once reckon'd one of the finest Men in a hundred Miles, is . . . now grown pale and lean, and one of the most melancholy" (2:389). Davys has reversed the usual romance expectation of the disguised heroine, and, instead, offers the reader both the masked hero and the sometimes disguised heroine, Abaliza. Even this early in the century, Davys is cognizant of the woman's position, and has her protagonist adopt disguises to suit her purposes and her search for fulfillment and self-identity.

At the conclusion of the tale, when she has been able to locate him, she "clapp'd on [a] Mask and then went towards him" (2:392), now she adopts the aggressor's role, declares her love, and minces no words as she describes her emotional state and commitment. By using the expected disguise at her discretion, Abaliza has been able to expose her own aggressive thoughts and thus invert the romance form.

Davys' ambivalence to the romance is evident in the conclusion. Abaliza is put in her place by her friend Lucy, who judges that both Abaliza and her conduct were "a little whimsical," "too pat"; her arguments "too weak"; "in fine, your whole Behaviour was a little too forward, which . . . is a fault in our Sex" (2:402). When she discards the submissive, subservient, feminine mask, she is condemned. So, although permitted to cast off the mask for a time and be aggressive, Davys's ambivalent feelings reassert themselves with the romance's happy ending.

*     *     *

Davys's *The Merry Wanderer* (1725),[10] a revised version of *The Fugitive* (1705), continues this sense of extreme ambiguity; in fact, its existence encapsulates and underscores the ambivalent position of the novelist herself. When the novel first existed as *The Fugitive*, it was a rebellious text; it displayed Davys's uncertainty about the future, her exile and isolation in Britain as an Irish person, and her general

discontent with her position as a female author. This tone of dislocation and disenfranchisement is greatly altered with the revision as *The
Merry Wanderer* (even the title change indicates the change in focus
and theme).

Rather than a tale of isolation and dislocation, *The Merry Wanderer*
is a story about masking, but it is disguise that leads to frustration and
deceit. The male protagonist is frequently taken in by the disguise, at
one time even discovering his mother beneath the prostitute's mask!
Pregnant women disguise themselves and try to seduce him; women
ridden with disease also try to abduct him. *The Merry Wanderer* shows
that disguise is a nasty game women play to trap men. Unable to be
themselves, women have hidden their true natures. Davys reveals this
ubiquitous ploy in the novel.

Coming so early in her career, *The Fugitive* is a troublesome piece
though. Not only is the disguise motif revealed in all its ambiguities,
but the piece itself that purports to be about unmasking is actually an
example of masking; the later version, *The Merry Wanderer*, is a
disguise of the discontent and unhappiness explored and vocalized in
the earlier *Fugitive*. Further, the novel involves several men disguised
as women—a tactic not frequently used by female novelists—with a
"message" that seems to be that men think it safer to be women in this
unstable world. Yet the feminocentric text reveals that it is unsafe to be
a woman.

In the female-centered texts of *The Familiar Letters, the Reform'd
Coquet,* and *The Cousins* Davys continues to explore this turmoil by
examining the romance fiction that masquerades as reality, thus supporting the controlling ideology of the age. In all three works, Davys
systematically strips the disguise from the romance fiction in an effort
to get at the true female self.

\*   \*   \*

Regarding Davys's *The Reform'd Coquet* (1720)[11] and *The Familiar
Letters* (1718),[12] Josephine Grieder observes that "What makes both
novels admirable is Mrs. Davys' understanding that psychology, not
sensationalism, gives fiction its substance."[13] It is just this understanding that allows Davys to unmask the ever-popular romance form,
review it, and revise it to make it her own. The promise displayed in
her earlier works, reaches full maturity here as she uncovers the
fatuous romance form while presenting a rich study of the masking
necessary and still undertaken by women.

*The Familiar Letters* provides, at first glance, a nonprovocative,
nonbiased examination of the correspondence between a male and
female friend. Much political cajolery is exchanged: she is a Whig; he,

a Tory. Comments are made about the foolishness of people in love. The first series of letters is heavy-handed with political matters, and finally Artander writes that he thinks their friendship so firm that "you will comply, when I beg of you to put a stop to this sort of Correspondence; and let your Letters for the future, be fill'd with the innocent Diversions of the Town: 'tis a pity Berina's Temper shou'd be ruffled with Politicks" (278). Berina's answer is direct:

> If Artander's Heart were not as hard as the Rock he has been scrutinizing into, he wou'd never have laid such strict Injunctions on my Pen, and robb'd me of my darling Pleasure; but to let you see how ready I am to relinquish every thing that gives you uneasiness, I have, in compliance with my friendship, laid by the Subject you dislike, and will, for the future, entertain you with something else. (280)

Davys here unmasks only to recover her female side. Berina will comply: she will mask her true inclinations and observations to please the man, but not before or without telling him what is truly on her mind. She will record the mildly soporific tale that he wishes, but she makes it clear that such tale telling is not her predilection.

Artander sends mixed signals. At first, he seems to want to know everything about her and develop a love relationship, but then he retreats and asks only for friendship; Artander masks his feelings. Berina, in my reading, seems to be clearer in her understanding of her true emotions; she is honest about stating her case: "Love is a thing so much against my grain, that tho' it be dressed up in a disguise of Wit, I see it thro' the Mask, and hate the base Imposture" (289). Berina indicates her nonpredilection for love as she remarks: "there is none so silly as this blinking God of Love: he makes mere Idiots of Mankind" (296). But it is really only a mask that she adopts to get Artander to declare his intentions, which he does in his letter of 1 January. He questions: "And is it sufficient Reason to withdraw your Friendship, because mine grows stronger? Don't Berina give me Cause to think you lie upon the Catch for an Opportunity to throw Artander off?" (301). Berina has it both ways. Although she wants romance to result (that is, marriage), she is unwilling to play the romance game.

The correspondence is refreshing, unguarded. For not only does Artander outline his steps of falling in love, thus unmasking this mysterious male process, but unlike the usually disguised, submissive woman, Berina speaks her mind as well. Perhaps *Familiar Letters* is the most important of Davys's works because of this clear-cut antiromantic attitude and feminine declaration. Berina is aware, though, that she must declare this state by masking her strong feminism in terms of masculine reference. As she writes:

> I shou'd despise a Husband as much as a King who wou'd give up his own Prerogative, or unman himself to make his Wife the Head: We Women are too weak to be trusted with Power, and don't know how to manage it without the Assistance of your Sex, tho' we oftenest shew that Weakness in the Choice of our Advisers. The Notion I have always had of Happiness in Marriage, is, where Love causes Obedience on one side, and Compliance on the other, with a View to the Duty Incumbent on both. (303)

Further, Berina is able to outline clearly what should be done concerning the mask that surrounds life. As she instructs Artander in one of the closing letters:

> But me thinks you are like a half-bred Player; you over act your Part: Then next time you put on the Lover, do it with an easier Air; 'tis quite out of fashion to talk of Dying, and Sighing, and killing Eyes, and such Stuff. (306)

Berina appears as the more rational and objective, more clear-sighted of the two; she is able to strip all the romances conventions to their essential points, and yet once this reduction has occurred, she slips back into the mask of compliance. *The Familiar Letters,* in the final analysis, is as bothersome as *The Lady's Tale* and *The Merry Wanderer,* for Berina, and through her Davys, ceases to mouth revolutionary statements at the end, and comes to support the male closure of the romantic, integrated ending. Yet she capitulates to such an ending only after she has subverted the form through the outspokenness of the heroine.

*  *  *

Still attempting to unmask the romance and find a voice, Davys begins *The Reform'd Coquet* ambitiously by declaring she will examine "the art of disguising" (2). The plot begins with the story of Callid and Froth, two would-be suitors to Amoranda, who plan to kidnap her to get her fortune. Their scheme is discovered by her maids, and Amoranda begins her own counterplot. In the meantime, she is directed by her uncle, E. Traffick, to attach herself to his old friend, Formator, who will serve as her guardian; he helps foil the plot to abduct her. Formator disguises himself as a toady to catch the culprits; they are dispatched and ultimately kill each other in a duel.

Formator takes over as her chief guide; "he made no doubt but one day he should see her the most accomplish'd of her Sex: in order to which, he provided a choice Collection of books for her, spent most of his time with her, diverted her with a thousand pleasant Stories" (53).

His name should announce his role: he is the "forming" agent, the molder, the hero in disguise.

As the hero in disguise it is generally assumed that he will get the woman at the end. What is more important in this romance is the movement of the heroine: from foolish, excluded, asexual maid, "giddy, thoughtless, inconsiderate . . . fit only for the company of those coxcombs I too frequently convers'd with" (160) to a mature, rational, marriageable woman. *The Reform'd Coquet* provides one of the earliest attempts at a female *bildungsroman* in the period that forthrightly traces the woman's romance journey of self-identity.

Davys's approach vis-à-vis the romance is different from her work in *The Familiar Letters*. Rather than discredit the romance by talking about it, expressing attitudes antithetical to its very raison d'être, she examines the form by placing a three-dimensional heroine against the typically romantic one-sided one. Amoranda is the new heroine.

To highlight her own role, Davys tells the "whinning romantick" (56) tale of Altemira, who has disguised herself as "a poor, thin, pale, meagre young Creature, hardly able to sit [a] Horse" (55), because she is running away from the advances of her brother. She is also duped by Lord Lofty, who tricks her into losing her maidenhead. He is helped in his schemes by the false Kitty. After he has had his way with her and absconds with Kitty for London, Altemira remarks: "my cruel Disquiet of Mind made so great an alteration in my Face, that when I came to look at it, I could not believe that I was *Altemira*" (74). To get her revenge, Altemira conspires with Amoranda to unmask Lord Lofty. Contrary to the expected passivity of the romance heroine, Amoranda takes affairs into her own hands and arranges an assignation for the summer house, carefully orchestrating the unmasking scene. Amoranda disguises Altemira as herself and arranges for a "marriage" to take place between "Amoranda" and Lord Lofty. In point of fact, he marries Altemira disguised as Amoranda, thus making Altemira an honest woman and righting his wrongs.

One treacherous plot is unmasked and is metamorphosed into something better. Unfortunately, the story does not end there. Berintha and an old school friend are introduced to Amoranda's household, and again the plot depends on disguise, for "Berintha" is a man who has fallen in love with Amoranda. She berates his "clandestine means" and by so doing presents Davys's own views on this surreptitious male method:

> Do you think, Sir, *said she, turning to him,* I am so fond of my own Sex, that I can like nothing but what appears in Petticoats? Had you come like a

Gentleman, as such I would have received you; but a disguised Lover is always conscious of some Demerit, and dares not trust to his right Form, till by a false appearance he tries the Lady: if he finds her weak and yielding, the day's his own; and he goes off in triumph; but if she has Courage to baffle the Fool, he sneaks away with his disappointment, and thinks nobody will know any thing of the matter. (108)

Davys continues: "Biranthus, for that was his True Name, was stung to the very Soul to hear Amoranda so smart upon him, but was yet resolved to disguise his Mind as well as his body" (108–9). Unable to cope with the new forthright woman, he can only resort to brute force: he kidnaps her and takes her to a deep woods. In good romantic fashion, she is rescued by Alanthus, the disguised Formator, her guardian and teacher, who subsequently reveals himself.

Masking here is used as a truth revealer, for she would accept the advice better from the "older" man, just as Amoranda would reveal herself, tell more of her love, to the man not loved. The conclusion brings about complete revelations and all the principals live happily ever after.

Davys's use of disguise is straightforward here. Because she does not have her heroine disguise herself, no great revelations of the interior female self can occur. Instead, we are privy to the machinations that the man adopts to gain and control the woman. Not only did Formator attempt to form her mind, but as Alanthus, he forms her love and emotional life as well. The coquet is reformed because that is the only way that the man can deal with her. Although Amoranda practices control—she engineers Altimira's wedding—it is a control carefully executed by the man.

The Reform'd Coquet displays Davys's great dismay with the eighteenth-century feminine world. The woman is trapped and controlled by the man who is the disguiser; she can only decipher as much as he permits. When the masks are discarded at the conclusion, it is to reveal a world that still forces the woman to hide her true self. Amoranda has been a pawn throughout the game played by the disguised men in the plot. She has only been allowed to react to them and their disguises; she has never been the instigator of the masquerade. (Even the "wedding" is a reaction to a male plot.) Yet great ambivalence exists here, for though the heroine must remain dumb to all the masquerading, the reader and author are allowed to see the face and motives beneath the mask.

*    *    *

Davys's preoccupation with unmasking is further exploited in her use of her critical prefaces and forewords; in them, she attempts to strip the disguise from the novelist's art and reveals the true state of romance writing. In the preface to *The Cousins* (1725) (revised in 1732 as *The False Friend*),[14] for example, she examines the state of the romance and tries to rescue it from the disuse and disfavor into which it has fallen. The romance, the relation of "probably feigned Stories," has fallen out of favor, she observes, because "the World's being surfeited with such as were either flat and insipid, or offensive to Modesty and good Manners; that they found them only a Circle and Repetition of the same Adventures" (407); "the commonest Matters of Fact, truly told, would have been much more entertaining" (408), she concludes, and so Davys tries to expose this romance mystique and tell the true adventures of love. This goal recurs in *The Lady's Tale*, *The Merry Wanderer, Familiar Letters*, and *The Reform'd Coquet*. In *The Cousins*, Davys once more strips away the mask of male hypocrisy as she tells the story of Elvira.

The doubting father, Gonsalvo, places his daughter Elvira in the care of his closest friend, Alvaro. When Gonsalva is forced to go away on business, "the other began his Wickedness; and, pulling off the Mask, he appeared bare-fac'd to the innocent Elvira, who had never defil'd her Thoughts with any thing so base as his Designs. He began by degrees to insinuate himself into her Favour, and first by one Stratagem, and then another, strove to work her into a liking of him" (418). But Elvira "was wholly unskill'd in the Art of Dissembling her self, and that made it the harder for her to find out [the] old Practitioner" (418). Her father returns, stops the rape, rescues her, and sends her off with her sister for a period of time. Then her aunt tries to engineer a love attraction with Sebastian, but Elvira falls in love with Emila's son, Lorenzo, instead. Many plot complications arise, but the final resolution finds Elvira united with Lorenzo and Octavio with his Clara; the unfaithful and deceitful, "false friend," Alvaro is punished for his ungenerousness, and the treacherous Portuguese, Sebastian, is equally punished.

Unfortunately, Davys relies more and more in the final pages of her text on just working out the love stories; her initial interest in eschewing the romance element is lost, and she is forced into telling a story that is similar to the French romance but with fewer plot complications. The promise offered to the reader in the preface does not seem to be fully justified in the text proper.

\* \* \*

With her last novel, *The Accomplish'd Rake: or, Modern Fine Gentleman*, Davys attempts, once and for all, to unmask the ambiguity of her age. On the surface, however, this story bears little resemblance to the romance. Davys is, in the last analysis, unable to achieve her goal, and the complex, feminine ideologies created by the male remain.

In her effort to uncover all the male mystique that governs her concepts of femininity, Davys creates a male protagonist, Sir John Galliard, and traces the making of him into a "modern fine gentleman," thus promoting the theology of the novel and the restoration of Sir John. Even this task is fraught with ambiguity, however. The first paragraph of the tale pleads for authorial license and imagination with the intermixing "now and then a pretty little lie" (241). Teachwell, Sir John's tutor, defines this new man:

> You are to kill your man before you can be reckoned brave. You must destroy your constitution with diseases ere you are allowed a man of gallantry; unman yourself by immoderate drinking to qualify you for a boon companion; blaspheme your Maker by execrable oaths and curses to avoid all show of sneaking religion. And if fortune forgets to be your friend, while the dice are in your hand, you must fling away your estate to some winning bully, lest you should pass for a man of prudence and thought. . . . and thus Sir John, I have described the modern man of honor. (262)

Yet it is an image that neither the characters nor Davys can comprehend. All he must do, it seems, is dress the part. When Teachwell dies, Sir John "is now left at London, sole master of his own actions" (277). In addition, "The first progress he made in modern gallantry was to get into the unimproving conversation of the women of the town, who often took care to drink him up to a pitch of stupidity, the better to qualify him for having his pockets picked" (277).

Sir John's education into the misrepresented role of modern fine gentleman continues as he romances Miss Friendly, the niece of his friend. He takes Miss Friendly and Miss Wary to the masquerade, where Miss Friendly tells him: "For my part, I intend to personate a sea nymph and dress in moss and shells. You, sir John, may appear like Neptune, because you know he is as much obliged to take care of the ladies of his own dominion as you are to protect me" (284). The masquerade, typically, allows the woman to exercise her hidden nature. Here, for example, Miss Friendly and Miss Ware exchange costumes to enjoy Sir John to the fullest. They indulge in a "double masquerade" (286). When he absconds with the supposed Miss Friendly to the bagnio, however, the deceit is revealed, and Miss Wary is dismissed summarily. While at the bagnio, Sir John encounters the masked "man" from the masquerade only to find that it is a woman in disguise, and a married one at that. She is retreating from a husband who cannot father an heir after eight years of marriage. Although they enjoy each other's company for the evening, Sir John is still intent on Miss Friendly. He continues to mask his lecherous designs on her, conveys an opiate to some macaroons, and quietly waits the most auspicious moment to give them to her. She is undone but totally unaware of the violation.

The story continues until Sir John is willing to claim the paternity of the son he begot with the drugged Miss Friendly. He is motivated to do so by Belinda, the only woman who is able to make him ashamed of his actions. He finally begins to think about his treatment of Miss Friendly, and the denouement of *The Accomplish'd Rake* quickly finds Sir John unmasking and becoming the "man of honour" (373) he was born to be. His villainy has been unmasked as shame, and the happy ending has been restored.

As is typical with these early eighteenth-century works, when confronted with the formidable male text, rhetorical strategy, and ideology, *The Accomplish'd Rake* supports the dominant power. The ambivalence that might have predominated in the novel's pages is reconciled, and male closure is assumed. The ideology of romantic love usurps its place, and the myth of female powerlessness is once more ensconced.

\* \* \*

As a novelist of the early decades of the eighteenth century, Davys demonstrates the complexity and the extreme ambiguity of these years. Within her novels, the clash between the two conflicting male ideologies—romantic love and female powerlessness—display themselves in all their ambivalence. Her early pieces, like *The Lady's Tale* and *The Familiar Letters,* define a position and a rebelliousness that Davys was unable to maintain in her later years. She makes clear statements that she is out to challenge the established, accepted romance ideology that sees each novel as a courtship story with the denouement predetermined as a marriage choice. Here the woman has no choice but is merely moved through a series of adventures until it is time for the hero to rescue her; she is left powerless. This type of resolution is not the case with Davys's early heroines, most especially Berina *(Familiar Letters)*. She controls their correspondence to a large extent and is vocal in expressing her likes and dislikes; she disrupts the typical narrative with her aggressive remarks that do not suit the ideology of the powerless woman. Davys herself is challenging enough initially to make statements about the value of the female life. Initially she attempts to unmask the pervasive and dominant romantic mode, but finds herself, as her career continues, trapped and hedged in by its conventions. Her last novel, *The Accomplish'd Rake,* is almost a

complete reversal, as it tells and supports the "male text." The protagonist, Sir John Galliard, uses masks throughout the work, as he
seduces and rapes numerous women who all remain in a position of
powerlessness to him. Davys tells *his* story and is hesitant to present
Miss Friendly's tale, the unwitting victim of his greatest hoax; therefore, the reader ultimately views the tale from the male perspective:
the powerful, romantic viewpoint.

Surprisingly enough for an early novelist, Davys was interested,
then, not in perpetuating the fatuous, oftentimes frivolous romantic
trappings of the popular form, but, like her contemporary Jane Barker, in unmasking the unrealistic, romanticized presentations found in
most popular fiction. In contrast to the scandal novels and the cloying
courtship novels, she presents unmasked heroines and undisguised
romances. Yet, her earlier tone of defiance sounded with *The Familiar
Letters* by the end has been translated into the more popular and
predominant voice of the all-powerful man. In the earlier works, the
female text had been able to insert itself within the pervasive male
story. But Davys solidifies herself as her work continues, and the
initial avant-garde position becomes more conservative. This new
position is marked in the text by her more standard use of the
masquerade until, in her last piece, she uses the conventional masquerade as part of the plot advancement technique in the story itself.

Considering her entire corpus, then, one finds that Davys does not
live up to the promise displayed in her earlier pieces, for the rebellion
announced in *The Familiar Letters* is finally masked in *The Accomplish'd
Rake* until little of the true feminocentric text is left exposed. Her
work, in actual fact, demonstrates exactly what the masquerade and
romance disguise are all about: capitulation to the controlling and all-
powerful male world.

# Chapter 7
# Mary Collyer

The 1740s witnessed a surge in antiromantic feeling, and by mid-century new attitudes had infiltrated the novel scene, specifically in the works of Richardson and Fielding. Critics today no longer claim *Pamela* to be the first English novel, yet in ways it still remains a watershed work. It is the attitudes Richardson propounded in his "new species of writing" that affect the work of the popular, minor female novelists. Richardson emphasized three things about his new rhetoric: writing to the moment, depicting familiar scenes, and inculcating moral values into the romance. It is the third point that is particularly pertinent to the female writers, especially those post-*Pamela*. We have seen since the earliest pieces that the female novelists have been using the romance form to express their concern and dismay with the eighteenth-century woman's position. With the novels before *Pamela,* however, this criticism was hidden in the disruption and distortion of the accepted feminine form, the romance, together with a corruption of the disguise strategy. Aubin, Barker, Davys, and Haywood make heroines of female protagonists who are treated anyway but the way a heroine, in the old school of romance, would be. With Richardson's inculcation of virtue and morality, a shift occurs in the presentation of the female romance. More value and merit is suddenly attached to the form; the authors become more morally prescriptive and instructive. Beginning with Mary Collyer's *Letters from Felicia to Charlotte* and climaxing in Sarah Fielding's *The Cry* and the many novels by Charlotte Smith, the romance form is openly examined and criticized, moral structures are probed, and women are able to explore their fate in a less disguised, less male-dominated way.

Samuel Johnson himself was aware of this shift in focus, and he notes in the *Rambler* that the "words of fiction, with which the present generation seems more particularly delighted, are such as exhibit life in its true state, diversified only by accidents that daily happen in the world, and influenced by passions and qualities which are really to be found in conversing with mankind."[1] Thus it is that the later female novelists explore and critique the very form they write. Like earlier female writers, they participate in the patterns established by the male figures: Richardson, Fielding, and Smollett, yet the second generation more consciously and meticulously examines these male patterns and finds them wanting.

The second half of the eighteenth-century novel scene finds Richardson, Fielding, and Smollett claiming a mimetic defense for their own work, a true-to-life approach that is absent in the high-blown romances of the continent and the earlier century works. Taking their cue from these male writers, the post-1740s female novelists also investigated this "realism" and found it to be the rationale of romance genre. In this context, they explored in their prefaces and the novels themselves the criteria of the romance and became preoccupied with defending the ethical utility of their works. Disguises were discarded except for pure plot machinations. After 1740 a spirit of moral earnestness enters the novel,[2] but it is a seriousness, unfortunately, that was applied to only the male writers. Dale Spender argues that around 1740 the notion of categorization occurs within the British fiction scene. She notes:

> Women who persisted with their literary endeavors were enjoined—implored—to confine themselves to what they knew. They were advised that their strengths lay in their exploration of women's world, in romance, the domestic scene. And once this categorization of women's writing ability was pronounced, it was soon achieved. If not in the writing of women, certainly in the minds of men. And so we have in the containment of women, a male romance, a "picturesque falsehood" constructed in male interest.[3]

Spender goes on to argue that this distinction is one based on sex and power. There would be no more *Pamelas,* in which a romance was invested with universal significance.

> Henceforward, women writers could be appreciated for their drawing room observations, their emphasis on manners, their attention to fine detail; they could be motivated by concerns of the heart. In contrast, men writers could be appreciated for their largesse and vigour, their emphasis on morals, their broad canvas of the wide world; they could be motivated by concerns of the mind.[4]

Women's writing is devalued. Even more, the form that most female writers use, that is, the romance, is similarly dismissed. The midcentury publication of *Pamela* causes a subversive and undercover evaluation of women's writing.

Female writers from the earliest part of the eighteenth century have been concerned with the frivolous nature ascribed to their writing together with their condition as writers and that of the average woman. Their concern becomes subversive, however. The insistence on nonhappy endings, the scandalously disruptive treatment of the female characters, the savagery of the description all point to the subversion of the supposedly typical female form. Yet, after the publication of *Pamela,* a romance with universal significance, and its extreme popularity, the female writers of romance could turn their attention to a more thorough investigation of the form and not be criticized. Collyer's *Letters from Felicia to Charlotte* is the beginning of a long and important subgenre whose members not only write romances but criticize them as well. The genre explodes. Suddenly everyone is talking about, reading, and writing romances. The disguise that the earlier novelists had to employ for criticism is discarded; a new, more forthright, open, and honest voice takes its place.

\* \* \*

Mary Collyer's (?–1763) midcentury work, *Letters from Felicia to Charlotte* (1744)[5] presents a transitional use of the masquerade topos and romance genre. This work combines the intense interest in masked truth telling and the revelation of the early-century works together with those late-century pieces concerned with unmasking the popular fiction in terms of its most predominant form, the romance. Collyer effectively manages to combine both concerns as she presents characters who, while they masquerade, comment on their disguise. They write romances as well as read them, and they are adept at hiding personal information under the cover of fiction.

Letter fiction itself is well designed to combine masking and revelation. It is a type that allows the women to unveil their inmost thoughts to each other and, therefore, to the female readership at large while discreetly disguising these truths in normal communication. Felicia sets the tone of the entire correspondence when she writes in her first letter to Charlotte:

> How agreeable is the thought, that as often as you hear from me, you will learn every thing that passes in the soul of your friend, whilst I in return shall meet with the same proof of an *open, undisguised* friendship from you! For my part, I intend to discover all the secret folds of my heart, and to *unbosom* myself to you without the *lest reserve,* as I am persuaded I shall never have any secrets which you have not a right to be acquainted with, and which I shall not be very ready to communicate. Pray do you follow my example; write with the *same unreserved freedom,* and *never disguise* those little affairs in which your heart is concerned. (1:2; emphasis added)

Collyer's argument for honesty governs her presentation of her characters. Like her foremothers in the early part of the century, she makes a strong statement about her ability to present a realistic picture. Yet, she cautions, her realism is tinged with "romanticism," a certain coloring of the imagination. Although she tells Charlotte in her third letter that the "sylvan diety . . . is a mere earthly being, as very a mortal as you or I" (1 : 17), it is "the native beauties of this rural retreat" that, she continues, "are so far from being heightened by my description, that were you with me, you would hardly think I had done them justice" (1 : 17). Felicia insists, however, that these scenes are not "the invention of a luxuriant fancy" (1 : 17), and she goes on to justify the realism of her vision.

Her entire attitude is down to earth. When the magnificent stranger enters, Felicia is quick to point out that he is "not much taller than I am: which by the way, is much too short for the hero of a romance" (1 : 22). He is fashionless enough to wear his hair "in natural curls" (1 : 22), and his thoughts center on truth and virtue so much so that he is insensible to the "idea of those fancied charms, those fashionable accomplishments which are necesary to form the character of the fine gentleman" (1 : 22–23).

Not only is Lucius unlike a romantic hero in appearance, but his deportment is equally unremarkable, that is, realistic rather than romantic. With a faltering voice and many blushes, he attempts to declare his interest in Felicia. Unlike the traditional hero of romance, however, his tongue is not gilded over, nor are his thoughts like so much honey; he does not know the romance jargon. When Felicia answers that she is not adverse to his advances, Charlotte, she expects, is waiting for the great crashing romantic crescendos:

> You are now ready to imagine that I shall describe him throwing himself at my feet, while with a flow of rapture, he admires my superlative goodness, blending his praises with two or three hundred adorables, transcended excellencies, infinite perfections, incomparable creatures, and abundance of other fine things of the same strain; and that to conclude his panegyric, he tells me how astonished he is, that a goddess so heavenly fair, can have the condescension to cast the lustre of her brilliant eyes, and raise to life a wretch so contemptible, so absolutely beneath her least regard.—But if [so you ]were extremely mistaken; for I did not hear him utter the least syllable of this sublime nonsense. (1 : 69)

Felicia, however, is nothing if she is not honest: she hides nothing. Her admiration of his realistic, nondisguised love declaration is soon dispelled when Felicia learns that she has just come into a considerable inheritance from her uncle in the East Indies. Such news is not good, however, because she will be separated even more from Lucius. Yet Felicia/Collyer is realistic and concludes in a very unromantic tone: "however romantic the Platonic friendship you propose may appear, I readily accept it, since that is all that either you or I ought to hope for" (1:87).

Felicia further unmasks the romance as she writes to Charlotte:

> From amaranthine bowers, and embrowning shades, from flowery lawns and all the silent, solemn scenes of peaceful innocence and harmless love, thy friend Felicia greets her other self, her dear, her most beloved Charlotte.
>
> Don't you think now, my dear, by this beginning, that I am tolerable well read in romance and have drunk deep of the spirit of those extraordinary performances. At least I think I ought to have some knowledge of them, since I seem to be writing one myself. My plot now begins to thicken; and I shall certainly, if ever these letters come to light, be considered in some future time, as a little heroine, while Lucius will have an undisputed claim to the honour of being the hero of my story. . . . but you need not be frightened, *here are no fiery dragons to conquer, or enchanted castle to storm.* . . . I will therefore leave these marvellous events to the doughty wonder-working champions of ancient date, and *content myself* with *sticking close to truth and nature;* and don't doubt but that in the rustic simplicity in which I spend my time, *I shall furnish a history as entertaining as theirs.* And indeed whatever name is given to my story, whether of rural adventures, novel, romance, I should be very well satisfied, though all the world thought it fictitious, might I at last . . . have it concluded, like the most celebrated pieces of imaginary scenes of love and gallantry, in a happy catastrophe. (1:122–23; emphasis added)

Collyer's candor is unparalleled in the pre-1740s pieces. Not until Sarah Fielding will we find such explicit exposure of the romance form. She even observes that they cannot learn from the romances:

> we have read novels, romances, and plays . . . but I believe we were neither of us form'd for intrigue, since with all our industry we can't yet invent any method to procure me the company of my lover (1:141).

Collyer's *Letters* is remarkable for the tact and sprightliness with which she invests the hackneyed romance convention. By using the "romance" plot but then uncovering it, Collyer is able to demonstrate the viability of the romance in the new age. The clearest example of this unmasking occurs with the subplot involving Mellifont, who tries to win her affections with his "spoils" of war. Collyer writes:

> When stamping with his foot, his trusty squire enter'd with the stuffed skins of several badgers, and other beasts of prey, the spoils of his hall,

when Mellifont bending one knee, laid them at my feet, and resting upon his spear, "See, fair Princess," said he, bowing low his head, "a knight renown'd for acts of chivalry, who lays at your divine feet the ravagers of the mountains and the vallies, but lower still he would lay his heart."

This set speech which he uttered with the utmost gravity and solemnity, he had doubtless studied before; I entered the room. . . . When struggling against a smile, I assum'd a smile, and looking down upon him with a lofty superiority and contempt, "Avaunt catif vile," cried I, "and think not to abuse my ears with thy audacious forgeries. Are these, wretch, the trophies of thy valor! where are the distressed virgins that thou hast delivered from the poisonous talon of fiery dragons, or the dreadful gripe of monstrous giants." . . . Here I turn'd hastily from him, and walking with a majestic stateliness seated myself at the other end of the room. . . . But I had no sooner turn'd my back, *than throwing away his masking ornaments,* he stepp'd up to me. . . . "Don't you think, Madam," cried he, "that *we have acted our parts to perfection? . . .* Madam, you are sensible it was *in disguise* that you made me a convert to love." . . . Here he paused, but instantly recollected himself, "O Madam," cried he, smiling and rubbing his hands, "I have a lucky thought; *permit me to assume another disguise;* as you first appeared to me a goddess, let me for once be disguis'd like a god. . . . *In his appearance who knows what wonders I may perform!*" (1:165–67; emphasis added)

Collyer further unmasks the romance plot when she has Mellifont, unable to win Felicia's affections, turn to Amelia, "a thing which however common in real life, is seldom or never heard of in romance" (1:181).

With Prudilla's unmasking (she had forged letters to Lucius from Felicia) and the reconciliation with her father, the plot complications of the first volume are concluded. The second volume of *Letters from Felicia to Charlotte* begins, unlike Felicia's first letter of the first volume, disclaiming all contact with romance and disguise; she tells Charlotte not

> to expect any more romantic adventure. I have nothing now to do, with the affecting scenes of fond distress, the pangs of jealousy, or the heart [to] incur . . . a father's displeasure. . . . regularity and order, peace and tranquility, have taken up their residence in our happy dwelling (2:4)

Because Felicia is a bride of three weeks, she expects only tranquility and reality. Yet her correspondence subtext changes. Felicia begins her twenty-eighth letter by apologizing for her three-month silence; she has been busy, she explains, being a wife. Much of the volume is taken up with Felicia's accounts of the rural people she meets. She shifts from the romantic, courtship presentation of the first volume to a realistic appraisal of life in the country. (See her thirty-second letter and her account of the country dialect). Like Richardson's *Pamela* and *Pamela II,* there is a distinct falling off in the action and in the presentation after the marriage occurs; marriage and romance seem to be antithetical. Romance is so unmasked in this volume that Lucius and Felicia learn the sordid truth of his liaison with Prudilla, the illegitimate child they produced; further realism occurs as Felicia and Lucius must decide what to do with the child.

The last letter of the collection further emphasizes this focus on realism, which the second volume especially trumpeted. It is written *from* Charlotte and includes her observations on everything she has read about and now seen. She writes of the difference between "frank behaviour . . . and all the low acts of disguise" (2:304).

Collyer has managed to examine fiction, the nature of fiction, and the nature of reality. Collyer's work points the way to the fiction of the second half of the century. The use of the romance topos continues to be the primary focus, and its investigation produces a group of novels that are even more frank and revealing than the disguise novels of the early years. The happy ending is almost forgotten as the later novelists examine the untruthful mask that the romance panacea oftentimes presents.

# Part 2
# Masquerading the Romance

Read me, and take me.

—Haywood, *The Masquerades* 2:21

# Chapter 8

# The Later Haywood

*The History of Miss Betsy Thoughtless* (1751)[1] following the success of Collyer's *Felicia to Charlotte* (1744) and Richardson's *Pamela* (1741) demonstrates, first of all, Haywood's chameleon-like ability to follow the popular form, in this case, the morally acceptable romance-novel. Richardson's emphasis on the educability of the feminine public in their moral awareness is echoed in Haywood's treatment of her own Miss Betsy Thoughtless.

Unlike Richardson and Collyer, however, Haywood's *Betsy Thoughtless* initiates a new era in the presentation and depiction of the female character. With Pamela and all those earlier Gigantillas, Baronesses, and Placentias, the reader is unable to detect any movement on the heroine's part: each begins and ends in the same moral position. With Betsy Thoughtless, conversely, the reader is actively engaged in watching the dynamics of change and learning a moral perception. Betsy becomes the first of many heroines who makes mistakes, learns from these peccadilloes, and is ultimately rewarded with happiness—she becomes a paradigm of the reformed heroine. Jane Spencer argues that this tradition is begun by women novelists and is followed by them exclusively.[2] It is an acceptable and understandable role for the female novelist, she continues, because it casts her in the role of "teacher," one of the few acceptable female occupations.

It is in just such a position that Sarah Fielding, Charlotte Lennox, and Charlotte Smith view themselves as well. Through their heroines, they are able to educate most of their female readership by presenting what they think is the morally correct position for women in the eighteenth century. Unlike female novelists of the earlier part of the century, they clearly and outspokenly define their position in their prefaces. Their stories are always about a fallible but unfallen heroine (Smith has one exception) who must learn to accept her position in life. In addition, almost all of them include an actual romancier or fiction maker/writer among their cast of characters who ends up speaking for the author herself; in several of the pieces, the authors actually speak to their readership in their own voices. Many have theorized about their profession and the romance writing that occurs in these post-1740 pieces, with the most important of these works being Sarah Fielding's *The Cry*. Even though the authors, and, subsequently, some of their characters are much more outspoken, some disguising of true sentiments and feminine thoughts in these later works still occurs. Yet, by and large, more candor and forthrightness emerges in these pieces.

Betsy Thoughtless, like every heroine before her, wants power. Her initial mistakes are precipitated because of her undisguised search for and desire for control and power. From the feminist viewpoint, what Betsy Thoughtless has to learn is not how to still want power but how to gain it subversively. The message has not changed—women still want control; it is just that they can now seek it in a more educated, less disguised way. The necessity of disguise together with the logic of the romance still makes up the prime instruments in this ongoing struggle. Now, however, less subterfuge exists on the novelists's part, and readers are aware of the educative value of what they read. As Haywood writes:

> Though it is certain that few young handsome ladies are without some share of the vanity here described . . . it is, however, for the sake of those who are so, that these pages are wrote [*sic*], to the end they may use their utmost endeavours to correct that error, as they will find it so fatal to the happiness of one who had scarce any other blameable propensity in her whole composition. (1 : 124)

Yet like all the other female writers of the period, a certain ambivalence exists, which also affects Haywood herself. Haywood can still ask: "Though it is certainly necessary to inculcate into young girls all imaginable precaution in regard to their behavior towards those of another sex, yet I know not if it is not an error to dwell too much upon that Topick" (1 : 7).

Haywood dwells on just that topic in *The History of Miss Thoughtless*. The popular "courtship" novel is brought to fruition here in the witty rendition of Betsy Thoughtless's move from an asexual, innocent ingenue to a mature, wise, sexual woman. It is *the* romance plot, but like the other writers in the latter decades, it is a romance that is studied, examined, and thoroughly analyzed. Even toward the end of her writing career, Haywood is still faced with examining the romance genre and female roles through the use of disguise. The age was still beset with ambivalent ideologies. Betsy Thoughtless physically and metaphorically masks her revolutionary tendencies from the conventional world only to have these disguises, ideologies, and principles reemerge during her fiction making and under the cover of her dreams. Disguise, here, is the educational tool that Betsy must experience before she is allowed to become an adult. Through masking, the adolescent Betsy is allowed to experience other selves, and through these masks, she forms and determines her own adult self.

In her later novels, Haywood openly discusses the fictions and masks that she had earlier viewed only in a disguised fashion. Betsy must learn, in other words, to stop making fictions that hide her state and, instead, confront her life as it really is. She must be taught the difference between appearance and reality; Betsy must learn to distinguish between the glittering but false fictions both women and men offer her as panaceas to her deplorably exploited state and the reality, ugly though it be, of her true position of being female.

*Betsy Thoughtless,* then, is about disguise; it is about the masquerading effects the man forces on the woman, her initial, passive acceptance of them, followed by a revolutionary rejection of these same fictitious, fallacious masks. The novel begins by stating such a concern; the title of chapter 1—"Gives the Reader room to guess at what is to ensue, tho' ten to one but he finds himself deceived"—emphasizes the idea of mask and deception. The reader, together with the protagonist, must sift out disguise from fact, reality from fiction. The inner fabric of the text is an interlocking narrative of rumors and false accounts. Like the characters themselves, the reader has to decide what stories to believe—that is, is Betsy really a prostitute just because tales have been spread about her loose behavior?

Betsy is not quite as thoughtless as Haywood would, I believe, first have her readers think. She is aware of the ultimate seriousness of the marriage game that she plays (in true romance fashion, *The History of Miss Betsy Thoughtless* is about Betsy's ability to find a husband) and is also conscious that her current, frivolous behavior is not conducive to forming a lasting relationship.

> She had too much good sense not to know it suited not with the condition of a wife to indulge herself in the gaieties she at present did, which though innocent, and, as she thought, becoming enough in the present state she now was, might not be altogether pleasing to one, who, if he so thought proper, had the power of restraining them. In fine, she looked upon a serious behavior as unsuitable to one of her years, and therefore resolved not to enter into a Condition, which demanded some share of it, at least for a long time; that is, when she should be grown weary of the admiration, flatteries, and addresses of the men, and no longer found any pleasure in seeing herself preferred before all the women of her acquaintance. (1:128–29)

This vanity, however, causes her to create fictions about herself and prevents her from seeing the reality both of herself and of Mr. Trueworth. She continues the flirtations with Mr. Staple and Mr. Hysom, noting that "Whoever thinks to gain me must be in a hurry, like Captain Hysom" (1:240). Betsy is besieged by everyone to accept Trueworth, and when Trueworth's aunt tries to find out the "truth" about their relationship, Betsy's fictitious accounts only cloud the issue.

> [His aunt] was extremely troubled to find their answers such, as were no way conformable to the idea Mr. Trueworth had endeavoured to inspire her with of his mistress' perfection. . . . Poor Miss Betsy, as the reader has had too much opportunity to observe, was far from setting forth to any advantage, the real good qualities she was possessed of:—on the contrary, the levity of her conduct rather disfigured the native innocence of her mind, and the purity of her intention. (2:86)

Although Betsy disguises herself, she is aware that underneath the facile mask, she is a sensible young woman; temporarily, however, she prefers flirting with the notion of romance and frivolity. So, too, Haywood reveals through her own exterior fiction mask a more serious interior. When Trueworth speaks in the dulcet tones of a romance hero offering Betsy a refuge from "the confused glare of pomp and public shews . . . in the shady bowers, or on the banks of a sweet purling stream" (2:89), Betsy's reaction is Haywood's:

> Shady bowers! and purling streams!—Heavens, how insipid! . . . you may be the Strephon of the woods, if you think fit; but I shall never envy the happiness of the Chloe that accompanies you in these fine recesses.— What! to be cooped up like a tame dove, or to coo,—and bill,—and breed?—O, it would be a delicious life indeed. (2:89)

Haywood and Betsy agree: no longer can the reality be covered over with romantic fictions—purling streams, insipid maidens, and shady bowers indeed! Through Betsy and her masking, Haywood will reveal the perception that is necessary for women to adopt, though it is a perception that ultimately must be adopted to a married state. *Betsy Thoughtless* does not (like some of Haywood's earlier works) preach a state of female singleness. It does celebrate marriage, but only when it can be entered into with no fictions, illusions, and romantic dreams.

Haywood finds that it is not just women who are at fault with this fictitious vision. Trueworth is a worse offender than Betsy. Initially he is almost incapable of viewing a truthful situation. When he and his friend, Sir Bazil Loveit, go to visit Miss Foreward, who with her "certain air of libertinism, both in her looks and gestures, which would have convinced Mr. Trueworth, if he had not been told so before, that she was one of those unhappy creatures, who make traffic of their beauty" (2:93–94), he finds Betsy there (she has come to visit her friend). Trueworth is shocked and almost convinced she has become one of "those" women herself. Trueworth, Haywood painstakingly points out, judges everything by appearance:

> fain would he have believed her innocent as she was lovely, but could not tell him to conceive there was a possibility for true virtue to take delight in the company of vice. . . . never were thoughts so divided,—so fluctuating as his;—his good understanding, and jealousy of honour, convinced him, there could be no lasting happiness with a person of Miss Betsy's temper. (2:98)

But then Trueworth reasons that once married, he will be able to restrain and teach her how to see his "purling streams, and shady bowers." Of course, Haywood is just as careful to show that his vision needs to be corrected as well. When Betsy explains that she and Miss Foreward are friends from boarding school days, Trueworth is slightly placated. The entire point of this incident, however, is to show that fiction and appearances often mask an important reality. Only Betsy is aware of the fabrications and lies that are involved with fiction, and she tells Trueworth: "Whenever I am convinced, that she is unworthy of my friendship, it must be by her own actions, not by the report of others" (2:105). Trueworth comes off the worse in this exchange. Later, after Betsy has more closely observed Miss Forward and the company she keeps, after she is attacked in the coach by one of Miss Forward's rakes, driven to a bagnio and "thought a common prostitue" (2:124), only then does Betsy see that Miss Forward has been masquerading as her friend and condemns her outrightly.

The entire framework of the novel is based on fictions and lies that must be exposed. The fault for all this fiction making, Haywood remarks, lies with men; it is their initial idolizing and fantasizing that makes women into something they are not. Miss Harriet tells Trueworth:

> It is an ill-judged policy, methinks, in you men, to idolize the women too much, you wish we would think well of you; if our sex are in reality so vain as you generally represent us, on whom but yourselves can the fault be laid. . . . I should think it would be sufficient for any man in his addresses to a lady, to tell her, that she happens to hit his taste,—that she is what he likes, without dressing her up in qualities, which, perhaps, have no existence but in his own imagination. (3:90–92)

Men have failed to recognize the reality that is woman and, instead, have created impossible angels and saintly forms that women are supposed to conform to, and women get caught. Interestingly enough, men try to catch women in this trap, but they also get caught themselves. Many of the farfetched incidents are purely the creation of the male imagination. Characters like Frederick Fineer, who acts like an Orlando Furioso in love, exhibit the extreme exaggeration of the romance form. Fortunately, his foppish state is uncovered by the real hero, Trueworth, and the plot is able to move to its truthful climax.

In the later, post-1740s novels the disguise ceases to be a physical one; instead, Haywood explores states of mind that are assumed and used as masks. Betsy disguises true emotions by the various frivolous, coquettish airs she adopts; for example, she never actually puts on a disguise, but she mentally assumes roles other than her true self. Thus, disguising true feeling, she becomes Mrs. Munden, which is a mask to her true self. Here, masks become verbal ploys, fictions created that must be addressed. Betsy is finally made aware of this insidious game that she plays (after Munden kills a pet squirrel that Trueworth had given her), and she casts off this "mental mask."

> In fine, she now saw herself, and the errors of her past conduct in their true light;—'How strange a creature have I been!' cried she, "how inconsistent with myself! I knew the character of a coquet both silly and insignificant, yet did everything in my power to acquire it:—I aimed to inspire awe and reverence in the men, yet by my imprudence emboldened them to the most unbecoming freedoms with me:—I had sense enough to discern real merit in those who protest themselves my lovers, yet affected to treat most ill those, in whom I found the greatest share of it.—Nature has made me no fool, yet not one action of my life has given any proof of common reason." . . .
>
> In summing up this charge against herself, she found that all her faults, and her misfortunes had been owing either to an excess of vanity;—a mistaken pride,—or a false delicacy:—the two former appeared only too contemptible in her eyes. (4:159–61)

It is this excess of vanity, this improper vision of self and reality that produced so many false masks. The remaining portion of the novel displays Betsy's new vision and her final reward: marriage to Trueworth.

\*   \*   \*

Although Haywood did not encumber her novels and romances with heavy preface material as did several of her contemporaries, she did attempt in her publication *The Female Spectator* (1744),[3] the first magazine by and for women, to investigate the new fictional domains. A fundamental moral seriousness is in the *Spectator* essays, and Haywood writes that with "an Education more liberal than is Ordinarily allowed to Persons of my Sex, I flattered myself that it might be in my Power to be of some measure both useful and entertaining to the Public" (1:6).

But her essays in *The Female Spectator,* in general, are more than merely entertaining; within the pages of the journal, she provides a survival manual for the midcentury woman. *The Female Spectator,* at times, reads like a collection of short stories, and we meet again many of the heroines who had graced the pages of her earlier fictions. The plots are reminiscent as well, for most concern marriage. Her aim throughout, even though her focus is on the "womanly concerns of courtship and marriage" is education. She wants her readership to be as knowledgeable as possible.

Haywood displays her own knowledge as she thinly disguises herself as the "female spectator" who is not a beauty, nor young; "I shall also acknowledge, that I have run through as many scenes of vanity and folly as the greatest coquet of them all" (1:2) she tells us. But her life and adventures have taught her well, and she is now able to anatomize all these "romantick" notions, which she does in the pages of the *Spectator*. She provides a blueprint of the romance—that is, she introduces a character, for example, Miss Tenderilla (1:7), tells her tale, then proceeds to give advice of how she should handle her story to make it work out correctly.

Many of the essays become treatises on education, and frequently the men are chastised for calling women "silly" and yet not endeavoring to do anything to help train their minds. "The world would infallibly be more happy than it is, were women more knowing than they generally are . . . all those little follies now ascribed to us, and which, indeed, we but too much incur the censure of, would then vanish, and the dignity of human nature shine forth in us . . . with . . . as much splendour as in the other sex" (2:195).

*The Female Spectator* provides the realistic context that is never directly addressed in the romances.

# Chapter 9
# Sarah Fielding

Sarah Fielding's (1710–68) interest is always in education. Not only did she write the first children's story, *The Governess; or, Little Female Academy* (1749), which is a fictionalized treatise on female education, but the underlying concern of each of her novels is how to teach women to read properly. *The Governess* and *The Cry* especially offer an invaluable program of how to read the romance. She teaches a gynocentric rather than an androcentric perspective,[1] which sees sexual harassment as the only way men know how to deal with women. Her goal, then, is to provide women with the proper vision and self-knowledge so that they can combat this sexual take-over.

\* \* \*

Fielding's first novel, *The Adventures of David Simple* (1744),[2] which she called a moral romance, sets the stage for her career-long examination of disguises and the art of the romance. It tells first the tale of Daniel's disguise as a kind, loving, dutiful son and brother, but goes on to uncover his villainy, "The Baseness of his Heart" (11), and his role in the forged-will scheme. David, his brother, disillusioned, leaves home seeking his fortune and a friend. His role throughout his "adventures" is to act as unmasker; he discovers a sinister world and uncovers the hypocrisy that exists in it. Although Fielding is concerned with the education of innocence by experience, her world view here is a decidedly dark one.

David is doomed to encounter masquerading people. His first love (and, he thinks, his last), Nancy Johnson, is soon revealed as a sham, when David overhears Miss Nancy voice her indecision whether to marry him or the rich Mr. Nokes. She can "play" at either disguise to get a man. Part of Nancy's indecisiveness, Fielding suggests, is due to her faulty education; she was brought up on romances, and thus, has an unreal vision of herself and her position in her middle class world.

Fielding continues her critique of the romance genre with Cynthia's story. Born with a natural curiosity, she observes: "If I was pleased with any Book above the most silly Story or Romance, it was taken from me. For Miss must not enquire too far into things, it would turn her Brain; she had better mind her Needle-work, and such things as were useful for Women; reading and poring on books, would never get me a Husband" (101). When she does marry, it is only to find disappointment, for her country gentleman husband cannot "make romantick Love" (109). He sees his wife's role as "his upper servant" (109), nothing more romantic. Cynthia declares she will not prostitute herself to him, thus masking her true feelings and accepting him as her husband, and she leaves him. Cut out of her father's will, she escapes destitution only by disguising herself as a "toadeater" (113) to a wealthy lady and living on these slavish wages. She learns quickly "how miserable it is to abandon one's self to another's Power" (117), but is finally saved when David rescues her.

Camilla's story, the other female protagonist, is just as fettering. She must deal with a shrewish, tormenting stepmother who rewrites the usual happily-ever-after, fairy tale script and will not allow Camilla to continue as dutiful daughter; her father's house, "which used to be my Asylum from all Cares . . . was converted by this woman's management into my greatest torment" (145). Livia, the stepmother, is presented as an archetypal fiction maker because she creates one falsehood after another to discredit Camilla and drive her away. Camilla finally escapes by disguising herself as a humpback: "[I] dyed my Skin in several places, with great Spots of Yellow; so that, when I look'd in the glass I was almost frighten'd of my own Figure" (166). But the disguise does not work. She is robbed and almost raped. Nothing is innovative in this presentation of the disguise topos, and we do not learn of any new ways to read the romance.

The first two volumes of *David Simple* are composed of feminine fictions—that is, Camilla's story, Cynthia's tale (with Livia's history contained within Cynthia's), and Isabelle de Stainville's history. These "histories" record the accepted, standard tale of the eighteenth-century woman and her plight of harassment, exploitation, and seduction. They present stereotypical vignettes of the feminine position with the predictable endings: "a happiness enjoyed by this whole Company" (302) finds Camilla and Valentine reunited with their father; Livia has died confessing her duplicity; Camilla and David, and Valentine and Cynthia have declared their love; and the second volume has ended with two weddings.

Fielding declares that it is left "to my Readers [*sic*] imagination to form them just as they like best: It is their Mind I have taken most pains to bring them acquainted with" (303); yet this promise is not fulfilled until nine years years later (1753) with the publication of *David Simple, Volume the Last*. Here, Fielding defines her lifelong goal of unmasking the masquerade and demystifying the romance for her readers and takes the first steps toward doing so.

\* \* \*

In the preface to *Volume the Last,* Haywood remarks that she takes up the story once again to put "known and remarkable Characters into new Situations" (310). She continues that "Her intention is not to shew [*sic*] how any Man, but how such a Man of a noble Spirit of Generosity and Beneficence would support himself under the worldly Misfortunes and Afflictions to which human-kind is liable" (311). She distinctly changes her comic notes to tragic ones as she begins this last exploration into the labyrinths of the mind, her favorite territory of exploration. But even more than a tragic investigation of David Simple's woes, the last volume is a deliberate exposure of the entrapping, romantic fictions that have ensnared the female characters.

The last volume unmasks all the bad characters who had disguised themselves as good, especially to persecute the women (for example, the Orgueils, Ratcliffs, and Draytons). It reveals Mrs. Orgueil first as the denigrator of romance reading (that is, she tells Mrs. Dunster that for little Cynthia "reading is not a proper Employment for a Farmer's Daughter" 328), and second as the creator of the type of fiction that is meant to keep the woman in her place. She "endeavour'd to teach the Children to be as artful and hypocritical as herself. For Mrs. *Orgueil* called governing the Passions, cunningly concealing them" (410). Mrs. Orgueil, as the prime fiction maker (that is, she tries to obtain guardianship of young Camilla to "educate" her after her mother's death), uses words for her own purposes. As Fielding notes: "Mrs. *Orgueil,* when she talked with little *Camilla,* endeavoured to intrap [*sic*] her, and drew such Conclusions from her Words as the poor Girl never thought of" (410). "Mrs. *Orgueil* had an art by dropping some circumstances, and altering and adding others, of turning any story to whatever purpose she pleased" (408). Orgueil's act is transparent, however; "this Fallacy of Mrs. *Orgueil* was plainly perceived by little *Camilla,* as it would have been by any grown Person" (410). Mrs. Orgueil's fiction, like her theory of education is stifling: woman must learn to keep her place.

Fielding's investigations into romance writing are, at first glance, timid. She is careful, both in the last volume and the earlier two books, to use the popular form even while she discreetly criticizes it. Thus, in the first volume, Isabelle's story is another example of romance making. Paradoxically, Isabelle is both a product of and a creator of fiction. She is an educator and she tells Julie: "it comes into my Head to tell a Story parallel to our Case" (198); in other words, she "makes us a story similar to the real situation in order to teach Julie . . . [who] immediately understood my meaning" (198). Although she "abhorred nothing so much as Dissimulation" (199), she is willing to use the romance topos to disguise her true, edifying intentions.

Isabelle's tale is complex and labyrinthean in its structure and plot. Her real emotions (and powers) are forever disguised: she must hide her love for Dumont because Vieuville, brother of her sister-in-law, loves her. Her tale envelops several other tales, again a masking ploy for her and especially for Fielding; with each further convolution of the text, Fielding is able to reveal the absurdity and ineptitude of the romance plot to examine true feelings.

Such convolutions characterize the main stories as well as the histories of Camilla and Cynthia. Fielding, however, is careful with her criticism; she bides her time. She waits until *The Cry* to blast this form entirely. In the meantime, she writes cautionary, educational pieces.

\* \* \*

Fielding's *The Governess, or Little Female Academy* (1749)[3] heralds the long-standing and ever popular tradition of the educational novel; this work can be read as a treatise about governesses and the proper form of female education. I submit that it is also an early Fielding treatment of the importance of female education vis-à-vis the so-called feminine art of disguise and romance. Fielding, again catering to predominant taste, is also capable of using a popular form to experiment with her own message. She uses the text to present her ideas about writing and reading fiction: "what is the true use of Reading? . . . to make you wiser and better" (vii).

Fielding observes that to enliven the serious part of her writing, she uses "those Methods of Fable and Moral which have been recommended by the wisest Writers, as the most effectual means of conveying useful Instruction" (iv). She follows Fenelon in his *Instructions for the Education of a Daughter* (1687), who advises that fables are an effective way of teaching. But the fable telling—and much of it occurs in the text—is placed under narrative layers, which gives the illusion of fact; that is, each tale begins with a physical description of the character, followed by a "Life" recital, after which comes the fable proper. It is an educational method presented in maternal terms—that is, Mrs. Teachum "mothers" each of her charges, and most of the accounts of their lives tell about the extended influence of their own mothers. Both Mrs. Teachum and Jenny function as surrogate mothers in the text.

In *The Governess,* the girls read to each other, and the eldest girl explicates the text, underscoring the moral. In much the same way, Fielding herself included the stories to comment on the entire notion of fiction and female learning.

*The Governess* is composed of "life accounts," histories of the main participants, and the fables told by these protagonists act as moral lessons for the reader. Jenny Peace tells the story of the Cruel Giant *Barbarico,* the good giant *Benefico,* and the little Dwarf *Mignon,* a tale of oppression and slavery that champions the weak, whose intelligence and faith triumph over the overzealous cruelty of the oppressor giant. Miss Dolly Friendly recounts the story of *Caelia* and *Chloe,* two orphaned girls, who set up a kind of female community with a widowed aunt and who, only at the last, admit a man to their special province. It is also a tale of deceit and treachery brought about by the man. The story does have a happy ending—the two women, once Sempronius is out of town, are able to talk freely of their emotions and their love. Chlore relinquishes all thoughts of a union with him, and Caelia and Sempronius are wed. Miss Suky Jennet reads a letter from her cousin Peggy Smith who died because of envy, and Patty Locket concludes: "What thanks can I give you? . . . for having put me into a way of examining my heart, and reflecting on my own actions; by which you have saved me, perhaps, from a life as miserable as that of the poor woman in Miss Suky's letter" (78). Jenny tells another fable ("The Princess Hebe: A Fairy Tale"), which addresses itself to controlling and ruling one's passions; she champions the virtuous, honest life though it be poor, noting that Hebe, through the teachings of the fairy Sybella, has learned contentment and peace: "the Moral of it is that whenever we give way to our Passions, and act contrary to our Duty, we must be miserable" (181). Again, like most of the stories told, it is a lesson learned while in the confines of the female community, though paradoxically, it is a tale of female treachery and deceit. Mrs. Teachum remarks that "A very good Moral may indeed be drawn from the whole, and likewise from almost every Part of it" (67).

Jill Grey in her introduction notes that "Sarah's choice of a school setting supplied the element of romance for the eighteenth-century readers, the majority of whom had never attended a school of any sort. This is the first example for the young of a dream-world in which the reader can picture him or herself" (79). She concludes: "Sarah's inclusion of fairy stories and oriental tales (though vehicles to convey her moral purpose) was a novelty to children starved of imaginative stories. While to those whose conscience forbade their reading romances and "idle stories" the use of the word "History" in her title made Sarah's book perfectly safe and useful. The title also suggests to

parents that *The Governess* would help in their daughter's education"
(81).

It is this overwhelming interest in education that holds all of
Fielding's work together. Although *The Governess*, on rereading,
seems to be a pale copy of the later *Cry*, both emphasize the importance of understanding the true workings of fiction and the fiction-
making process.

*The Governess* teaches how to read the fiction. It also teaches the
principals of self-examination, for each character has had to record her
life story. Then Mrs. Teachum critiques each version, pointing out
positive and negative qualities. Fielding hopes to teach through example The ultimate moral that *The Governess* preaches: "there is No
Happiness but in the Content of our own Minds" (223).

\*   \*   \*

Fielding's *The Cry: A New Dramatic Fable* (1754)[4] is her most
definitive examination of the use of disguise and romance in her fiction
and real life. She unmasks the entire genre as she anatomizes the bare
bones of the romance convention, thus making *The Cry* her most
sophisticated treatment of this ubiquitous archetype.

She begins immediately in the preface by expressing her interest in
"paint[ing] the inward mind" for her readers rather than "amus[ing]
them with a number of surprising incidents and adventures" (1:11);
this interior exploration involves unmasking the romance genre. This
psychological interest is presented through a focus on words. *The Cry*
investigates the use of language seen through the disguise of male
words and idioms forced on the woman; Fielding investigates how the
man corrupts the language he teaches the woman. (Interestingly
enough, Portia's father insists that she learn "as many languages as my
memory could retain"; 3:109.) It is a psychological examination bent
on uncovering all the false thinking and rhetoric that exists in the
world and is reflected in literature. *The Cry* becomes a battle between
truth and the fictional untruths often used to cover it over.

Fielding begins by defining the cry as

> all those characters in human nature, who, tho' differing from each other,
> join in one common clamour against Truth and her adherents. By bringing
> all such characters together, we would wish to dive into the bottom of
> their hearts, to shew what must be their sentiments, and how carefully they
> ought to be avoided. (1:20)

"The *Cry* . . . puzzle and perplex themselves, and twist everything a
thousand different ways, but all in vain" (1:130–31). They act as a

"Chorus" (1:201). Una, or simple Truth, is in opposition to this fatuous crowd. The major conflict, on one level, is between Una and The Cry, between truth and disguised truth. In a long passage, key to her entire critical theory, Fielding explains how she unmasks the usual romance writing through an examination of language. First she describes the "usual" story:

> If the heroine of a romance was to travel through countries, where the castles of giants rise to her view; through gloomy forests, amongst the dens of savage beasts, where at one time she is in danger of being torn and devoured, at another retarded in her fight by puzzling mazes, and falls at last into the hands of a cruel giant, the readers' fears will be alarm'd for her safety; his pleasure will arise in seeing her escape from the teeth of a lion, or the paws of a fierce tiger; if he hath conceived any regard for the virtuous sufferer, he will be delighted when she avoids being taken captive, or is rescued by the valour of some faithful knight; and with what joy will he accompany her steps when she finds the right road, and gets safely out of the enchanted dreary forest! (1:12–13)

Fielding explains this "male story" to her readers; it is the usual tale of sexual exploitation, female vulnerability, and masculine control. It is not, she continues, the whole story, which she will tell "in plain English" (1:32):

> But the puzzling mazes into which we shall throw our heroine, are the *perverse interpretations made her words; the lions, tigers, and giants, from which we endeavor to rescue her, are the spiteful and malicious tongues of her enemies.* In short, the design of the following work is to strip, as much as possible, *Duessa* or Falsehood, of all her shifts and evasions; to hunt her like a fox through all her doublings and windings; to shew [*sic*], that let her imitate Truth ever so much, yet is she but a phantom, and in a word, to expose her deformity, in hopes to persuade mankind to shun so odious a companion. Nor can this be effected, unless we could awaken the judgment to exert itself, so as to reject all the alluring bribes which the passions, assisted by the imagination, can offer. . . . *Thoroughly to unfold the labyrinths of the human mind is an arduous task;* and notwithstanding the many skilful [*sic*] and penetrating strokes which are to be found in the best authors, there seem yet to remain some intricate and unopen'd recesses in the heart of man. *In order to dive into these recesses, and lay them open to the reader in a striking and intelligible manner, 'tis necessary to assume a certain freedom in writing,* not strictly perhaps within the limits prescribed by rules. Yet we desire only to be free, and not licentious. We wish to give our imagination leave to play; but within such bounds as not to grow mad. . . . let it be remember'd that human Nature is the picture we intend to paint. (1:12–14; emphasis added)

She continues by giving an example of just how this language control works: she creates a scene "of a young gentleman paying his court to a young lady" (1:66). The woman is a "goddess," seated "at the shrine of her altar," listening to his "flattering speeches" (1:69), which, translated into plain English are:

> Madam, I like you . . . and it will conduce much to my pleasure and convenience, if you will become my wife: that is, if you will bind yourself before God and man to obey my commands as long as I shall live. And should you after marriage be forgetful of your duty, you will then have given me a legal power of exacting as rigid a performance as I please. (1:70)

It is to solve just this female language difficulty that Fielding writes.

Fielding, then, does two things simultaneously in *The Cry*. Invoking the reader's "fertile fancy" (1:21), Fielding tells the complicated romance stories of Portia, Melantha, and Cylinda; she covers these stories with her special use of language. *The Cry* is both a romance and a book about romance language.

In *The Cry,* she presents a two-tiered story, simultaneously giving us the male and female text. On the male level, we read of Portia and of her adventures and misadventures; of her father Nicanor; of the twins, Cordelia and Ferdinand; and of Oliver, the elder son; and so on. On a second and female level, *The Cry* is a book about language, writing, and the interpretations given to the word. (Fielding writes that the images in the mind govern the language used; see 1:113). Portia frankly admits this focus when she writes:

> I must quit mankind and lead the life of a hermit; for to be always studying what words I may utter, or what I must stifle; in short . . . to be afraid to say my very soul is my own, for fear somebody should lay a plot to rob me of it, is too painful a task for me ever to undertake. (2:40–41)

Portia's realization of the importance of words provides a bridge for the two levels, the two stories. In effect, Portia is discussing the necessity of masking, hiding one's true thoughts and emotions to reach a position where words can be used truthfully and realistically. She cannot say what she truly wants to, for *The Cry* misinterprets every word that she utters. For example, the following exchange, in which Portia is describing her love for Ferdinand, is symbolic of many scenes in the novel:

> It would, I confess, be the highest joy of my life, to know myself instrumental to his happiness but if [it] was deny'd me, all I could do would be

to take care that by behaviour I became not the cause of his misery. Was the man I love even to marry another woman, so far should I be endeavouring to injure that woman, that I could not be inspired with the least degree of hatred towards the real object of his choice, and perhaps the cause of his happiness. *The Cry* could hold no longer, but from every mouth burst forth—*was ever heard such romantic stuff?* such affectation! such refinement! . . . concluding at last in full chorus, that *Portia* had positively declared, that she should be better pleased to have her lover marry any other woman than herself. . . . And Portia retorts: *"It is not in the power of the most labour'd eloquence, fairly to extort such a conclusion from my words. . . . I said only . . . that his wife could not be the object of my hatred, nor could I rejoice in any misfortunes that might attend the man for whom I have an affection. Such wrestling false conclusions from the plain and simple expressions is your refuge, O ye foolish Cry, from beholding Truth."* (2:51–52; emphasis added)

Such an exchange is possible because Portia has already established the "real use of language" (2:19) with her group of "turba" characters, signifying "all the evil passions turmoiling the mind of man" (2:17) and the "dextra" characters, who emphasize "rightness of mind" (2:18) and tranquility. Her characters are designated by the language they speak, for their choice of words unmasks their minds (2:200).

To emphasize the importance of words, large portions of *The Cry* are dialogues (designated as scenes) between Portia, Una, and the Cry discussing and defining words. Both Portia and Fielding want to strip the person or word to its very essence. As Portia notes:

It is a simple mind alone that can penetrate a single character; and in most companies, the best mask you can wear is always to appear barefaced. For there are such numbers amongst mankind who will not believe but the whole world is so much of a masquerade that no one chuses [*sic*] to appear in it without a disguise, that whoever dares to shew [*sic*] his face, or rather his mind, in its own natural colours, without a mask, will gain the credit (such as it is!) of making use of a more artful refinement in putting on his disguise: and most probably every one of his acquaintance will form a different judgment of him, and each will privately rejoice in the thought of being alone able to trace his real character. (2:140)

Yet *The Cry* is not a pondersome, dull collection of critical views. The "story" of *The Cry* revolves around the romantic triangle of Portia, Ferdinand, and Melantha. Portia, as ingenue, is in love with the upstanding Ferdinand, but Melantha is jealous and discards her old lover so that she can have Ferdinand.

Melantha is not alone in her villainy. Book 4, volume 2, introduces

Cylinda, a woman of learning, who, in this volume, recounts her love for Phaon, who dies of a fever, and then her search for a man to love, finding him in Cato. But "the loss of Liberty which must attend being a wife, was of all things the most horrible to my Imagination; and the absurdity of my losing my liberty from my admiration of *Cato,* was too glaring to escape my observation" (2:320), and she refuses him. She has an affair with Millamour instead, and Fielding uses this encounter as another way to expose "romance." As she notes:

> For it is easy to make the world believe, that the days of romance are so far returned, as for admirers to dangle after their adored mistresses, many for the honour at last of kissing the hem of their garments. And *Millamour* often said, that as he did not chuse [*sic*] the reputation of a man of intrigue, he had frequently been deterred from making his addresses to women he liked, from seeing them possessed of so foolish a vanity, that it would be impossible for him to keep an amour with them a secret. (3:13)

When Millamour tries to force marriage, however, again she would rather get rid of the lover than gain a husband. (Fielding's morality is extraordinarily modern and outspoken.) Then she meets and lives with Nicanor for five years. This sojourn is followed by residence with Artemisia and her daughter, Brunnetta, and her brother, the married Eustace.

In a sophisticated manner, again with an emphasis on language, its male and female components, Fielding dexterously follows Cylinda's recital with Nicanor's version of the same affair—one plot: two versions.

The plots, however, are all united in Portia—with Ferdinand's eventual winning of her love and his proper use of language to her. Securing Portia's love is tantamount to unmasking, for it is in this concern with truth that the two plots merge: Portia's romance with Ferdinand and its negative, parallel one of Cylinda's affair with Nicanor; and the second concern with language and creating words. For telling the truth—be it lover or reader—involves stripping the falsehood from self and from words. Portia and Una must reeducate the reader and the Cry so that both can understand the new vocabulary and romance. They have given fresh meaning to the word romantic:

> The application of the word *romantic* . . . took its rise from the great love young girls formerly had to reading those voluminous romances, in which the heroine is represented as thinking it the highest breech of modesty to give the least hint of having one favourable sentiment for her lover, till he hath passed many years of probation, and given innumerable proofs of

being capable of adoring his mistress even to madness. The poor deluded readers of such romances, who thought it a fine thing to imitate these exalted heroines, and expected of their lovers such service and adoration, were very properly ridiculed by the name of romantic, and 'tis no more than an act of kindness to laugh them out of such absurdities. (1 : 60–61)

Portia and Fielding lead the way with the laughter.

*    *    *

Fielding continues to provide new definitions as she reinvents and revitalizes the historical biography with *The Lives of Cleopatra and Octavia* (1957).[5] Here she investigates the "Lives of Persons who have really made their Appearance on the Stage of the World" (iii) in an effort to get at the "Truth" once more. Her introduction to *The Lives of Cleopatra and Octavia* is an important critical document in her continuing examination of the reader's "insatiable Curiosity for Novels and Romances." She notes:

> Infatuated with a Sort of Knight errantry, we draw these fictitious Characters into a real Existence; and thus pleasingly deluded, we find ourselves as warmly interested, and deeply affected by the imaginary Scenes of Arcadia, the wonderful Achievements of *Don Quixote,* the merry Conceits of *Sancho,* the rural Innocence of a *Joseph Andrews,* or the inimitable Virtues of *Sir Charles Grandison,* as if they were real, those romantic Heroes had experienced the capricious Fortunes attributed to them by the fertile Invention of the Writers. (xlii)

To uncover these "Works of Fancy" (iii) and "to inform, and give us juster Notions of ourselves" (iii), she turns to the famous "Amours of *Anthony* and *Cleopatra,* which presents characters "like true mirrors," "the real Images of our Persons" (xliii).

And yet Fielding's attempts to present raw reality are still covered over,

> for as the modern Relish for Works of Imagination would almost tempt her to despair of Approbation, without some Mixture of Romance, she has, in Compliance to this Taste, introduced the Lives of those Ladies, as supposed to have been delivered by themselves in the Shades below. By which Method the Reader may at least expect a more impartial, distinct, and exact Narrative of their several Adventures, and of the Motives they were influenced by. (xliv)

Fielding is writing fictionalized biography with *The Lives;* it is a direct outgrowth from the critical stand taken three years earlier in *The Cry.* Once again she takes great pains to separate fantasy from fact, and her intention here, at least, is to reduce the mythic, larger-than-life stature of the famous lovers "through the Assistance of an Eastern Sorcerer or Magician" (xliv).

Fielding begins this uncovering process by having the protagonists speak in their own voices, thus unmasking themselves. Cleopatra, for example, initially confesses the difficulty of this task "to reveal those secret Motives of my Actions, which were once so little known to myself, that I was almost as much the Object of my own Deceit, as were either of my powerful Lovers" (1).

History has proved Cleopatra to be one of the arch dissemblers of all times, and her recital becomes one long narrative account of disguise. She frequently hides her body in a disguise, and Venus-like, is quick to point out that "I had Art enough to be sensible on what Trifles sometimes depends a Woman's gaining or losing a Conquest" (12). She is the hunter looking "on Anthony as my Prey" (9).

Cleopatra not only becomes the chief masquerader, but she also indulges in romance creation as well as revealing how she engineered the first meeting with Anthony, setting the scene like a romance novel. Reminiscent of Placentia's tactic taken to seduce Philidore (Haywood, *Philidore and Placentia*), Cleopatra writes: "I placed myself in pensive Posture, with my Head reclining on my Hand. . . . the first moment it was apparent that I saw him, I arose with an Air of such Alertness . . . that my Foot slipped, as it were by Accident, and I fell on my knees" (13–14). Even her "fall" is staged, and Anthony "little imagined how this was in Reality an Omen, that by Tricks and Deceit I should rule him for the Remainder of his Life" (14).

In this first-person narrative, Fielding has given the reader a recital and revelation of the female delusionist's art. Cleopatra, though a historical figure, is, for all intents and purposes, a female romancer who creates fictions and outrageous characters; she calls herself "a Woman of Art" (17); instead of writing an all-consuming romance, she creates herself as a character and lives out the fiction. Like other female novelists, she is interested only in the result: "I omitted no one in my Power to increase his Flame; for as I had not Passion for him, my Judgment was cool, and enabled me to turn his Passions to my own Advantage as I pleased" (15). She is, like other female novelists, an image maker, a controller. "I had, in Plain Truth, no other Value for this great Hero, than he was the *means of my Power* and the Instrument of my Ambition" (18; emphasis added). Cleopatra is reminiscent of the notorious Haywood protagonists such as the Baroness de Tortillée or Gigantilla, who do anything to control.

Cleopatra continues to engineer their relationship. She devises entertainments to keep Anthony enslaved and even persuades him to dress up sometimes as "Gods and Goddesses," and sometimes she "like an ordinary Woman, and *Anthony* in the Disguise of a Servant" (26). Not content with physical disguises, Cleopatra is able to wear her "Affectation, like a loose Robe I could turn and wind it, so as to lace it in that Light which I thought best fitted to dazzle and blind the eyes of the Man whom I intended the Honour of being my Dupe" (86). She governs by seeming not to, "by continually putting him in mind that one is too weak to govern him" (133).

She continues:

> During this Year which *Anthony* spent with me, I so accustomed myself to Treachery and Deceit, that at last I could not live a Day without inventing some new stratagem to impose on Anthony; and even sometimes, when I had no sort of Purpose to work out of it, but the mere Pleasure of the Deceit. To exult in the Thought, and gratify the glorious Ambition of knowing it was in my Power to deceive, was often the only End of my Artifice; and I could not help thinking myself much greater than the greatest hero. (33–34)

This statement is the archetypal one of a dissembler and controller. Cleopatra concludes: "I . . . could raise what Picture I pleased in his Mind, and make him see them in that Light only which would lest serve my Purpose" (51).

Octavia's portrait is the complete opposite: "She had an excellent Understanding, but never exerted it in artful Tricks to impose on Others; it was honest and sincere, wore no Disguise herself, nor was apt to be suspicious of it in others" (59). Like Una, in *The Cry,* Octavia is the voice of truth; she would not lead a "life of Deceit or Hypocrisy" (148); "where Art was required to preserve a Man's Affections, it was impossible but I must lose them" (171). Yet her role is limited here, for no disturbing, rowdy, lying crowd is to be stilled. Octavia cannot compete with the glitz and glamour of Cleopatra; truth looks dull in this work. Cleopatra's flamboyance makes disguise popular. It is only with her next full-length work, *The History of the Countess of Dellwyn,* that Fielding attempts to counter the true force of the masquerade, as she painstakingly details the rise and fall of one of the most magnificent dissemblers of feminine eighteenth-century literature.

\* \* \*

In the preface to *The History of the Countess of Dellwyn* (1759),[6] her longest and most detailed novel, Fielding continues her practice of unmasking the novelist's art; She delineates the characteristics of the writer who has "the capacity of penetrating that peculiar Quality, which hath taken such strong Possession of the character he would represent to his Reader" (1:x). The writer is a searcher "into the inmost Labyrinths of the human Mind [who] . . . penetrate[s] the Force of the different characteristic Bent[s] of the various Dispositions of Men towards their Conduct in Life" (1:xvii). She continues to be concerned with "the Purity of language" (1:xx), admonishing writers not to use words "so equivocally, as to be made applicable indifferently to what is either vicious or virtuous" (1:xx).

This investigation of "Disposition" and language in *The History of the Countess of Dellwyn* causes Fielding to examine the "Circaean transformation" (1:88) of the country-educated, unaffected Miss Lucum into the sly, insidious, haughty, duplicitous Countess of Dellwyn. It is a study paradigmatic of her entire career, for Fielding here investigates and uncovers what makes a woman, who initially "had not Art enough even to appear indifferent" (1:54) into one "who was now overwhelmed with black Clouds and tempestuous storms" (1:62) of untruths and guises. Fielding likens her to an "Amphisbena . . . a Creature so unfortunate as to be formed with Two Heads; the one continually striving to lead it forward, and the other as strenuously endeavouring to drag it backward" (1:62); she becomes the arch dissembler. Fielding here, once and for all, unmasks the aggressive woman who reads Homer and Ovid as romance writers, thus trying to find some employment for her strong imagination (see 1:93).

After Miss Lucum has been transformed into the Countess of Dellwyn, "she was in a manner under an Obligation to live a Lye; not only her Language, but every Look. . . ." Her life becomes one continual masquerade. When Dellwyn decides to remain in the country, his "Lady was again metamorphosized from the gay, fluttering, admired young Woman of Quality [the Form she had last appeared in at London] into a lamenting Niobe" (1:98). She masks her disappointment and guards her tongue.

She no longer has "any Relish for her once favourite Amusement of Reading; and mostly she disliked those Authors who have penetrated deeply into the intricate Paths of Vanity in the human Mind; for in them her own Folly was continually brought to her Remembrance" (1:102). She will only indulge her taste in romances to continue to feed her romantic and masquerading nature, for romances placed her in the position she now occupies: "Reading was like setting a Glass before her, which represented her to herself in so many deformed Lights, that she could not bear the disagreeable View" (1:103).

To avoid any self-confrontation that would be highly disagreeable, and, anxious not to participate any further in her sham "matrimonial

Dialect" (1:218), the Countess, especially in the second volume, indulges in constant masquerading, disguising this obsession as a competition with her former friend, Lady Fanny Chlegen née Fashion to procure lovers. Certainly it is a game that Lord Clermont knows how to play—too well—and the greater part of the second volume is taken up with the Countess's intrigue with Lord Clermont and with Captain Drummond's attempt to reveal this affair to her husband. The Countess thinks she will be able to keep the truth from her husband; her plan fails, and they are divorced. The Countess plans a grand European tour. She disguises under her former title, Countess of Dellwyn, deciding "that a Countess, with half a Reputation, would meet with a more favorable Reception in the Metropolis of many Kingdoms . . . than a plain Gentlewoman of Virtue more un-blemished than Lucretia's" (2:226). Yet, her "story" does cross the channel, (she has already become a "fiction"), and soon Paris is abuzz with the true history of the Countess of Dellwyn. Deciding to mask this tale, she encourages D'Orville's attentions and affections; "she hoped to bury all her Misconduct in this change of name; and that the Faults of Lady *Dellwyn* might be forgiven Madam D'Orville" (2:242).

But at the last, she is unmasked; her history is discovered. She flees to France, and D'Orville returns to England. "All Places were now become irksome to her. She found it impossible to fly from Infamy, unless she could at the same time fly from herself" (2:273).

The novel unmasks the artful, aggressive woman: the interior female side. Fielding uncovers the inner workings of the romantic myth—those initial allusions and fantasies gathered from romance reading that Miss Lucum had translated into the mask of the Countess of Dellwyn. But these dreams, these romantic trappings are stripped and exposed in the pages of *The History of the Countess of Dellwyn;* the fairy tale does not exist. At the end, she can no longer sustain the facade; she can no longer invent words, stratagems, and mind-sets: "She could not film over the Odium of her own Actions, by applying to them the Words Gallantry, Intriguing, Coquetting, with many other softening terms" (2:50). Without benefit of either the Cry or Una, Charlotte Lucum, the Countess of Dellwyn, uncovers the truth, exposes the romances, and learns a vocabulary suited to herself.

*   *   *

Fielding's last novel, *The History of Ophelia* (1760),[7] combines the critical theories of *The Governess* and *The Cry* together with the unmasking techniques of *The Countess of Dellwyn* in a first-person narrative that anatomizes, for the last time, the vagaries of the romance topos.

*Ophelia* is about life and literature. The story begins as Ophelia's aunt recounts her thorough disillusionment with men: she had believed the old "tale" told by the soldier, had secretly married him, and had gone with him to America. When she learns of the existence of another wife, she decamps with Ophelia (Ophelia's mother has died, and the aunt raises her) and settles in Wales. Because she had been so thoroughly disenchanted, "The Books she had brought into Wales were chiefly Books of Divinity, and such Histories as served to enlarge and instruct the mind of the Reader, without informing him of the existence of Vices, which a Pure Imagination, untaught by Observation and Experience, cannot represent to itself" (1:12). Ophelia, however, learns to view life as it is a romantic interlude despite her aunt's efforts. For example, her first encounter with Dorchester is overlaid with a romantic coloring. Dorchester calls out: "Stay! beauteous angel, stay!" (1:14) and bends toward her "in the most suppliant Posture, with Gestures, which I thought almost prophane to address to a Mortal Being" (1:14). Ophelia is hoodwinked and readily accepts the adoration. When Dorchester discovers her essays and annotations of the books in their library and reads her "Confession" (1:22), "he could scarcely believe all he had seen was any thing but Enchantment" (1:22–23). He is not allowed to break the spell. And Ophelia records: "I have since been told, that my Aunt would not suffer him to stay, but on Condition, that he should say nothing which might tend to lessen my ignorant Simplicity" (1:23). His presence interrupts their country idyll, and Ophelia owns that her "former Amusements became less pleasing to me; I found less Attention to what I read" (1:25).

Not only does Ophelia unmask reality from the earlier idyllic perception she had of it, but when Dorchester appears, masked, and abducts her, she notes: "Hypocrisy was a Crime of which I had never heard; this was my first acquaintance with Deceit; and Hatred sprung up with it; (1:29–30). Her entrance into the masked, real world is as abusive and threatening as the abduction. She is instantly forced to adopt a disguise, that of the melodramatic heroine, and she is propelled into a world of deceit that she does not know: money, power, and control. Her exposure is painful until she learns the rules of this society—that is, how to masquerade the true self in order to "be" the prevailing and popular role. The more she hides her true being and plays the heroine, however, the more vulnerable she becomes; she is even mistakenly abducted once again. Although she is capable of putting a mask on, she is not well versed enough to be able to read others through their disguises, and she believes professions and declarations at face value.

Ophelia has not learned to disguise her feelings, and so she is highly vulnerable to attack and exploitation. "What my Heart innocently felt, I thought my Tongue might unreproachably utter" (1:140), she thinks. Nor can she tolerate such disguised hypocrisy in others: "to conceal a Truth, which, if known, may hurt, and can be of no Service, may be a Duty; but to pretend an Affection we do not feel, I esteemed criminal; and to express what we know will not, and what we did not intend should be believed, appeared to me an excessive Folly" (1:148). Her candor is excessive.

Her critique of people who "effect" different characters is also extended to literature (and it is here that Fielding merges the two popular topoi):

> I have been convinced by Observation, that Plays and Novels vitiate the Taste: I allow many of them to be extremely diverting, some very fine; but by the multiplicity of Events, mixed with a good deal of the Marvelous; they learn the Mind and Dissipation even in Reading. . . . In short, I esteem such Reading as bad for the Mind, as high Meats are for the Stomach; they may create a false Appetite, but will pall a true one, and make all proper Food appear insipid, till by long Use even they grow tiresome, and the true Appetite being vitiated, all alike disgust. (1:159–60)

And yet, Ophelia already masquerades, for though she says she does not and cannot abide hypocrites, she becomes one herself as she disguises herself to retain Dorchester's love. (One must consider the whole book, however, her unmasking process, for told retrospectively, it is an explanation of her actions.)

It is in this new, disguised role that she attends her first masquerade:

> in Absurdity it exceeded what my Expectations had formed of it. The motley phantastick Crew seemed to me more like what the Imagination represents to us in Sleep, when the Body is disordered than any real Objects that ever appear before our Eyes. . . . Masquerades are the Produce of a strange Excess of Fancy, an overheated Imagination, set to work by a wild desire of Amusement. (1:217–18)

She continues:

> A Masquerade, by no means, answered my Expectations. . . . before half the Evening was spent, I found that Wit, the great Requisite to make them so, was a scarce Commodity; and that after the Wearer was once dressed,

he thought as little of the Character he had assumed, as he did of the Propriety of it when he chose the Habit. Thus one sees a Harlequin limping with difficulty across the Room; an old woman skipping and dancing more nimbly than any of the Company; a *French Petit Maitre* pensive or sleepy; a Fortune-teller dancing a Minuet; a Bear exercising the Height of solemn Politeness; a Shepherdess bold and impudent; a nun coquettishly frisky; a *Turk* drinking wine, and a *Spaniard* easy, gay and familiar. (1:223)

Unwilling not to unmask this form, Fielding continues her great uncovering and observes much as she had done earlier with Ophelia's remarks about literature, and as she had done throughout *The Cry:*

The Variety of shocking Forms terrified me, till use had a little familiarized them; and I found that this Assembly, in the opinion of most People, received its Terrors, *not from masking the Faces, but unmasking the Mind.* When I learned that the English were such great Enemies to Sincerity, that none dared practice it *bare-faced,* I allowed there was some Excuse for thus defending themselves from the ill Effects of so uncommon an Indulgence of that Virtue. I should imagine some relaxation from the painful Exercises of Dissimulation and Flattery necessary; and might be productive of general good. But the Divine Countenance of Truth is so seldom seen here, that if, by Chance, she does appear, she is often mistaken for ill Nature. (1:218; emphasis added)

Continuing her observations to Lady Rochester, she replied,

That she looked on a Masquerade as the *English Saturnalia;* and as People of Fashion here were more abject Slaves to ceremonious forms than the *Roman* Domesticks were to their Masters, it was but reasonable, that they should have their Days of Liberty to declare their Disgust with Impunity, and revile those they disapprove. (1:220)

Yet the revilement is all Ophelia's; Fielding offers the revelation. As she continues to study the English and their great masquerade custom, Fielding/Ophelia uncovers what has been hidden for too long and observes:

I soon perceived that I should acquire more Knowledge of the true Dispositions of Mankind at three of these Assemblies, than by living three Months in the polite World; for it was the first Time I saw People *in their natural Characters; the Mind was now apparent, the Face only hid;* and, as the Company I was with, were much used to these Entertainments, *they could see thro' the Masks, which would have concealed many of my Acquaintance from my less discerning Eyes,* and by their Assistance I perceived the forced Prude indulging in Coquetry; the affectedly Grave giving a loose to Mirth and

Pleasure; the fawning, pert, and impertinent; great Statesmen condescend-
ing to be trifling, and Philosophers, to be foolish; all laying aside those
Parts, which Interest, the love of Power, or of Fame induced them to act in
publick. (1 : 221; emphasis added)

Yet Ophelia reveals her own bias and need for a mask as she watches all
the maskers and unmaskers when she tells Lady Cambridge

that this Diversion seemed an Emblem of Death; it laid all Hearts open,
and put an End to all Dissimulation and Pretence; and if the Resurrection
was not so quick, I should be more on a Par with the rest of the World,
since I was not one of the Number who durst not appear without an
internal Mask, unless I had an external one to conceal me. (1 : 222)

But, unbeknownst to her, Ophelia does have a mask: that of innocence, and it is this pristine truthfulness that both protects her and
provokes others to try and strip her. Thus, following the masquerade,
she is abducted by the Marchioness of Trente, who tries to buy her off
from Lord Dorchester; she is guarded by Mrs. Herner but eventually
does make her escape and returns to London where she is kept from
Lord Dorchester and Lady Palestine.

Ophelia is not allowed to unmask, however; her "departure" is not
read correctly by Dorchester, who believes she has abandoned him.
Lady Trente was responsible for all this upset and is understanding,
yet she disguises her own role in the abduction by placing the blame
on Ophelia. The Marchioness is still unable to capture Dorchester's
affections because her language of deceit betrays her. Predictably,
Dorchester and Ophelia are able to reconcile their differences and
soon have returned to their earlier, affectionate state.

Unfortunately, though Ophelia is healed romantically, her physical
condition continues to decline, and a trip to Bedlam (as curative)
occurs. Like the masquerade, the asylum provides another metaphor
of the illusionary and disguised state of the woman. It provides a
topsy-turvey world that defies the laws and conventions of the mundane world. It provides the lesson that all should heed: "If People
once suffered themselves to deviate from Reason's Path, who can
pretend to fix any certain Bounds for their misguided steps" (2 : 106).

The second volume attempts to correct all the fallacious disguises
and missed steps of the first volume; plot intricacies are uncovered,
villains revealed, and so on. Most important, Lord Larborough unmasks Dorchester and his intentions vis-à-vis Ophelia. She learns that
Dorchester "waits impatiently to find some Moment, when [her]
Virtue shall be off its Guard" (2 : 162). Ophelia is shocked.

To uncover the truth of Larborough's accusations, Ophelia agrees to play the hypocrite. She will hide in a strategic position after dinner and listen to the conversation between Larborough and Dorchester. Thus "as soon as Supper was over I left them, but went into a Closet, the Door of which I had purposely set open" (2:170). With much bating, Larborough gets Dorchester to reveal his deep love for Ophelia and yet still declare his great aversion to marriage itself. Dorchester goes on to reveal how he has controlled her imagination to maintain her innocence in his schemes. He and Lady Palestine covered over her true past so that "her Reputation has hither continued unblemished" (2:181). But he has been unable to perpetuate his schemes. "I thought I had only a Woman to resist me; who would have expected an Angel should be hid in a cottage, while we frail Mortals inhabit Palaces?" (2:183).

Ophelia has heard enough. Shocked at his unmasking, she plots how she will escape. She dissimulates and "tried to conceal [her] grieved Heart under a smiling Countenance" (2:188). Ophelia, however, has been taken in once again; Larborough engineered the entire scene to deceive her.

Because Fielding has been concerned with masking Ophelia, the author allows the work to finish in romantic fashion, and "like all other Romances, [this one] must end with Wedlock" (2:266). Yet it is a tepid ending at best. Ophelia's penultimate decision—to "go where I shall be secluded from Mankind, where Virtue makes every Action open and intelligible; there I am capable of living happily, without learning the Arts that hide her every real thought" (2:237)—tempers the happy resolution that comes so close to the conclusion. Further, I think that Ophelia could have managed on her own; this marriage was not totally necessary for her, nor for Fielding and the denouement of her masquerade investigation.

\* \* \*

Fielding has succeeded in unmasking the romance; her unique combination of masquerade together with the highly detailed examination of words, their use and power, and the romantic text justify the importance attached to Fielding's position in the eighteenth-century, feminine canon. It remains for Charlotte Lennox to make the most comprehensive transition from masquerade to romance. Fielding, however, took the first all-important steps.

# Chapter 10
# Charlotte Lennox

Charlotte Lennox's (1720–1804) career presents the clearest picture of the transition from the novelist's simplistic use of disguise as a coding device of self-discovery to the manipulation of the disguised romance genre as the ultimate encoded instrument for self-examination. Comparing her first novel, *The Life of Harriet Stuart* (1750), with her famous, second work, *The Female Quixote: or, The Adventures of Arabella* (1752), the reader first encounters a heroine who disguises herself while she acts out the romance story; her disguises are for protective purposes and enable Lennox to advance the plot. Arabella, conversely, does not physically masquerade, but she is disguised mentally as she cloaks her thoughts in romance vernacular and action. The two novels become companion pieces, with *The Female Quixote* oftentimes operating as a commentary on the first book as both disrupt standard theories about disguise and romance in an effort to help the female discover her identity.

Lennox's third novel, *Henrietta* (1758), attempts to present a solution to the ambiguity of the first two pieces. If Harriet Stuart is the typical heroine who is controlled and exploited by the man (an example of the ideology of female powerlessness), and Arabella is the heroine who can control because she is fictional (and, therefore, has paper power only), Henrietta combines the positive qualities of both women and provides the least ambiguous figure in the Lennox canon. She manages to explore the ideology of powerlessness and romantic love while remaining both powerful, in love, and her own person. Henrietta hides under assumed names, thereby protecting her true self and exercising freedom and power because men cannot determine who she is. But she views disguise as dependency and is gladly ready to discard such untrue efforts and cover-ups.

By her last novel, *Euphemia* (1790), Lennox has discarded masks completely; it is a novel that draws a fine line between fictional and autobiographical presentations. In the letters exchanged between Miss Harley and Mrs. Neville, one finds the true Charlotte Lennox voice.

Much like Charlotte Smith, here Lennox takes reality and only thinly veils the true facts with a fictional disguise. Like Smith, her novels tell of unhappy marriages, money difficulties, and general despair; she weaves many of her own mishaps into the lives of her characters[1] and thus unmasks the true Charlotte Lennox as well. She proves that the woman can have both power and love, thus disproving the reigning ideologies.

\*    \*    \*

Lennox's first novel, *The Life of Harriet Stuart* (1750),[2] is a seriatim account of Harriet's life from youth to marriage, which she writes to her friend and confidante, Amanda. The reader finds that Harriet is not one to mask her feelings; her account is sometimes painfully honest, yet it is an honesty that she has to work at. In the beginning, she is very much a disguising heroine of the eighteenth-century romance.

*Harriet Stuart* is an example of the popular educational novel that teaches woman her place. Harriet learns to be a romance heroine, who is submissive and passive, learns to mask her intellect, kowtow to her emotions, and be sentimental. During the crossing to America (her father is posted there), she is instructed by the romantically inclined Mrs. Villars, who tells the reader that Harriet is a natural coquet. And when *I compared my adventures* with some of those I had read in *novel and romances,* [I] found it *full as surprising*. In short, *I was nothing less than a Clelia or Statira*" (1 : 8; emphasis added).

Like other Lennox heroines, her romance training will be her undoing. When her mother presses her to marry Mr. Maynard, Harriet prodigiously declares her lack of interest in him, and her mother concludes: "These horrid romances . . . turned the girl's brain. The heroines of these books are always disobedient: and I suppose she intends to copy their example" (1 : 29). But it is not so much a copying of their example as just absorbing the sort of personality and plight of the eighteenth-century woman, when the only models are the romance heroines who are the causes of Harriet's behavior. Thus, like them, she falls in love with the man of her choice, Dumont, and like all romances, it will take two volumes and many plot complications until she is able to sort out the relationship and make it work, thus living happily ever after.

Her first encounter with the "fantasy of romance" is the doomed romance with Bellmein; she believed his romantic lies and was hoodwinked. Her father will not let her wallow in this sentimental claptrap, and he urges her to marry Maynard, but the "fear of being forced to

marry Maynard, and the tender remembrance of Bellmein tormented
me" (1:80); Harriet stalls for time. Her mother says she is aware of
her stratagems:

> I begged them (with tears in my eyes) to grant me a few months delay;
> promising to endeavour (in that time) to obey them with less reluctance.
> My mother (who was extremely obstinate) fearing lest this artifice, as she
> called it, should incline my father to grant me the favor I asked: possessed
> him with an opinion, that I was mediating some new strategem, and
> possibly had intelligence with Bellmein. This so incensed him that he
> protested he would give me to Maynard, tho' he was immediately after to
> follow me to the grave. (1:83)

She tries to escape; instead, Bellmein, disguised as an indian, kidnaps
her, further emphasizing her pitiful, heroine's plight. His disguise—
his indian savagery—is an externalization of the true male interior.
Such savagery frightens Harriet; she scorns his proposal and escapes
from him, returning to her family.

Volume 1 continues with even more hair-raising adventures and
narrow escapes that force Harriet into the role of heroine. In volume
2, Lennox focuses on more subtle forms of masquerade; much subterfuge, hiding, and lying occurs. Also, volume 2 contains two long
histories—one of Lady Louise and the other of Mademoiselle Bell-
ville—further illustrating the romance-disguise form that Lennox explores so adeptly. Through her characters, Lenox discovers that
disguise often reveals a truth that the characters did not want examined. For example, when Harriet pretends to be Lady Louisa to test
and ascertain the love of the Earl of L____ for herself, she discovers
that

> in the person of the Earl of L____, I soon recollected the same Lord
> S____ I mentioned in the beginning of my history, who, by the service he
> had done me, while I was yet a child, had filled my young bosom with the
> first tender emotions it had ever felt. (2:33)

She masks her recognition, however, and "assumed an appearance of
unconcern; and affect[s] not to have the least knowledge of him"
(2:33). Harriet finds the disguise more than uncomfortable, however,
as the earl declares his fondness for his memory of "Harriet."

Disguise does lead to truth, but not always a truth that is wanted.
Most of the disguise stories in the second volume involve the unmasking of the men; each of the case histories presented is an uncovering of
yet another cad; their disguises are adopted only to trap women.

The history of Mrs. Dormer (volume 2) is a representative example of this ubiquitous male deceiver. In her youth, she falls in love with her father's enemy's son. They marry secretly, and he leaves for Paris. "For two months he continued to write constantly to me by every post; but I could not help observing, that he carefully avoided the stile of a husband, and never once acknowledged, by the most distant hint, that I was his wife" (2:64).

Several years later, still not having had contact with her first husband, she falls in love with Mr. Clayton. When she confesses the state of her love and life to Mr. Clayton, her father hides himself in the nearby closet and hears it all and immediately disclaims her. Mrs. Dormer, however, wins our approval; even when her husband dies (killed by Clayton), she does not marry the man she loves, but lives alone throughout the remaining years, thus exhibiting great virtue and fortitude. The story unmasks the hypocrisy of man and the abiding veracity of the woman.

Feminine veracity as noble as it is, does not save Harriet, however. Her story continues as she is abducted by Dumont's retainers and is taken to Paris and placed in a convent; she is given a false identity and is told that Dumont has married. She is rescued from the convent by the Count de R____, who takes her to the Earl of L____; he has procured a *lettre de cachet*. She is detained in the marchioness's house and is camouflaged once more: "I . . . suffered the officious French-woman to dress me as she pleased only to the vermilion, with which she would have daubed my cheeks" (2:166). Harriet is rescued from this entire situation that the men have created around her because of their desire to possess her by another woman. As her rescuer explains: "known, I am a woman, and have only taken this disguise in order to accomplish my design" (2:172). How clever of Lennox to effect the great salvation of the besieged, seduced, abducted maiden by another woman. It is Madam Danville who changes identities with Harriet so that Harriet can escape.

Like Haywood's Idalia, Harriet experiences heroine adventures and vicissitudes; she staunchly faces kidnappings and abductions. Harriet Stuart is different from her predecessors and the more famous Arabella because the latter only invents and imagines the fantastical, romance adventures; she experiences mundane occurrences. Harriet, conversely, experiences the real kidnappings and abductions. Although her plight is frightful—and she faints in terror frequently—such actions are the standard fate of the heroine. Arabella's terror, on the other hand, is of a frightening and more insidious kind. She controls the fantasies; her plight demonstrates the degree to which her mind is controlled by and committed to these fantasies. Her fate is more serious. Harriet is still controlled by the man; it is the man who abducts her and forces her to comply with his desires. Arabella conversely makes her conscious self a thrall to her unconscious, aggressive self. *The Female Quixote* is the more sophisticated rendering of the plight of the woman, because it is female initiated and controlled. Her terror has been internalized.

*        *        *

This "terror" does, indeed, continue in Lennox's next novel, *The Female Quixote: or, The Adventures of Arabella* (1752),[3] which combines heroine disguise and romance criticism in a unique pastiche of masquerade and love structuring itself on the contrast between the novel and the romance, ultimately demonstrating that the romance is excessive fiction. Arabella is not only the chief protagonist, the female quixote, the much harassed, frequently disguised heroine, but, as Langbauer suggests, she is also "the ideal reader, completely given over to the sway of the text, attesting to the power of romance, a power the novelist desires for her form too. . . . she tries to cast out from her writing exactly the power which she also envies and wishes to usurp."[4]

*The Female Quixote* is about the nature of female power. It explores whether female power is possible in real life or just exists in romance fiction. *The Female Quixote* is structured on the contrast between the romance (female power) and the novel (male power) and the archetypal two plots. Lennox explores the ideology of power in her text as she examines the marginality of female control in the gender-based form both in terms of her character and her self. Realistically, Lennox must educate Arabella out of the romance frame of mind and toward a realistic viewpoint, one that is necessary for the mental survival of a woman. To believe in the male romance's ideology is not to know one's self as a woman. This task becomes a symbol of Lennox's own struggle as a writer. Paradoxically, while using the romance to empower herself and her art, she must simultaneously uncover the male ideology that governs the romance form and renders a woman powerless, expose it, and recode it for her own use. Lennox has the difficult task to see if she can make the romance form empowering, not imprisoning.

Ultimately, Arabella will learn that she cannot exist in the liminality of the romance text. She learns the novel language, and at the end, Arabella/Lennox adopts the male voice that the clergyman teaches her; both she and Lennox assume the male language. This take-over not only gives the male power, but, with Arabella's adoption of nonromance (that is, real language and literature) at the conclusion of the story, the reader is left with the unpleasant notion that Arabella is not freed but trapped by male power in a male literary form. Although she will no longer read romances, one assumes that in her wedded bliss, she will still try and pattern her marriage on the romance model. Therefore, the most important section of the novel is Arabella's insistence that Lucy learn how to tell Arabella's story: *the woman's story*. Arabella explicitly instructs Lucy in rhetorical strategies, proper vocabulary and so forth.

Like her own creator, Arabella indulges in fantasy creation, to be sure, but she also writes women's history. The key scene when Arabella instructs Lucy how to tell the female story illustrates this point, for it is the symbol of the book:

> Here, instead of my desiring you to soften those Parts of my History where you have greatest Room to flatter; and to conceal, if possible, some of those Disorders my Beauty has occasioned; you ask me to tell you what you must say; as if it was not necessary you should know as well as myself, and be able, not only to recount all my Words and Actions, even the smallest and most inconsiderable, but all my Thoughts, however instantaneous; relate exactly every Change of my Countenance; number all my Smiles, Half-smiles, Blushes, Turnings pale, Glances, Pauses, Full-stops, Interruptions; the Rise and Falling of my Voice; every Motion of my Eyes; and every Gesture which I have used for these Ten Years past; nor omit the smallest Circumstance that relates to me. (135)

One reads *The Female Quixote* for this woman's history.

Arabella and Lennox have become one. The emphasis in the text has been on dialogue, dialect, learning the correct romance rhetoric. Lennox and Arabella have tried to uncover the form, and by so doing, reencode the romance for the new enlightened female reader and her new understanding of self. This new feminine identity is part of a larger female awareness. *The Female Quixote* celebrates female networking. Thus, though it uncovers the romance form, it also uncovers the necessity of telling the romance's tale.

The story begins innocuously enough with the Marquis of _____'s banishment from court and his retirement to the country. Time is telescoped, and soon the reader is introduced to his teenaged daughter, Arabella, who "supposing Romances were real Pictures of Life, from them she drew all her Notions and Expectations" (7). By them she was taught to believe, that "Love was the ruling Principle of the World; that every other Passion was subordinate to this" (5). She thinks of herself only in terms of the heroine; she is "kept in a continual anxiety by a vicissitude of hopes, fears, wishes and disappointments" (7), for Arabella is "a strict observer of romantic forms" (14).

Numerous illustrations of Arabella's "romancing" of the story occur, all attempts on her part to get at the woman's story, her story, that
needs to be told. For example, she is out riding as is Mr. Hervey, an
early suitor; his previous attempts to talk to her have proved unsuccessful:

> While he was considering how he should accost her, *Arabella* suddenly
> seeing him, and observing he was making up to her, her Imagination
> immediately suggested to her, that his insolent Love had a Design to seize
> her Person; and this Thought terrifying her extremely, she gave a loud
> shriek. (21)

Hervey is apprehended as a highwayman because of Arabella's behavior. Arabella's fantasy is a bid for power, but it is also a true picture
of how the woman views herself in relation to the man. She wants to
control; by assuming the romance heroine's role, she is able to subvert
the form and use it for herself. She shifts the power from Hervey to
herself, and she tells him:

> A little more Submission and Respect would become you better, *you are
> now wholly in my Power;* I may, if I please, carry you to my Father, and have
> you severely punished for your Attempt: But to shew you that I am as
> generous as you are base and designing, I'll give you Freedom, provided
> you promise me never to appear before me again. (22; emphasis added)

Hervey leaves for London, and Arabella,

> in order to be completely generous, A Quality for which all the Heroines
> are famous, laid a Command upon her two Attendants not to mention
> what had passed, giving them, at the same time, Money to secure their
> Secrecy; and threatening then with her Displeasure if they disobeyed. (23)

Not only does being a heroine involve adventures, danger, and power,
but secrecy—the prime ingredient of disguise—is also an important
quality for the heroine. Her power, so she thinks, must be kept
hidden.

Being a romance heroine allows Arabella to act in a fashion diametrically different from her real self. As heroine, she has power. As
she remarks, when she learns that her father has arranged for her to
marry his nephew, Glanville:

> The Impropriety of receiving a Lover of a Father's recommending ap-
> peared in its strongest Light. *What Lady of Romance ever married the Man
> that was chose for her?* In those Cases the Remonstrances of a Parent are
> called *Persecutions; obstinate Resistance, Constancy and Courage;* and an

Aptitude to dislike the Person proposed to them, a noble Freedom of Mind which disdains to love or hate by the Caprice of others. (29; emphasis added)

She flatly refuses to be even civil to Glanville, and though he immediately falls in love with her, violating all the romance forms, Arabella scorns him. Glanville, because he "had never read Romances . . . was quite ignorant of the Nature of his Offence" (36). He does not understand her aversion and scorn; he does not understand the romance game. Arabella, disguised as heroine, is beside herself with anger and fury at having her will—her power—disobeyed:

> she thought it both just and reasonable to provide for her own Security, by a speedy flight. The Want of a Precedent, indeed, for an Action of this Nature, held her a few Moments in Suspense; for she did not remember to have read of any Heroine that voluntarily left her Father's House, however persecuted she might be; but *she considered, that there was not any of the Ladies in Romances, in the same Circumstances with herself who was without a favoured Lover,* for whose sake it might have been believed she had made an Elopement, which would have been highly prejudicial to her Glory . . . she thought there was nothing to hinder her from *withdrawing from a tyrannical Exertion of parental Authority,* and the secret Machinations of a Lover, whose Aim was to take away her Liberty, either by obliging her to marry him, or by making her a Prisoner. (38; emphasis added)

Patterning her behavior on "*Statira, Parisatis, Clelia, Mandana,* and all the illustrious Heroines of Antiquity" (1:78), Arabella resolves to run away. Her father's untimely accident prevents her escape, and when Glanville returns, she is more civil to him—lecturing him about the heroines of old. She instructs him and asks him to read about Cleopatra, Cassandra, Clelia, and The Grand Cyrus; she even suggests he try a romance rhetoric. Glanville is dismayed at the length of these romances, however, let alone the new jargon he is asked to adopt. "Therefore glancing them over, he pretended to be deeply engaged in reading, when, in Reality, he was contemplating the surprising Effect these Books had produced in the Mind of his Cousin" (54). When her father learns of her addiction to these romances, he gathers them all together to consign them to the fire (59). Heroically, Glanville saves them from destruction, and, for the moment, is in her good graces.

Arabella continues her romanticizing so single-mindedly that Lennox is able to point out the absurdity of such a disguise, for Arabella has not yet learned the importance of her disguise vis-à-vis her female colleagues. One of the most ludicrous scenes in the novel occurs when Arabella thinks the "gardener" is coming to be an insolent lover to her and to take her away. She and Lucy, her maid, engineer an "escape," hoping a "Knight" or "Cavalier" will save them.

When she sprains her ankle, faints, and is supposedly deserted by Lucy, who in reality had gone for aid, Arabella finds herself in dire straits; recovering, but still thinking she is pursued by Edward, she flags down a passing chaise and begs for aid.

> *Arabella* suffering no Apprehensions from being alone with a Stranger, since nothing was more common to Heroines than such Adventures: all her Fears being of *Edward,* whom she fancied every Moment she saw pursuing them. (151)

But she is discovered, rescued and returned, much to everyone's happiness.

Fortunately, Glanville is able to see beneath the foolish romance mask that she wears:

> Every thing furnished Matter for some new Extravagance; her character was so ridiculous, that he could propose nothing to himself but eternal Shame and Disquiet, in the Possession of a woman, for whom he must always blush, and be in Pain. But her Beauty had made a deep impression on his Heart: He admired the Strength of her Understanding; her lively Wit; the Sweetness of her Temper; and a Thousand amiable Qualities which distinguished her from the rest of her Sex: Her Follies, when opposed to all those charms of Mind and Person, seemed inconsiderable and weak. (128)

Yet, though Glanville truly understands the interior Arabella, he is incapable of dealing with the fatuous facade that she presents to the world; however, Glanville knows that he must, if he intends to marry her. It is interesting to note that the power here is all the man's. He must cure her "of her romantick passion" (128). The ideology of the romance has not changed at all—it is the man who controls. Glanville just cannot disguise his maleness and his power. Sir George, conversely, can and does. The contrast between the two suitors is important to the female concerns of the novel; both illustrate the necessity of a proper rhetorical language.

Sir George, for example is adept at dealing with frivolous masks; he is well read in romance himself (see 49ff.),[5] and he decides to beat Arabella at her own game; he will approach her only through romances and their rhetoric, patterning his entire argument on the orations of the French romances.

Predictably, yet foolishly, Arabella is captivated by his approach.

Glanville notes her reactions and tries to disguise his own sincere love in this romantic jargon. For example, when out for the hunt:

> *Arabella* expecting he would begin to talk to her of his Passion, could not help blushing at the Thoughts of having given him such an Opportunity; and Mr. Glanville, endeavouring to accommodate himself to her Ideas of a Lover, expressed himself in Terms extravagant enough to have made a reasonable Woman think he was making a Jest of her: All which, however, Arabella was extremely pleased with. (236)

Volume 1 ends with Arabella, still misinterpreting and misusing her power, and still deeply disguised as the romance heroine.

The second volume of *The Female Quixote* continues Lennox's investigation of the romance genre as Arabella and her cousin, Miss Glanville, indulge in the niceties of romantic heroine behavior. Arabella, at first thinking that it is quite fit for her to abandon Sir George Bellmour, to his deathlike fate because she will not marry him, who is dying of love for her, suddenly recalls the history of the fair Amalzontha, who, though refusing to marry the person chosen by her father, when he was dying, did condescend to visit him. Throughout, Arabella patterns her behavior on the historical heroines. Perhaps, Arabella reasons, she should visit Sir George. Her behavior is criticized by Miss Glanville, but Arabella is shocked at Glanville's seemingly innocent yet highly provocative conduct toward the man.

In an effort to educate Miss Glanville and the reader, much of the second volume is composed of "lectures" on historical heroines. One can learn by following their actions, Arabella insists, and she instructs Miss Glanville. The Countess of _____, however, feeling great compassion "for the fair Visionary . . . she resolv'd to rescue her from the ill-natur'd Raillery of her sex . . . and acknowledg'd, that she herself had, when very young, been deep read in Romances" (230); she teaches Arabella and painstakingly points out how times have changed. Although heroines did wander "thro' the World by Land and Sea in mean Disguises," were "carry'd away violently out of their Father's Dominions by insolent Lovers," were "confin'd in Castles, bound in Chariots" (235), such behavior is no longer demanded or indicative of the heroine's state and fate. In other words, the countess must teach Arabella the new, survival rhetoric of the romance. She teaches her the paradoxical language she must adopt. "The Countess's Discourse had rais'd a Kind of Tumult in her Thoughts, which gave an Air of Perplexity to her lovely face" (240), but Arabella continues her overimaginative behavior. Thus, her views of and deportment in London and environs are all governed by this imaginative vision. She glides through the town heavily veiled, ponderously and foolishly acting like a heroine. She is convinced that a prostitute is a heroine in disguise, that two women in Richmond are masquerading royalty. But she goes too far. "Mr. Glanville who had never heard her in his Opinion, talk so ridiculously before, was so amaz'd at the incomprehensible stuff that she utter'd with so much Emotion, that he began to fear her Intellects were really touch'd" (275). Arabella is examined and thought to be mad; she sees villains everywhere and even jumps in the Thames to avoid certain destruction, but catches a fever from this ill-timed swim.

Although her plight, by now, is ludicrous in the extreme, there is actually something of merit that is going on beneath this disguise of romantic masks. Much like Doody's argument in her article, "Deserts, Ruins and Troubled Waters: Lennox's Female Dreams in Fiction and the Development of the Gothic Novel," the focus on the absurdities of Arabella's imagination suggest the true panic that the woman is constantly threatened by. Her dreams and fantasies are only a replaying of her innermost fears. The female story being told is important here. Arabella's madness is real—it is the mark of sheer terror that is the result of the power that the male wields. Hers is the controlled madness exhibited by all the heroines from Barker and Davys to Smith. It is only in the language of the romantic fool that she can expect to be heard.

\* \* \*

Henrietta, unlike Arabella, does not need a decoder, nor does Lennox as the author of *Henrietta* (1758),[6] her third novel, as she speaks out forthrightly about the woman's fate in the eighteenth century. It is a disrupting text; even the plot is unsettling as Miss Henrietta Courteney attempts to procure a seat in an already fully occupied Windsor Stagecoach as the story begins. She is running away from an arranged marriage with a man, Sir Isaac Darby, whom she hates, and is "going to London, there to conceal [her]self from the search . . . for me" (8). Confessing her plight to one of the female passengers of the coach, Miss Courteney begins a "romantick" friendship. Her chosen confidante assures her that they will correspond daily, every hour in fact. "Oh! what a ravishing pleasure it is to indulge the overflowings of one's heart upon paper!" (8). Miss Courteney is to be called "Clelia." Miss Woodby becomes Celinda, thus masking their true selves.

Disguising is something new for Henrietta. Lennox observes:

Though she was naturally communicative, even to a fault, yet she did not think proper to disclose herself farther, than to tell [Mrs. Eccles, the landlady], that she had been obliged to come to London upon some affairs of consequence. (13)

Her openness is further revealed when the narrator tells us that she has no interest in the *New Atalantis,* Manley's scandal novel; it "did not suit her taste" (14). Nor does she want any of Mrs. Haywood's novels, which, Mrs. Eccles assures her, "are the finest lovesick, passionate stories" (14). Henrietta prefers Fielding's *Joseph Andrews,* though she has already read it three times. Her reading tastes, in general, smack of the realistic and the moral. She learned to read the journal her mother left her and the moral "little narratives . . . and just reflections and useful maxims" (24). She has been taught a realistic rhetoric that will not allow her to get caught up in Miss Woodby's language.

Henrietta's view is refreshingly unclouded with romantic notions. For example, when discussing shepherds and the pastoral mode, Henrietta unmasks "Celinda's" romantic version and tells her of true shepherds:

> I happened to be at the house of a country gentleman, who managed a large farm of his own. One of the servants saying something about the shepherd, my heart danced at the word. *My imagination represented to me such a pretty figure as we see on the stage in the dramatick pastoral entertainment of Damon and Phillida,* in a fine green habit, all bedizened with ribbons, a neat crook, and a garland of flowers. I begged to be permitted to go into the fields to see the shepherd. . . . but how was I disappointed— the shepherd was an old man in a ragged waistcoat and so miserably sunburnt, that he might have been mistaken for a mulatto; the shepherdess looked like a witch. . . . How diverting it would have been to have heard this enamoured swain sigh out soft things to this lovely nymph. (24; emphasis added)

It is just such candor and down-to-earth observations that characterize Henrietta. Unlike Harriet Stuart, she is not victimized, nor does she fantasize, like Arabella. As she rationally explains to her aunt, even though courting her disfavor, she will not marry Sir Isaac Darby. "I would rather submit to the lowest state of poverty, than marry a man whom I could neither love nor esteem, or, change the religion in which I was entirely satisfied" (50). And, so she runs away. (She has also learned of the alternative plan to incarcerate her in a French convent.)

> I walked peaceably out of a door, not without some trepidation however, which arose less from the fear of a pursuit, than the consciousness that I was taking a step which every young woman of delicacy will if possible avoid. (47)

Henrietta has two guides throughout her adventure (who do read "romantically")—Miss Woodby and Miss Willis. Miss Woodby, or the favored Celinda, is easily taken in by a romantic situation. She is adept at participating in romantic escapades. She reveals "Miss Benson's" true name to Lord B——. And for just a moment, "she reflected that she had been indiscreet, and revealed too much of her friend's situation; but being incapable of taking any great interest in the concerns of another, this thought did not affect her much" (58). She is only interested in the romance. Mrs. Willis, her second landlady, conversely, is a truthful, unimpassioned friend. She counsels Henrietta and warns her about Mr. Damer's plots. Both Damer and his lordship, thinking they have unmasked her because of Miss Woodby's candor, are anxious to betray and seduce her. Damer has made up a story of "extra lodgers" that will force Mrs. Willis to evict her, while Lord B. will be the recipient of her favors. As Damer explains, it is war:

> This is a bad world . . . a very bad world: nothing but stratagems and designs, fraud and cunning. Our sex . . . is in a state of war with yours; our arms are sighs and vows, and flattery and protestations, and (as in all other warfares) we fight to destroy. (79)

To clear her name from all the false stories Miss Woodby has told, Henrietta tells Mrs. Willis that she wants to go into service:

> Henrietta, whose imagination was naturally lively, and not wholly free from these romantick notions, which persons of her age readily admit, began to consider her transformation from the niece of Lady Meadows, and a presumptive heiress, into the waiting maid of a cit, as one of those caprices of fate which never fail to produce surprising effects. *She could not help fancying herself the future heroine of some affecting tale, whose life could be varied with surprising vicissitudes of fortune;* and that she would at last be raised to a rank as much above her hopes, as the station she was now entering upon was below all that her fear had ever suggested. (84; emphasis added)

Henrietta clings to a mask of self-righteousness and is determined to clear her name. She has listened to Mrs. Willis who tells her with "plainness" (71):

> you cannot possibly be married against your own consent; and you have it always in your power to refuse. As for the convent, you cannot be cheated into it . . . since you know she had such a design, and may guard against it. (73–74)

Unfortunately, Lennox allows the plot to take over at this juncture, and Henrietta is soon embroiled in Mr. Freeman and Mr. Melvil's peccadilloes. The two English gentlemen masquerade as Freeman (her brother) and Melvil (the Marquis of _____) to accompany Henrietta and Miss Belmour to Paris, where Belmour hopes to bring her lover, Mr. Morley, to his senses by her departure; she thinks her absence will cause his heart to see correctly. Meanwhile, Melvil falls in love with Henrietta and grows "quite romantick" (132); Henrietta in her turn, is equally in love with him. But the lover, because of false pride and misplaced honor, does not get together with her, and Henrietta continues to hide behind her mask. Finally, in an effort to unite the lovers, Freeman unmasks; when he inadvertently hears that "Miss Benson" is Miss Courteney, he discovers his sister. And when he reveals her true identity to Melvil, he ardently declares his love. Predictably enough, Henrietta and Melvil live happily ever after.

In her investigations of disguise and romance *Henrietta* has moved beyond the more facile observations made in *Harriet Stuart* and *The Female Quixote;* the move displays Lennox at the height of her creative, investigative powers. She has examined the masquerade topos and has anatomized the romance: Harriet and Henrietta have unmasked, and Arabella has ceased to view life with romantic spectacles. It is altogether fitting, then, that *Sophia* (1762),[7] her next novel, displays a side of Lennox's talents heretofore unexhibited.

*     *     *

*Sophia* is interesting because of Lennox's experimentation with disguise and romance characteristics. She imputes the "constant course of dissimulation" (1:20) usually attributed to the fair sex and its dealing with the male gender to Sir Charles Stanley instead. (He clearly foreshadows the sensibility of *The Man of Feeling*.) Much of *Sophia*'s plot, then, revolves around Sir Charles's romantic disguises. Early on he shifts his attentions from Miss Harriet Darnley to her younger sister, Sophia, initially, because she is better looking and because a better financial settlement is made on her. "The secret upbraiding of his conscience disquieted him" (1:43), but Sir Charles does not alter his intention to pursue the younger sister. He is a rake, and Lennox gives the reader another *Pamela:* reformed rake and innocent, impoverished heroine.

*Sophia* teaches a lesson in correct, realistic perception. Throughout, the reader remains as disguised and mystified by Sir Charles's actions as do the characters in the book. Only Sophia sees through Charles's hoodwinking actions (see 1:90, 92); late in the second volume, she can still question "his real or imputed faults" (2 : 143) and be unable to stop her love for him.

Whatever other qualities one attributes to Sophia, she is the heroine with "an imagination lively as hers was, and a little romantick" (2 : 164). Yet Lennox's investigation is not primarily concerned with the heroine and her romantic vision and capabilities. Instead, the focus in *Sophia* is on those who have a corrupted imagination, like Mrs. Darnley and Harriet who believe only "in the mean disguise" (1 : 9) and treat romanticism skeptically if at all as well as those who supposedly mask but actually do not, such as Charles and Sophia.

*Sophia* is a novel that presents a black-and-white picture of the eighteenth-century world and its inhabitants: those who masquerade and those who do not. Sophia and Mr. Herbert belong to the party that does not need to hide or disguise true feelings under the cover of a masquerade, whereas Mrs. Darley, Harriet, and Sir Charles initially belong to the party that dissembles. In a less dramatic and romantic fashion than her previous works, Lennox delineates the masker and the nonmasker. Lennox makes an attempt to place Sophia in a romantic escapade, but it soon falters, and the interest in other characters— because of their extreme black or white identities—is not great; it is allegory in eighteenth-century form.

Lennox appears to have taken a page from Fielding's text and her directives in *The Cry:* her presentation here is in an effort to paint the inward mind. A minimal interest exists in romantic, exterior adventures. Instead, she concerns herself with disguising lovers in a plot that is far less complex than her usual pieces.

In *Sophia* Lennox has told a tale of unmasking. It is her only novel that does not deal directly with romance and the masking of the romance. The entire story is built around the exploits of a character who will not disguise.

\* \* \*

Her last novel, *Euphemia* (1790),[8] continues her investigation of the female psyche and its predilection to compose romance stories as a way to demonstrate and exercise female power. In *Euphemia* Lennox continues to investigate feminine perception and the nature of reality. She traces the effects of the "romance" perception on one's "real" perceptions in most of her pieces. In *Euphemia,* however, she eschews the expected romance tale and presents a starker, more realistic version of the woman's story in the letters exchanged between Maria Harley and Euphemia Lumley Neville. *Euphemia* is an epic story; it is also an "American" novel, set in the Albany, Schenectady, and Hudson River area. It tells the saga of growing up female in a society that forces its women to grow down and undercuts many of the romantic assumptions made in both her earlier fiction and in that of other female novelists of the period.

The tale begins as Maria writes that she had expected, with her return to England, to be able to converse in person with her dearest friend, Euphemia, now Mrs. Neville, but Euphemia is about to leave for America, and so their long correspondence must continue transatlantically. On the surface, the story then traces the fortunes and misfortunes of Euphemia in the New World. As Maria Harley queries in her second letter:

> But tell me, my Euphemia, by what strange fatality have all these things happened? When I went to France, I left you rich and happy; the reputed heiress of a large fortune, both your beloved parents alive, and every prospect brightening before you. What a reverse, in the space of a few months! An orphan! your inheritance lost! married; and in consequence of that marriage becoming an exile from your country, doomed to waste your days in America. (1:5)

The questions really being asked here, without the least romantic overlay, are those concerning the woman's true fate: issues of motherlessness, exile, dependence, financial insecurity, and so forth. Euphemia's move to America allows her to become a new persona, and Lennox is impelled to break away from the popular, romantic heroine to present a more realistic, less romance-blinded protagonist in the New World setting: she investigates more contemporary and necessary modes of female survival. Gone are the flamboyant romantic trappings; in their place are realistic patterns of behavior. Euphemia would never imagine that a gardener in America is anything but a gardener.

To be fair, Euphemia's story initially smacks of the romantic. It glamorizes the New World and presents sparkling vignettes of life there.[9] The continuation of feminine enslavement and harassment is not new in America, however. Yet as the journal progresses, neither Maria nor Euphemia "fantasize" their account; instead, they present bone-chilling realistic pictures of the married woman's true fate. Euphemia's theme is one of frustration and despair on the part of the long-suffering and exploited wife who is required to be loyal and dependent on a husband for whom she has long since lost respect and caring. Neither heroine has time or inclination to turn to romance for escape; they grapple with the reality of life instead.

At first, Euphemia has to contend with the "romance image" that has been built up around her. Maria (much like Anna Howe in Richardson's *Clarissa*) tells her:

You are above all praise; therefore, without incurring the guilt of making you vain, I may venture to tell you how we talk of you here in our set. "She is a woman," said Mr. Grenville, "either lifted up by her own strength above the passions of her sex, or Nature hath exempted her from them by a peculiar privilege." (1:166)

Euphemia must learn to submit to loss of power (that is, a loss of a romantic overview); she acquiesces and marries to please her mother rather than herself and is faced with loyalty to a boorish, stupid husband. She initially surrenders all claims of power and control:

Destined to live under the control of another, I find obedience to be a very necessary virtue, and in my case it is an indispensable duty. I am a wife; I know to what that sacred tie obliges me: I am determined, by Heaven's assistance, to fulfill the duties of my station. (1:58)

The rest of the novel challenges this bold assertion and details Euphemia's working out of this loss of power, of a romance vision.

Maria Harley is also faced with learning to live in a nonromantic world. She had been the darling of her uncle (see 1:7–8), but he remarries. "Lady Harley was a true stepmother, and contrived to alienate my uncle's affection from me by artifices which imposed upon us both" (1:8). But Maria ultimately is able to exert her power; her uncle wills her a "deed of gift . . . amounting to about twenty thousand pounds" (1:108), and Maria is able to oust the unscrupulous Lady Harley. The money gives her power, and Maria is even able to see through the romantic frippery of Harley's suit to her, and thus accept him, not as a hero of romance but as a man. As she writes to Euphemia:

he actually, my dear, threw himself at my feet with the air of an Orondates. The place, his posture, his language, had all so romantic an air, that I could not help smiling as I desired him rise. (2:44)

Euphemia also learns about power and control not through the subversion of the romance, but through the reality of survival in the New World. She triumphs. Just as the female writer controls the romance form, so Lennox turns the New World setting of male prowess and courage into a feminized locale that permits the woman to continue to tell her tale, only now it appears without disguise. In *Euphemia*, Lennox's final examination of the romance genre, the heroine has learned to live realistically, not romantically—she survives!

*   *   *

Lennox's final statement, then, is one in support of truth. She will not support such frivolous, romantic foolishness as Arabella practices, nor will she believe a real woman can be as beset as Harriet Stuart. At the end, she points to the candor that is the hallmark of Charlotte Smith's romances.

Lennox's career presents a representational perspective of the movement in the use of the masquerade topos and the romance form, and exhibits how the female novelist comes to grips with the ideology of romantic love and female powerlessness in the course of eighteenth-century fiction. Her work provides a minihistory of the female novel in the eighteenth century.

With *Harriet Stuart,* she presents a full-fledged romantic heroine who must indulge in the popular form of masquerade—disguise as protection—to save herself. Her story is one of female powerlessness and unawakened selfhood; the major episodes in the story focus on the man as cad, threatening and frightening the innocent woman. Each of the histories told in the tale, especially in volume 2, reveals the man as a rogue. It is a novel that explores the romantic masquerade topos and uncovers the fallacies at the base of the disguise and ideologies propounded by the man.

Her second novel is an examination of the popular romance topos: Arabella read real life as if it were a romance. Disguises are assumed here not for protection but to assist the woman in moving against her powerless state; for as a woman, she has no power, but as a disguised heroine, she has quite a lot. Arabella becomes the antithesis of Harriet Stuart. Considered together they provide a portrait of the archetypal, disguised, romantic heroine.

With *Henrietta* and *Euphemia,* Lennox has moved away from the ideology of female powerlessness toward realistic, fictional presentations of the female state. Henrietta does not willingly disguise herself. With *Euphemia,* her last novel, Lennox has finished exploring the question of disguise and fiction and here presents an autobiographical, only slightly disguised tale that explores the epic adventure of two women in the latter part of the century both in Britain and the United States. It is a novel that finally offers a solution to the nagging question that has been the focus of all this fiction. And it is a novel that shares the limelight with the work of later novelist, Charlotte Smith; this writer almost immediately discards the mask and endeavors to present a realistic tale that shows the solution, from the female view point at least, to this ideological ambivalence that is part of the eighteenth-century state of being female. Lennox masks the autobiography of Euphemia; Smith openly avows her autobiographical connections.

Chapter 11

# Charlotte Smith

In 1723, Jane Barker's Dorinda, the heroine of *A Patch-Work Screen for the Ladies,* was so blinded by the romantic mask presented in the popular fiction that she married her footman, thinking him a prince in disguise. Seventy-five years later, Miss Goldthorp, one of the protagonists of Charlotte Smith's *The Young Philosopher* (1798),[1] could muse about her "rescue" by the novel's hero, George Delmont, "that heaven had performed a miracle in her favour, and sent an hero to her rescue, such as fables feign when they tell of demigods and knights endowed with supernatural powers" (1:109). The narrator evaluates this extreme romantic susceptibility and concludes that:

> Miss Goldthorp was a young lady naturally of a very tender and susceptible nature, and who . . . was very deeply read in romance and novels, by some one or other of the heroines of which she occasionally "set her mind," so that with a great versatility . . . she rarely appeared in her own [character]. (1:110)

A great difference does not exist between Dorinda and Miss Goldthorp's perception; yet seventy-five years have passed, and numerous romances have been written and read. Have the intervening novels, and the hard work of the novelists been for nought? Are the heroines, the female readers, and the novelists themselves still imprisoned in the ambiguous, emotional, ideological bonds of the early years of the century? Resoundingly not, *Masking and Unmasking the Female Mind* has attempted to argue. Yet vestiges of the "romantic panacea" were still offered to the public, and so characters like Miss Goldthorp were still lessons for the late eighteenth-century reader. The novelist in the latter years of the century still had to contend with the soporific views of women's miserable lives, yet the novelists themselves were much more articulate with the opposition and criticism of their fate.

Charlotte Turner Smith (1749–1806), writing in the last decade of the century, offers the most personal answer to this entire issue of disguise and romance. Specifically, rather than employ the masquerade only for her characters, Smith adopts the disguise for herself, thus writing quasi-autobiographical tales. She has taken the romance and disguise to its most logical conclusion: total self-identity. For example, in *Ethelinde* (1789), she is Miss Clarenthia Ludford; in *The Banished Man* (1794), Mrs. Denzil. In both, she is the novelist writing about her craft. In effect, she explodes the whole notion of fiction by examining it from the inside, in some cases, by satirizing the views of the novelist (Ludford), and in others by exposing the horrors of her own fate (Denzil). Thus the repressed, aggressive tendencies that have been latently obvious in the earlier novelists here are openly manifested. Her novels are autobiographical to a much greater extent than we have observed in other writers; *Montalbert* (1795) and *Marchmont* (1796), especially, are based on her own real-life situations of financial loss, legal mishaps, and chicanery.[2]

For example, Smith was married when she was only fifteen years old because her father decided to remarry, and the stepmother chose not to be encumbered with an adolescent daughter. Her marriage to Benjamin Smith was disastrous. Not only was he himself inconsiderate, irresponsible, and chauvinistic, but Charlotte was forced to contend with similar attitudes in her mother-in-law, with whom they lived. Smith, however, was on good terms with her father-in-law, though the extraordinary complications of his will (he died in 1776) caused her much anxiety and heartache. These difficulties coupled with her husband's inability to secure and maintain employment made her life extremely difficult, culminating in her husband's seven-month imprisonment for debt. It was during this time, in an attempt to assuage the family's debt, that she first found her way into print with *Elegiac Sonnets and Other Essays* (1784).

None of her efforts succeeded in financially straightening their circumstances, however. In 1786 she left her husband, and, until her death in 1806, she supported herself and her children through her writing.

Her novels display two kinds of disguise. First, most of her novels contain a humorous parody-type character like Barker's Dorinda who imbibes romance aesthetics with her mother's milk and who thinks that the romance will teach her "life"; Smith "unmasks" the foolishness of such a belief as she examines, through her second mask, the poet-novelist, the conventions of romance, and romance writing. It is in this character that Smith unmasks herself, and speaks in her own voice as she shows what novel and romance reading should provide; she unmasks by presenting this novel character in a satiric light thus revealing, in reverse fashion, the true state of the art. Further, through a "creative" character (either a man or woman who fashions the fabric of the story), she examines the nature of her craft qua novelist. Unlike midcentury novelists, she is not solely concerned with examining romance writing through manipulation of the actual plot of the romance. Indeed, by producing euphoric, happily-ever-after texts, she allows herself a large degree of latitude in studying the critical issues of novel-romance writing and reading in general. Although disguised under her artful mask of the romance, her novels are highly educative treatises that examine, perhaps once and for all in the eyes of the eighteenth century, the state of the romance and the mask.

*    *    *

Smith's first novel, *Emmeline: or, The Orphan of the Castle* (1788),[3] took the novel-reading public by storm; its first edition (a run of fifteen hundred copies) was soon exhausted, and a second edition (probably of five hundred copies) appeared before the end of the year, and a third edition was called for by June of the following year. Not only popularly acclaimed, *Emmeline* also received scrupulous notoriety from fellow novelists. Anna Seward writes to Mrs. Hayley on 11 January 1789 that she is embarrassed and upset by the obviously autobiographical characters, Mr. and Mrs. Stafford: "Whatever may be Mr. Smith's faults, surely it was as wrong as indelicate to hold up the man, whose name she bears, the father of her children, to public contempt in a novel. . . . how sickening is the boundless vanity with which Mrs. Smith asserts herself, under the name of Mrs. Stafford" (viii, note 3).

But Smith was innovative not just in her *own* unmasking: the main plot of *Emmeline* not only details the titular heroine's exploits (which include a breach of engagement to Delamere), a plot that is half over before the hero even appears, and Emmeline's harassment by other suitors and her discovery of true love with Godolphin but also incorporates the story of Adelina who willingly marries her seducer and destroyer. *Emmeline* also presents a new rhetorical strategy in the fiction of the period; Smith has included her own poetry within the prose narrative and has created characters who claim to be accomplished poets. They provide the mask that Smith will use in her next nine novels. This "creative mask" allows her to continue her experimentation with the novel-romance form and prepares the reader for the explicit discussion about novels as well as for the experimentation with the form that she will attempt in her endings. Like Jane Austen who supposedly was an avid reader of Smith's novels,[4] Smith is concerned with the genre and her contribution and relationship to it.

Her handling of such forms here in her first novel is not as sophisticated as it would become later. Because *Emmeline* is an early novel, there is more typical use of the disguise topos than in the later novels and much of the plot hinges on the éclaircissement of who is in love with whom. The characters act out scenes of exaggerated emotion. For example, Delamere histrionically tells Emmeline: "No . . . if you determine to push me to extremities, to you only will be the misery imputable, when my mistaken parents, in vain repentance, hang over the tomb of their only son, and see the last of his family in an early grave. It is your power only to save me" (1:97). Emmeline "shuddered at the picture he had drawn of his despair" (1:97) and granted his request.

Delamere is not the only creative one (even if he is the one who engineers the plot). Emmeline draws portraits and paints miniatures, but she is unable to disguise her feelings, and her attempts at creativity are pure representational art. Her realistic philosophy is important. This painful honesty is further emphasized when Smith writes that she tells only an unvarnished tale; in recounting the events for Lord Montreville, her "account of all that had happened, [was] written with such clearness and simplicity as immediately impressed its [*sic*] truth" (2:181). Unlike other popular heroines, she does not need to seek fulfillment through disguising. In fact, Emmeline does not seem to be interested in the fictional escape offered by romances at all; Delamere "went out, and returned with some volumes of novels, which he had borrowed of the landlord's daughter; of which Emmeline read in some a page, and in others a chapter, but found nothing in any way, that tempted her to go regularly through the whole" (2:169). She had been instructed early on by the realistic Mrs. Cary, and Emmeline has no romantic delusions. Emmeline is well aware of her own mental prowess. She tells Montreville: "I have a mind . . . which is infinitely superior to any advantages such a man as Maloney [the steward] can offer me" (25) and refuses to be gotten rid of in so high-handed a romantic fashion. She countermands all romantic attempts by Montreville and Delamere, and forthrightly tells Godolphin that she "found, indeed all attempts to dissimulate, vain; the reserve she had forced herself to assume, gave way to her natural frankness; and having once been induced to make such an acknowledgement of the state of her heart, she determined to have no longer any secrets concealed from him who was its master" (4:455). Further she becomes the protegé and companion of Mrs. Stafford, another woman who reads a great deal, but is not swayed by romantic fiction (see 1:43).

Further, when Lady Adelina assumes the disguise of Mrs. St. Laure, Emmeline forcibly appears as only herself. With her inability to disguise, Emmeline is an interesting "first" heroine for Smith to have created. From the beginning, then, Smith reveals her no-nonsense approach to fiction writing and reading. Both Emmeline and Smith believe in the truth-telling power of fiction. Here, Smith does not have to explore or question its function in her prefaces like her male and female predecessors. Instead, she creates characters who speak her beliefs for her and act out her message of realism.

Smith displays some ambiguity, however, in her first novel. Even though she takes the romance characteristics away from her heroine, Smith is not able to discard them entirely; instead, she assigns these qualities to one of her male characters, Lord Delamere.

Lord Montreville is afraid for his son, Delamere; if he becomes involved with Emmeline Mowbray he might act romantically (that is, foolishly). Lord Montrveille knew his son very well, for Delamere does, indeed, cast himself in the role of romantic hero. Early on, for example, when he learns through his valet that his father is having Emmeline sent away, Delamere bursts into her room, throws "himself at her feet, and [pours] forth the most vehement and incoherent expressions that frantic passion could dictate" (1:32). His behavior immediately forces Emmeline into the role of heroine: she is too terrified to speak, becomes insensible to her surroundings, and faints. Further, Delamere forces Emmeline to be a heroine when he abducts her in the coach, thus setting loose the entire chain of romantic escapades.

For a first novel, *Emmeline* is increasingly complex, for Smith is already exploring and exploiting the romantic form. The romantic action is seemingly controlled by men: first Lord Montreville, then Delamere. Smith is sophisticated with her strategy here, for she lets the men control, yet she undermines this very domination through Emmeline. As Montreville remarks early in the novel: "Pride and self-love seemed to resent that a little weak girl should pretend to a sense of rectitude, and force of understanding greater than his own" (1:122–23), yet she does and so inadvertently controls her plot.

Smith's iconoclastic approach goes even further as she tells the story of Adelina Trelawney, whose unloving, but financially expedient se-duction and marriage was the accepted fate of the eighteenth-century heroine; further Adelina's intimacy with the loving Fitz-Edward is also considered routine. Having his illegitimate child is acceptable as well. But her willing desire for a union with her beloved seducer and an abandonment of her brutish husband is totally outside the accept-able fictional patterns. Although Trelawney is a tyrant, societal mores forced her to remain with him.

From the beginning, then, Smith displays her tendency toward unmasking and realism. She uncovers several romantic conventions in *Emmeline* and introduces her major concerns (that is, realism and feminine power) in the numerous narrative threads of the narrative.

Emmeline's creative ability paves the way for Smith's continued interest in feminine fiction.

* * *

In *Ethelinde, or The Recluse of the Lake* (1789),[5] Smith masks her interest in novel writing under the disguise of a new, novel-writing character. She creates Miss Clarenthia Ludford, a budding novelist-romanciere, and in the character of the gullible Ethelinde, Smith examines the effect of romance on the seemingly average, young woman who "reads . . . every book that is to be had at a circulating library" (2:129). In both characters, Smith disguises her own self. Likewise, the characters themselves adopt disguise costumes. Clarenthia frequently appears "drest like the shepherdress of the Alps, the tender and unfortunate Adelaide" (2:123), and Ethelinde masks herself as a self-sacrificing heroine.

From the beginning, Ethelinde is presented as a different, sensitive, feeling young woman. Motherless since twelve years of age, she prefers solitude and books to lively entertainment, and "the circumstances of her life had taught her to think and to feel" (1:8). She is sensitive and has a well-honed imagination, for, Smith writes, Ethelinde "had learned to see the face of nature with the taste of a painter, and the enthusiasm of a poet" (1:33). The realistic presence of the hero, Montgomery, does not curb her imaginative zest.

> Montgomery still appeared the most interesting figure on the canvas; she *saw* him, *in her imagination*, sitting pensively on the banks of the Lake, or on the fragment of rock where they had last conversed; she heard him sigh over the recollection of the few but decisive moments they had passed together; she *fancied* him lamenting that destiny which tore them for ever from each other; and she *beheld* the concern with which his mother watched his desponding looks and altered spirits. (1:237; emphasis added)

Her imaginative sensitivity is a characteristic she shares with Smith. But she is also the creative product of Smith, and it is as heroine that Smith can note:

> To feel herself thus strongly and suddenly attached to a person of whom she knew so little, was exactly that *romantic infatuation* which she had so often condemned as weakness when it had occurred in real life, and as of dangerous example when represented in novels. But it was in vain she felt all its impropriety; and her reason served to shew her the danger of her situation without affording her the strength to extricate herself. (1:238; emphasis added)

Ethelinde is the female protagonist of the piece, but she also makes herself the "heroine" of the story. She is called the "romantic Princess" (5:55); she is frequently put in heroine-harrowing, disastrous positions. For example, Lord Danesforte takes her to the Lake but is so violent in his rowing demonstration, that Ethelinde is thrown overboard; she is rescued by Montgomery, who is immediately cast as the hero:

> The expression of his countenance was so ingenious, so interesting, and his form so perfectly answered every *idea of an hero,* that had her eyes only been consulted it was impossible to deny him the preference to all the men she had ever seen. (1:103–4; emphasis added)

Fortunately, Montgomery has a "natural taste and poetical enthusiasm" (1:107) and "wishes, wild and romantic as they certainly are" (2:49) similar to her own. Ethelinde freely and imaginatively creates scenes of heroes and heroines, of Montgomery and herself:

> Disgusted by the useless and unmeaning parade with which she was surrounded, and weary of society where friendship and sincerity were forgotten, she suffered her imagination to wander towards scenes more adapted to her taste, and more soothing to her heart. . . . To be the wife of Montgomery!—she dared not trust herself with an hope *so romantic*—so enchanting—*so impossible!* She tried to drive it from her; but her *busy fancy* was still in spite of herself employed *in dressing scenes of visionary happiness,* from which she returned to feel with *awakened anguish* the melancholy and depressing circumstances of her *real situation.* (2:28; emphasis added)

The "romance" plot of Ethelinde, then, involved conquering all the opposition that separates Ethelinde and Montgomery and will not allow them to be hero and heroine. (That is, she is pursued first by Sir Edward, then by Davenant. She must face family debts, debtors' prison with her brother's extravagance, and so on.)

In point of fact, Ethelinde and Clarenthia are really two sides of the same person; Ethelinde almost becomes like Clarenthia's created romantic heroines, and Clarenthia herself oftentimes envisions herself in a heroine's light: "she has a fine romantic name for an adventure; and will, probably, by dint of reading plays and romances, fancy herself the heroine of a novel, and find one of her father's clerks for the hero" (2:128). And Ethelinde

> greatly feared, that the greatest charm Clarenthia found in having a *attachment,* was in having so placed it, as to be sure of an opposition from her family, and to have laid a plan for such imaginary miseries as might

establish her own opinion the "heroine of a tale of sympathy," not unworthy the place she contemplated with the most pleasure—a modern circulating library. (5:84–85)

Clarenthia turns to novel writing herself, she tells us, because of her displeasure with contemporary novels:

they are too probable, and I fancy myself reading what is true. Now the thing I like is to be carried out of myself by a fiction quite out of common life, and to get among scenes and people of another world. (2:166)

She then goes on to catalog *her* romance story.

My heroine falls in love with a young man; quite a divine creature of course, who is obliged to go [as an] Ambassador to Tripoli. She knows not what to do, but at length determines to hire herself into the family of the Tripoline Ambassador here, to learn the language, and accompany her love as his *valet de chambre*. This plan, by help of walnuts to change her complexion, and a pair of black mustacios, she accomplishes; then she meets with an amazing number of adventures in France, where she kills two or three men in defence of her love; and her sex being discovered, a French nobleman becomes enamoured of her, and carries her away by force into a chateau in a wood. But I will not tell you a word more of it, because I will surprise you with the catastrophe, which is quite original; only one event is borrowed from the Arabian nights, and one description from Sir Charles Grandison. Rupert, indeed, says, that with a little application, my pen will become truly Richardsonian. (2:167–68)

The adventures almost read like Ethelinde's own (at least with all the plot complications) or, even more to the point, like so much of the midcentury fiction (I am reminded of numerous Haywood plots that could be synopsized thusly).

Smith has it both ways. First, she can make Clarenthia look foolish and her novel techniques even more so when the plot is described so inanely. Yet, the very inanity disguises some sophisticated, important issues that will continue to interest Smith in her later novels. Clarenthia's story, the fiction she makes, is the surface one of female exploitation (that is, the male story); yet feminine aggression also occurs (that is, the female story). Her heroine kills men—certainly a desire of the women protagonists since Penelope Aubin. She disguises herself as a man and lives, for awhile at least, the freewheeling life of one. Although Clarenthia's story is fiction, she unmasks what is at the heart of women. Further, by claiming to study or imitate the Richardsonian style, she indicates that what is of concern here is a psychological novel that probes the inner female psyche. On closer inspection, one sees that the vaporish, overly imaginative heroine that Ethelinde is sometimes close to becoming is *not* the Clarenthia Ludford heroine type at all. Clarenthia's own position as "a young lady of science" (2:123) affords her a seriousness that in some ways Smith supports. Clarenthia's own take-charge attitude has to be contrasted with ones like the following about Ethelinde to appreciate Clarenthia's positive aggression:

> The heart of Ethelinde had long been irrecoverably Montgomery's; but too well persuaded that it was impossible she ever could be his wife, she endeavoured, not to conquer her affection for him, for that was not in her power, but to subdue her mind to her situation; to dedicate her life to the service of her father, and her brother, and of her heart to Montgomery; never to marry, since death would be preferable to an union with any other man; but to content herself with loving him and seeing him happy. (3:22–23)

Yet Ethelinde is not without a backbone. A tenaciousness and stubbornness about her becomes evident as the story progresses. Most important, Ethelinde demonstrates that heroines who have imagination can succeed. In one of the most trying, touching, and important scenes in the novel, after she has made her escape from the imprisonment and torture forced on her by the Woolastons, who are in league with Lady Newendon and who want her to marry Davenant, we watch as Ethelinde repairs a letter and creates a life (Davenant had ripped the letter during a struggle with her). Initially, she was too upset to deal with the letter:

> Montgomery's letter, however, the fragments of which she had folded up in a sheet of paper, and put into her bosom, she now anxiously took up; but too much agitated to attempt to *re-adjust* the pieces and *decypher it,* she could only kiss the torn relicts, and bathe them with tears. (2:63; emphasis added)

Smith continues:

> she began with painful pleasure to put together Montgomery's letter, which had been written on several sheets of long paper; *Some pieces were still wanting;* but these *Ethelinde by her imagination supplied,* and read with satisfaction, that as his departure became inevitable his mind had acquired courage to bear his separation from her with more calmness. (2:71–72; emphasis added)

So, too, Smith pieces together the fabric of her own story. In fact, this picture becomes symbolic of Smith's entire corpus. Her own imagination supplies the missing facts from the pages of real life, the raw material with which she works. Smith concentrates on this concept so much in Ethelinde because she does not include a preface with this novel and, therefore, cannot critically explore these notions. Her criticism, then, takes the form of characters. *Ethelinde* presents several types of women (who unlike Emmeline) actively try to control their fate.

In the novel, Smith experiments with several female voices. Unlike *Emmeline* in which first Montreville, then Delamere, and finally Godolphin create and control what happens to the heroine, here the women, especially Ethelinde and Clarenthia, make their own fate. For example, half of the first volume is Mrs. Montgomery's story (128ff.), a tale that defines the assertive woman—for example, she goes to the battlefield to find her wounded husband. She also takes a realistic view of life, telling her son: "Ethelinde . . . would be content with any lot, however humble, that was your election. . . . the romantic idea of love in a cottage, which has distracted so many young heads, is too wild and chimerical for you to encourage yourself in dreaming of, or for you to wish that Ethelinde should imbibe" (4:86).

Further, as a counter to the take-charge Mrs. Montgomery and Clarenthia, Smith offers Lady Newendon, "a pretty, insipid doll, whose mind was a mere blank, and whose person was fitted only to exhibit to advantage feminine fineries" (1:5). Smith continues: "Lady Newendon, on whose education great sums had been lavished, had learned everything, but could do nothing; nor had she the least ambition to be anything but a very pretty woman" (1:23). Yet Lady Newendon is wise; she consciously chooses to be "female." Note her reaction to Ethelinde's mishap in the boat: "Lady Newendon insisted upon fainting but as nobody seemed dispos'd to attend her, she very prudently contented herself with the appearance of it only" (1:83). She is untrue to her marriage vows and repeatedly seeks a union with Dannesforte and a divorce from Sir Edward. Mrs. Royston also seeks control by disregarding her vows and subsequently chases Montgomery.

These women and their lives disprove the typical male retort that Harry makes to his sister Ethelinde:

Upon my life, Ethy, I wish you happy, and therefore I wish you could get this whining romantic nonsense out of your head about inviolable friendship and everlasting love: stuff that you have picked up from the novels and story books you are eternally reading. In real life such things are not. (5:195).

Smith's concern with the fabric of fiction enables her in the next six novels to examine the very process of weaving this fictional fabric. I believe these novels are the most exciting, for Smith has discarded (with the exception of Mrs. Denzil in *The Banished Man*) the sardonic mask of the novelist and, instead, investigates the notion of creativity and fiction writing itself. Unfortunately, she does so under the guise of a male hero, who plays the creator. Is this a bid to cover her own aggression under a paternalistic guise? Does the male mask still offer a protection that she thinks is necessary? Does she need male sanction and approval to investigate the creative principle? One's immediate and spontaneous answer is no. Her concern continues to be the nature of fiction, the creative process, and what the romance form does to the creative talent. She desexes the form and deals with raw power.

\* \* \*

*Desmond* (1792),[6] like so many of Smith's novels, investigates creativity. Because it is her only novel to use the epistolary method, as she writes "a work, so unlike those of my former writings" (i), a more immediate quality exists in the work, for the reader watches the creation of fiction firsthand as the letters are written, read, and critiqued. Most of the correspondence is between Lionel Desmond and Erasmus Bethel, but in the second and third volumes, many letters are exchanged between Geraldine Verney and her sister, Fanny Waverly. As chronicled in the letters, the characters not only read fiction, but they write, examine, and talk about it as well.

*Desmond* is Smith's most extensive study of her craft. Her use of mask here, though seemingly simplistic, is actually very sophisticated. For example, Desmond writes to Bethel toward the close of the last volume: "Never, my dear Bethel, did the most feverish dreams of fiction produce scenes more painful, or more terrific; than the real events to which I have been a witness, and in which I have been an actor" (3:243), which echoes Smith's own claim, made in the preface, that she has "not sacrificed truth to any party" (viii). Desmond goes on, in his role as creator-letter writer to recreate the scenes for Bethel, thus casting the "true" events in a prose form. Desmond is the masculine mask for Smith. He is "romantic" (1:10) and capable of using his imagination, and easily pictures Geraldine in his mind's eye (see 1:161).

Desmond is the romantic composer of this piece. Early in the correspondence, he writes to Bethel telling him about receiving the first letter from Geraldine:

With what delight I retrace every word she has written; with what transport kiss the spaces between the lines. . . . But you . . . will smile contemptuously at it, as boyish and romantic folly—My dear Bethel, why should we call folly that which bestows such happiness, since, after all our wisdom, our felicity depends merely on the imagination? (1 : 102)

Desmond quotes Sterne about the efficacy of the imagination, for it is through its workings that one can see through to the most valuable of human values. Desmond casts himself in the role of hero through the power of "the strange phantoms that haunted my imagination" (1 : 216):

> I *believed* myself at the same window as where I stood to observe the storm; and, that in the Count's garden, immediately beneath it, I saw Geraldine exposed to all its fury. . . . I hastened, I flew, with what velocity we possess only in dreams, to her assistance: I pressed her eagerly in my arms—I wrapt them round her children—I thought she faintly thanked me. (1 : 216–17)

He wants to be the romantic hero and savior. In reality, he is able to act heroically, for he saves Geraldine's house by offering the money needed, and he saves her brother's life in a duel and his fate from a bad marriage.

Geraldine also is a creator and also casts herself as heroine. Geraldine, like Desmond, has

> recourse to my pen and my pencil, to beguile those hours, when my soul, sickening at the past, and recoiling from the future, would very fain lose its own mournful images in the witchery of fiction. (3 : 162)

Fiction for Geraldine becomes a "mask" in which she can hide from the present exigencies, and yet, paradoxically, it also unmasks her innermost thoughts, as she records in her "Ode to the Poppy" that "No more I'd sue, that thou shouldst spread, / They spell around my aching head" (3 : 165–66) and, instead, reveals her true feelings. For example, in her imagination she sees Desmond wounded, and she heroically saves him (2 : 7). Both Desmond and Geraldine imaginatively see themselves as heroic. According to Smith they are able to do so because their "passion [is] so generous and disinterested as to seek only the good of its object" (ii). Smith here strikes at the very roots of creativity.

In *Desmond* Smith examines the entire fictive process of masking as she uses characters, seemingly real, who themselves adopt masks in the fictions they create. That is, in their letters, they tell the "truth," yet within the letters themselves create fictions. Further, she examines the nature of fiction because these same characters indulge in a critique of the romance genre. Perhaps even more telling is Smith's creation of

Fanny Waverly, who is Geraldine's chief correspondent. Fanny is unable to project herself as heroine because she has no text. Geraldine puts restrictions on what she may write (2 : 145); her mother controls her reading (2 : 146). Novels and fiction are banned:

> Novels, it is decided, convey the poison of bad example in the soft semblance of refined sentiment—One contains an oblique apology for suicide; a second, a lurking palliation of conjugal infidelity; a third, a sneer against parental authority; and a fourth, against religion; some are disliked for doctrines, which, probably malice only, assuming the garb of wisdom, can discover in them; and others, because their writers have either, in their private, or political life, given offence to . . . prudery . . . and thus I am reduced to the practice and finesse of a boarding-school miss. . . . I must confine myself to such mawkish reading as is produced, "in a rivulet of text running through a meadow of margin." (1 : 145–47)

Geraldine is dismayed;

> How long, my dear Fanny, has your reading been under proscription?— We used to read what we would, when we were girls together, and I never found it was prejudicial to either of us. . . . But if every work of fancy is to be prohibited in which a tale is told, or an example brought forward . . . that the errors of youth may be palliated, or the imagination awakened—I know no book of amusement that can escape their censure; and the whole phallanx of novels, from the two first of our classics, in that line of writing, Richardson and Fielding, to the less exceptionable . . . must be condemned. (2 : 164–65)

Geraldine questions the harshness of everyday life (and clearly she is very capable of such an estimate because of what has happened to her):

> And since circumstances, more inimical to innocence, are everyday related, without any disguise, or with any disguise, or with very little, in the public prints; since, in reading the world, a girl must see a thousand very ugly blots, which frequently pass without any censure at all—I own, I cannot imagine, that novel reading can, as has been alleged, corrupt the imagination, or enervate the heart. (2 : 166)

Geraldine, in the guise of Smith's true voice and unvarnished assessment of romance, then goes on to remark:

> as to others, those wild and absurd writings, that describe in my inflated language, beings, that never were, nor ever will be, they can (if any young woman has so little patience and taste as to read them) no more contribute to form the character of her mind, than the grotesque figures of shepherd-

esses, on French fans and Bergamot boxes, can form her taste in dress. (2:166–67)

She concludes that she finds the playhouse more objectionable than novel reading (2:170).

Perhaps the most important part of this section that examines creativity and the novel, however, occurs when Geraldine unmasks completely and discusses her own preferences in novel reading. Smith unmasks herself in a sly but important fashion when she writes as Geraldine:

> I got up into my own room, and devoured with an eager appetite, the mawkish pages that told of damsels, most exquisitely beautiful, confined by a cruel father, and escaping to an heroic lover, while a wicked Lord laid in wait to tear her from him, and carried her to some remote castle. Those delighted me most that ended miserably; and having tortured me through the last volume with impossible distress, ended in the funeral of the heroine. (2:173–74)

Geraldine's unmasking of her fictional tastes is tantamount to Smith's own revelations. At this juncture, then, I think, it is important to note the advances that have been made in the "women's story" since the early years of the century. Although still adhering to the proper fictional "forms," Smith need not distort them as much as say Haywood did in most of her romances. Smith is freer to voice her opinion. Thus, unlike Haywood, who could only articulate her anger and aggression about the plight of the woman through disrupting the romantic text and exploiting the accepted, euphoric, love story, Smith can express her feelings about fiction and about women in the fiction itself in a less antagonistic way. She creates characters who critique the very sort of fiction that Haywood was writing and simultaneously writes a euphoric text. Smith enters her fictional world unlike any of her predecessors.

\* \* \*

Her success with *Desmond* was followed in 1793 with *The Old Manor House*,[7] reputed by some scholars to be her best novel.[8]

It is, naturally enough, a four-volume romance that details the love story of Orlando Somerive and his Monimia Lennard. It is a euphoric romance: the lovers are united at the end; the man inherits the wealthy, family estate, the woman presents her adoring husband with a son. The Somerives are well on their way to establishing a socially acceptable "new world." After the extraordinary candor and revelation that occurred in *Desmond, The Old Manor House*, at first glance, is disappointing. Smith does not engage in much self-unmasking here; instead, she adopts the voice of the hero and explores the necessity of creativity through the male voice.

From the beginning, it is Orlando's story; he casts himself in the role of hero. Initially, his character has equal parts of reason and feeling:

> Naturally of a warm and sanguine temper, the sort of reading he had lately pursued, his situation, his very name, all added something *to the romantic enthusiasm of his character;* but in the midst of the *fairy dreams which he indulged,* reason too often stepped in to poison his enjoyments, and represented to him, that he was without fortune and without possession. (1:53; emphasis added)

Orlando's guise of hero is an important one. His brother frequently addresses him as "Sir Knight" (2:277; 3:150), or as the "most fortunate and valorous Orlando of the enchanted castle" (3:207). He is the "knight of romance" (1:65), whose "figure and face" exactly "correspond with the ideas of perfection" (3:121) one derives from reading novels.[9] He fashions himself as Pyramus or as Galatea with Monimia his Pygmalion:

> The books he had given her, the extracts she had made from them, and her remarks, afforded them conversation, and gave to Orlando exquisite delight. He had animated the lovely statue, and, like another Prometheus, seemed to have drawn his fire from heaven. The ignorance and the prejudices in which Monimia had been brought up, now gave way to such instruction as she derived from Addison and other celebrated moralists. She understood, and had peculiar pleasure in reading the poets, which Orlando had selected for her; and when she repeated, in a fascinating voice, some of the passages she particularly admired, Orlando was inspired with the most ardent wish to become a poet himself. (2:125–26)

Orlando does, in fact, try his hand at a sonnet or two.

Smith's attribution of the typical romance qualities (usually assigned to the woman) to Orlando makes *The Old Manor House* unique in the author's canon. She writes:

> Sanguine and romantic in the extreme, and feeling within himself talents which he was denied the power of exercising, his mind expatiated on visionary prospects, which he believed might easily be realized. (2:53)

Orlando's father chastises him for reading too much, for such frivolous stuff has only exaggerated Orlando's romanticism. Orlando even goes so far as to suggest to Monimia that they gaze at the moon, though separated, at the same time for "romantic satisfaction" (3:87).

Monimia is only a pale copy of these romantic qualities. She tells us, "Though I had often ridiculed the stories in novels where young women are forcibly carried away, I saw great reason to believe some such adventure might happen to me" (4:230). Yet all her reading has been directed by Orlando. He has made her the "sweet nymph of the enchanted tower" (3:201).

Yet he is not free. Although Orlando envisions himself as the creator, he is still a product and prisoner of the very system he claims to control. Unlike Desmond, he does not actually control or make his fiction; he merely plays his part as the hero. He does not so much "create" Monimia as he "allows" her to be the heroine, just as Smith allows him to be the romantic hero. *The Old Manor House* is a cleverly crafted novel, but it does not explore the intricacies of authorship and creativity that Smith had begun in *Desmond.* The novel does not allow Smith herself to unmask; instead, it imprisons her in the grip of the male tradition, and Smith tells a traditional and acceptable love story that casts hero and heroine into the accepted roles.

∗   ∗   ∗

Smith begins *The Banished Man*[10] with a preface, the first to appear in her novels. It is a formal piece of unmasking, for here Smith directly speaks of her personal dilemmas: "The work I now offer to the Public has been written under great disadvantages . . . at a time when long anxiety has ruined my health, and long oppression broken my Spirits" (A3). Her financial predicaments continue, she tells us; the lawyers have confiscated most of her grandfather's estate, and she and her children continue to be poverty stricken. Smith claims that she still tries to correct this injustice, but in the meantime, she must survive and does so by writing fiction, by yoking together the two plotlines of realism and romance. Her preface assures the reader that it is the realistic story that is the most important. As she writes:

> I have in the present work, aimed less at the wonderful and extraordinary, than at connecting by a chain of possible circumstances, events, some of which have happened, and all of which might have happened to an individual, under the exigencies of banishment and proscription (1:xv).[11]

Because she is concerned with truth telling, she discourages the hidden quality inherent in the very nature of disguise. (One need only recall her first heroine, and Emmeline's inability to "decorate" the truth to see this attitude reflected.) She still employs a certain coloring of the imagination that she casts over the piece to make it fiction, but the fact remains that Smith disguises her concerns "as novelist" in only a cursory fashion. (She also includes as the preface to the second volume a dialogue between author and friend.)[12]

After the revelations of the preface, Smith begins her story, which concerns the exploits of the Chevalier D'Alonville to regain his lost fortunes. Disguised as a peasant, he is befriended by the Baroness de Rosenheim and her daughter, Madame D'Alberg, and the volumes record his arduous search to save his dying father's life and estate (throughout much of the novel, he is a wanderer and a fugitive). He is also befriended by the Englishman, Edward Ellesmere and, together, they journey across the continent and Britain in an effort to right the wrongs of the revolution, thus championing realism over an outdated romantic view of class and economy.

There are predictably enough, love interests: D'Alonville for Angelina Denzil, and Ellesmere for Alexina Carlowitz, a Polish emigre; at the conclusion of the four volumes, both pairs are successfully wedded. This euphoric romance story only provides a vehicle that enables Smith to investigate her true subject: the art of fiction. As she writes:

> One great objection to novels is the frequent recurrence of Love scenes: which readers of so many descriptions turn from as unnatural, or pass over as fulsome; while, to those who alone perhaps read them with avidity, they are said to be of dangerous tendency. (2:56)

Her focus is creativity, not love. One of the most memorable characters in the novel is Charlotte Denzil, poet and writer; she is the magical figure, who, by her own admission, acts like Prospero (2:216), uniting the diverse strands of the story. Mrs. Denzil is Charlotte Smith.

> Driven from my home twelve years since, with a large family wandering without any fixed plan, was long a matter of necessity and may now, for ought I know, be grown into habit, and be a fault of temper. (2:220)[13]

The "disguise" is successful—is it Mrs. Denzil or Smith herself? The answer is not important. It is important to note that this material is transferred to the character and is not confined merely to the revelatory preface material. Smith does not hide. Mrs. Denzil is harassed by creditors, Mr. Thomas Tough and Humphrey Hotgoose. Because of all the financial worry, she becomes sick. It is not just Mrs. Denzil who is ill, however; Smith, too, is the victim.

Thus harassed by pecuniary difficulties, driven about the world without any certain home, she experienced, from day to day, the truth of the adage, "That the ruin of the poor, is their poverty," for she was thus made liable to much greater expenses, than would have happened in a settled establishment; perplexed by creditors, and sickening from the sad conviction that her power of supporting her family by her literary exertions must every year decline, while her friends become more and more weary of her long continued sorrows. (4:117–18)

No mask is used here; Mrs. Danzil and Smith are one and the same person.

Through Mrs. Denzil, Smith catalogs and examines the trials of being an author. The disguise is barely perceptible. For example:

After a conference with Mr. Tough, she must write a tender dialogue between some damsel, whose perfections are even greater than those "Which youthful poets fancy when they love," and her hero, who, to the bravery and talents of Caesar, adds the gentleness of Sir Charles Grandison, and the wit of Lovelace. But Mr. Tough's conversation, his rude threats, and his boisterous remonstrances, have totally sunk her spirits; nor are they elevated by hearing that the small beer is out; that the pigs of a rich farmer, her next neighbor, have broke into the garden, rooted up the whole crop of pease, and not left her a single hyacinth or jonquil. . . . Melancholy and dejected, she recollects that once she had a walled garden well provided with flowers, and the comforts and pleasures of affluence recur forcibly to her mind. She is divested from such reflections, however, by hearing from her maid that John Gibben's children over the way, and his wife, and John himself have all got the scarlet fever; and that one of the children is dead on't, and another like to die. She is ashamed of the concern she felt a few moments before for a nosegay, when creatures of the same species, and so near her, are suffering under calamities infinitely more severe. . . . compassion for these unhappy persons is now mingled with apprehensions for her own family. . . . With the earliest dawn she sends her servant . . . to enquire at their door how they do? (2:225–26)

This passage is important not only because it uncovers the thin disguise that Smith has adopted as Mrs. Denzil, but also because of what it reveals about the novel and fiction. The romantic exploits and escapades of the hero and heroine seem far removed from the everyday reality that faces her readers. Such detailing of her existence, then, supports the entire notion of romance's raison d'être: necessary disguise. To deal with the awfulness of life, one disguises in a romance both author and character. The romance provides escape for both writer and reader. As Smith records following her bout with the infectious neighbors:

The rest of the day is passed as before; her hero and her heroine are parted in agonies, or meet in delight, and she is employed in making the most of either; with interludes of the Gibbin's family, and precautions against importing the infectious distemper into her own. (2:229)

*The Banished Man* is an important work in the Smith corpus, and eighteenth-century feminine fiction because of the thorough unmasking that occurs within the novel, both of the novelist and the romance. She is aware of the pitfalls of the romance, and she quickly glosses over them. She is careful in her narrative to avoid such scenes and part of the lugubrious quality of the novel results from this loss of the usual, expected, romance trappings. By anatomizing the romance, and then not using its standard pieces, she unmasks the genre and calls into question its very being. She exposes men and their pretentions to help women and female writers. Nothing is left sacred; by the end of her examination, men, the art of novel writing, and the romance have all been exposed.

*    *    *

*Montalbert*[14] (1795), like *Marchmont*[15] (1796), which renders the facts of her life in yet another fictional guise, continues the exposure of *The Banished Man*. Though bearing the name of the titular hero, *Montalbert* is really a book about women's history. Oddly enough, it is a story of mothering—of the loss and then the discovery of a mother figure—and "mothering" as a sense of female history. Both Rosalie Lessington and Mrs. Vyvian, Rosalie's biological mother, must learn how to read the female text. They must learn how to read the romance—between the lines. Their story is offered in between the male text, yet even here Smith eschews the expected form, and a major portion of the tale focuses on Walsingham, who is not the hero.

In *Montalbert,* the emphasis is on story and reader. Rosalie Lessington naturally enough, is a reader; she enjoys the "odd volume of *The Tatler,—Robinson Crusoe*—Nelson's *Feasts and Fasts*—Harvey's *Meditations*—a volume of Echard's *Gazeteer*—Mrs. Glass's *Cookery*— and *Every Lady her own Housekeeper*" (1:18). Such a list is not typical reading matter for a heroine, but it is insightful, for it is a "male" list supporting the male ideologies of female submission and powerlessness. It is a reading list that supports romance reading, for romances keep woman in their place. Her father, for example, has arranged a marriage for her with Mr. Hughson, but "Her soul abhorred the idea of receiving Hughson as a lover" (1:61). Her mother, unaware of the covert lessons of rebellion inherent in the romance text, tells her daughter: "It would be some thing new, Rose, and altogether unlike the heroine whose adventure you have studied, if you should happen to like the man recommended to you by your friends, and in every respect eligible" (1:59). Rosalie is forced into an exploited heroine role, and she is compelled to participate in the usual submissive tactics—"Dragged to a scene, where she considered herself exposed as an animal in a market to remarks and purchase of the best bidder, it was with extreme reluctance that Rosalie entered the ball-room" (1:81); she has, however, refused to regale herself in the feathers, flowers, and ribbands of the ballroom masquerade.

Rosalie's refusal to comply places her on the side of Smith's aggressive heroines. Yet it is an aggression that she does not fully comprehend at first. Rosalie instinctively does not act the heroine's part: she marries Montalbert secretly, and she keeps a journal. She has to learn not to act the heroine's role consciously; she must learn about women's history and female texts.

Initially, Rosalie is a product of male exploitation. Supposedly the fourth and youngest daughter of the Reverend Joseph Lessington, master of arts, vicar of Cold Hampton, and curate of Barlton Brooks, she was actually surrendered by her real mother because of her illegitimacy and her mother's unsanctioned liaison with Mr. Ormsby. To quote Rosalie, the ten years she spent living with the Vyvians, her surrogate family, "were my days of an alloyed felicity; it was my golden age, and every scene has imprinted itself deeply on my memory."

*Montalbert*, like *Ethelinde* and *The Old Manor House* is about the loss of that golden age; it is a loss soon turned to advantage. Smith leads Rosalie through this deceptive "age of innocence," created and maintained by the man to control the woman, and shows how, paradoxically, the woman can recreate and restructure what she learned then, so that it can still offer her solace and aid. *Montalbert* becomes a living lesson on how to read the female text.

Mrs. Vyvian, Rosalie's real mother, is also a victim of the break-up of the female, Edenic paradise and of a misreading of the text. Her mother observes: "He knew I neither did nor ever could love him—for I told him so when I married him. He was contented to possess my fortune and my person" (2:10). The only area the Vyvians had in common was their religion, and when Vyvian abandons Roman Catholicism and adopts the Anglican church to get a seat in Parliament, Mrs. Vyvian becomes a solitary, an "isolated being in the midst of her family" (1:13). In the meantime, she lost her heart to the youthful Ormsby; "he was not an artful seducer; but I had no mother, I had no friend, and those who candidly reflect on my situation will surely [be] compassionate, though they may not perhaps acquit me" (2:28). Her father has Ormsby banished, though rumor has it that he had Ormsby killed. When her daughter, Rosalie, is born, Mrs. Vyvian disguises the entire affair and pretends that Mrs. Lessington, her closest, dearest friend, had twins (1 : 107). Rosalie "Lessington" is born amid deception and intrigue, and immediately is forced into following the female pattern her mother has set for her.

Patterns of the mother are, indeed, visited on the daughter and Rosalie's marriage to Montalbert "seemed rather like the fictions of romance than reality" (3 : 105). She still has not learned how *not* to read the male romance story. The "romance" element is enhanced as she is abducted and imprisoned—somewhere in Italy—and rescued by Montalbert's best friend, Walsingham. Rosalie takes after her *real* mother, Mrs. Vyvian, who led the life of a heroine; her surrogate mother, Mrs. Lessington, has none of the romance heroine qualities in her. As she tells Rosalie vis-à-vis her acceptance of Hughson: "Let us have no more romance, Rosalie, it will answer no purpose, but to irritate your father without changing his resolution" (1 : 75).

Returning to England after her imprisonment, Rosalie learns of her real mother's death. In an attempt to define and understand herself, Rosalie turns to her journal and almost all of the third volume is a record of her personal reflections on her imprisonment, her search for her mother, and an understanding of the female text.

*Montalbert* is an indictment of mothers, that is, an indictment of not teaching female history. None of the mothers seems compelled to establish patterns for their daughter. All three of the mothers presented—Mrs. Vyvian, Mrs. Lessington, and Mrs. Montalbert—all capitulate to male demands and thus fail as female models for the daughters (daughters-in-law) involved. Neither Mrs. Montalbert nor Mrs. Lessington provide Rosalie with anything but further chains and prisons. They have been so indoctrinated by men that they willingly prepare Rosalie as a victim. Smith shows by these awful stereotypes what monsters men have made of women: Mrs. Lessington, who boldly offers her daughter for sale, a thoroughly acceptable contemporary practice to meet the demands of Mr. Lessington; Mrs. Montalbert, "who had projected a marriage for [Montalbert] with the daughter of a friend of her own" (2 : 3) and who places restrictions—financial, national, and religious—on her son's choice of wife; and Mrs. Vyvian, who married to provide a father for her illegitimate child—all exhibit the capitulation of female decency to unworthy male demands. In abrogating their duty, the older generation create most of the difficulties the younger generation experience. When Mrs. Vyvian tries to excuse herself, explaining that she was easily seduced by Ormsby because "I had no mother, I had no friend, and those who candidly reflect on my situation will surely be compassionate, though they may not perhaps acquit me" (2:18), she is unaware of the extraordinary truthfulness of her observation. Without strong, independent mothers, the next generation of women is almost certainly doomed to remain under male control. Smith's use of the legal term "acquit" is important; in *Montalbert* mothers are on trial. Although her primary text tells of Rosalie's romantic adventure, her subtext examines the role of teaching, the role of mothers.

The second text of *Montalbert* is the male one, the story of the hero's search for self—the no one from no place who becomes someone from someplace. The male text is really a tale of fathers, and as such it portrays a rather horrific tale of tyrannical, obsessive fathers—for example, Rosalie's surrogate father tries to force her to marry Hughson, and Mrs. Vyvian's father forced her to take the blame for Ormsby's imprisonment and deportation to India. Mr. Lessington ignores her and dies. Even Montalbert comes in for criticism, for he abandons Rosalie in the early stages of her pregnancy, thus denying his fatherly role.

Female "bildungsroman," not the male story, is important in *Montalbert*. After two volumes detailing the detestable position women are forced to assume, the third volume presents a blueprint for self-examination in the journal Rosalie keeps during the imprisonment. Ostensibly she keeps an account so she can tell Montalbert of her trials; in fact, she records the workings of a female mind, what she calls "this monotonous account of lingering anguish" (3:8). Not since *Desmond* has Smith's writing been so immediate or enthralling.

Smith uses Rosalie's entire experience to examine the nature of illusion making, to probe the mysteries of fiction. She has Rosalie observe:

> The objects, formerly so familiar to her, brought back the days of Rosalie Lessington, and the strange vicissitudes that had happened since seemed rather like the fictions of romance than reality; she was then the daughter of a village curate; humbled by her supposed sisters, and shrinking with terror from parental authority, which seemed likely to compel her to marry a man she disliked. Her present situation formed a strong contrast to that she was then in; but was it better?—She was now the daughter of parents who did not own her, a wife without a husband, and the mother of an infant who seemed to have been born to misfortunes. (3:105)

Smith emphasizes, however, that illusions of paradise and Edenic pleasure merely masked the exploitation that she was subject to even as a child.

In the third volume Rosalie's real mother, Mrs. Vyvian, dies, leaving her again without a role model. (Before her death, Rosalie has learned of her true parentage and thus was able to consider Mrs. Vyvian in her real role.) Rosalie spends the entire novel looking for the part she is meant to play. Although Smith has flirted with realistic presentations as she, one by one, takes away Rosalie's props and supports, the restoration of husband and son returns the story to the familiar male-dominated world. *Montalbert* succeeds because Smith embedded her realistic, often brutal analysis and revolutionary, feminine probing within the popular romance form.

Thus, the expected "romance quest," at the last, leads Rosalie to Montalbert. The usual romance nobody becomes a somebody, again overtly detailing the feminization of the "orphaned" Rosalie into Mrs. Montalbert; more meaningfully, under cover of this fiction, is the finding of the female self.

\* \* \*

She continues this female investigation with *Marchmont* (1796) and its critical preface, which not only codifies her novelistic theory but simultaneously reveals the real Charlotte Smith. It is her most personal work, her most thinly disguised. It contains the most "facts" turned into "fiction" and is, I think, Smith's most sustained attempt to understand her fate.

In the preface, she speaks to the reader both as an ordinary woman beset with domestic problems and tragedies and as a novelist, an artist trying to create a believable story in the midst of humdrum reality. The preface is a true scene of unmasking, and no one who reads it cannot hear the besieged voice of Smith. She observes that this is her thirty-second volume presented to the public; she writes "from necessity and by no means from choice" (vi). Smith apologizes for the state of both *Montalbert* and *Marchmont* and goes on to explain that "these volumes, therefore, have been written under the disadvantages of wanting a friendly critic on those errors of judgment which occur in every long work entirely dependent on the imagination" (x). Further on in the preface, she disclaims the use of the imagination and notes that she teaches morality and reality:

> It is a fault frequently imputed to novels, that they are directed to no purpose of morality, but rather serve to inflame the imaginations, and enfeeble by false notions of refinement the minds of young persons. I know not what share of those faults may be found in the present production, but my purpose has been to enforce the virtue of fortitude: and if my readers could form any idea of the state of my mind while I have been writing, they would allow that I practise the doctrine I preach. (xv–xvi)

*Marchmont* becomes a story of fortitude and patience as it tells of Althea's long and arduous struggle to win Marchmont and of the almost insurmountable difficulties of their married years.

Althea, the protagonist, was raised in the country by her aunt, Mrs. Trevyllian. She is not allowed the luxury and peace (and freedom) of such an idyllic, independent existence for long. Her halcyon days end abruptly with Mrs. Trevyllian's death and Althea is forced to go to live in London with her father, Sir Audley, and stepmother, Lady Dacres. Her father tries to force her to marry the scurrilous lawyer, Mr. Mohum, but her "native integrity, her soul revolted at the idea of selling herself to any man, and Mohun was in his person, manners, and morals equally disagreeable to her" (1:151). Later, she muses, that had she married him,

> Privileged by her sex, he might have dissipated my fortune, and his own, and possibly have beat me, or locked me up; or sold me if he could have met with a purchaser, to give cause to his brutal humor or contribute to his selfish indulgence. (4:279–89)

Sir Audley, like many of Smith's male characters, is a tyrant and is not used to having his demands ignored:

> he could not endure to find opposition where he thought he had a right to implicit obedience. . . . The refusal of his daughter . . . seemed the most unpardonable offense that ever was committed against him. . . . Therefore in very angry and peremptory terms he declared to her, that though he had first condescended to speak to her rather as a friend than as her father, she should find that he would be obeyed. (1:152–53)

Part of Smith's purpose here is to learn how to deal with autocrats, despots, and tyrannical father. Althea's fate is the typical one of the eighteenth-century woman. She is homeless, without money, and motherless (because of the death of Mrs. Trevyllian). Although cut from the same cloth as so many of the age's heroines, Smith writes that she struggled to make Althea interesting:

> How difficult then is it for a novelist to give to one of his heroines any very marked feature which shall not disfigure her! Too much reason and self command destroy the interest we take in her distresses. It has been even observed, that Clarissa is so equal to every trial as to diminish our pity. Other virtues than gentleness, pity, filial obedience, or faithful attachment, hardly belong to the sex, and are certainly called forth only by unusual occurrences. Such was undoubtedly the lot of Althea, and they formed her character; for in the hard school of adversity, she acquired that fortitude

and strength of mind which gave energy to an understanding, naturally of the first class. (1:178–79)

She must learn how to avoid the matrimonial pitfalls Sir Audley arranges for her and how to keep herself until such time as she can become as free in person as she is in mind.

The reader watches Althea develop her own self. On a textual level, it is these trials and tests that make her adventure interesting, the plot so entangling and entrapping. Subtextually, Smith probes the female psyche to see exactly how much suffering, how many near violations a woman can endure. *Marchmont*, like *Montalbert* and her last novel, *The Solitary Wanderer*, is less outwardly revolutionary; the focus is on the interior state of mind and how the inner being deals with the frustration and violence that is so much a part of life. *Marchmont* teaches strength of mind; Althea is able to turn her exile and punishment into a positive state:

> Accustomed insensibly to her solitude, Althea passed her time without murmuring. Her mind compelled thus to exert his strength at so early a period, and her education having been such as had not enfeebled while it ornamented her excellent understanding, she not only became reconciled to a situation which to most young women would have been intolerable, but every day learned to rejoice at the election she had made, and compare the melancholy tranquility of her present situation with the splendid wretchedness to which a union with Mohum would have condemned her. (2:2304)

This is the strength of mind and character that she learned from Mrs. Trevyllian; Smith would have her readers adopt this mind-set as well.

With these heroines of her later novels, Smith offers alternatives. She is trying to show her readers that they do not have to accept the lies men offer, that they have a right to their own minds, selves, and lives. Smith probes the facade of the "typical" romance, the fiction that women have come to believe is true, and like Haywood and Fielding, she exposes the myths that have proliferated in the pages of the century's fiction. She dispels notions of female dependency and gothic entrapment as she reveals these notions for the fabrications that they are. Here in *Marchmont*, she will not allow her hero to be romantically, unrealistically, heroic; instead, he is chased by creditors, poverty stricken, and homeless. Despite such obstacles, he proves himself. Althea is not cast in the heroine mold either; although homeless, poor and incarcerated in a country estate, she is living alone and happy.

To emphasize her support of the independent women, Smith creates Lucy Marchmont, who is, like Althea, governed by "Good sense and courage" (3:156) and that desire of independence, however humble, in which true and laudable pride really consists" (3:157). Lucy has a commonsense attitude toward life that is applauded by Smith and Althea. She accepts her condition for what it is and continues to make the best of it:

> I am not ignorant that young women totally destitute of fortune as we were have no chance of marrying. Well! it is very sad, to be sure, to be predestined old maids; but a million of these . . . live single; and I am sure there are such who are living happier, and more quietly and comfortable than many women who have families. (3:158)

Making the best of life seems to be the theme of *Marchmont*. Lucy Marchmont, Althea, and even Marchmont himself repeatedly voice their acceptance of a fate far from romantic and ideal. Beset with financial problems, inheritance legalities, individual rights, and so on, these three characters manage to present examples of how one can triumph.

A great amount of covert tale telling does not occur in *Marchmont*. Because the story so closely follows Smith's own life, the overt fiction itself tells an exceedingly rebellious story, she has no need to resort to "hidden" meanings. No female novelist character exists because Smith herself has figured so prominently into the text of the novel. Like *Desmond* and *Marchmont*, however, her concern remains that of creativity.

*   *   *

Smith continues her anatomy of the romance genre in her last novel, *The Young Philosopher* (1798), remarking "that my intention in this has been *to expose* the ill consequences of *detraction*" (vi; emphasis added). Again, she is concerned with romance and reality. More than in her earlier works, Smith truly spells out romantic conventions. She pits the overly zealous Miss Goldthorp, an example of the romance writer gone to seed, who was so "very deeply read in romance and novels, by some one or other of the heroines of which she occasionally 'set her mind,' . . . that with a great versatility of character she rarely appeared in her own" (1:110), against Laura and Medora Glenmorris, who show the proper mix between reason and fantasy.

Through the exposure of the romance genre through Miss Goldthorp's antics, Smith is able to outline and write her own romance. Laura and Medora not only tell a romantic tale, but they become romance heroines themselves.

The tale, however, begins with Miss Goldthorp, who "was one of

those young women, of whom it is common to say, that they are
'highly accomplished'" (1:137). Her female accomplishments, however, support her frivolousness, and she quickly adopts the role of
coquet. She sees Delmont as the hero and quickly disguises herself as
the lovesick maid. "Tears filled her eyes, she sobbed, and hid her face
(though not her blushes) in the bosom of her friend" (1:169). By her
own admission, Miss Goldthorp has learned to play the hypocrite and
disguise her true feelings to get her man; the appellate attached to her
throughout is "the romantic Miss Goldthorp" (1:171). Yet her romanticism rings false. Her escapades exist only in her mind, and her
whole being adopts romanticism only to give pleasure to herself. She
does not even create novels for others.

To counter all this artful chicanery, Smith creates the Glenmorrises,
mother and daughter, who exist without disguise. Laura Glenmorris
becomes Smith's spokesperson as she clearly and succintly outlines the
true function and purpose of romance. Unlike the foolish, selfish
fancies that control Miss Goldthorp, which are really lies and cheap
tricks, Laura Glenmorris defines romanticism as a life philosophy that
is positive and fulfilling. Indeed, this passage is key to Smith's entire
oeuvre as well as that of Barker, Davys, Haywood, Fielding, and all
the female novelists considered in this study. Mrs. Glenmorris explains:

> Oh! what romantic stuff! is a common exclamation, if any one ventures to
> feel or to express themselves out of the style of common and everyday life.
> But why is it romantic? I should be sorry, it is true, that a daughter of
> mine, suffering her imagination to outrun her reason, should so bewilder
> herself among ideal beings as to become either useless or ridiculous; but if
> affection for merit, if admiration of talents, if the attachments of friendship
> are romantic; if it be romantic to dare to have an opinion of one's own, and
> not to follow one formal tract, wrong or right, pleasant or irksome,
> because our grandmothers and aunts have followed it before; if not to be
> romantic one must go through the world with prudery, carefully setting
> our blinkers at every step, as a cautious coachman hoodwinks his horses
> heads; if a woman, because she is a woman, must resign all pretentions to
> being a reasoning being, and dares neither look to the right nor to the left,
> oh! may my Medora still be the child of nature and simplicity, still venture
> to express all she feels, even at the risk of being called a strange romantic
> girl. (2:13–15)

This attitude is the unwritten creed of the romance writers. From
Barker to Smith herself, each romanciere-novelist has studied and
considered how to use the romance form in the most profitable
fashion for her readers. It is in this role as instructor-creator that Laura
Glenmorris presents her story.

The stories of Laura and Medora form the bulk of *The Young Philosopher.* Both Laura and then later her daughter live out the role of the romantic heroine. For example, Laura elopes with Glenmorris, and her "girlish imagination delighted itself with the prospect of the wild romantic solitude which love only was to embellish" (2:77). Like a heroine, she is captured by pirates, by vengeful and tyrannical relatives, and so forth. Unlike the fictional heroines that we have read of in the pre-1740s fiction, however, Laura creates herself and her tale as heroine and retells the tale as an example for, first, her daughter, and second, her auditors. Laura unmasks the heroine's antics as she exactly outlines romantic perils; here, for example, her ultimate exploit is her incarceration in a madhouse through the operations of her own mother, who unromantically wants to deprive both Laura and Medora of any family money. Laura's exploit moves beyond the normal frivolousness of the heroine and attempts to underscore the true state of the eighteenth-century woman. Laura becomes less the romantic heroine and more the mask for Charlotte Smith herself who writes out her own anguish through her realistic characters.

Further, Medora Glenmorris underscores this shift from romance to realism. Like Smith, she forgoes being a romantic heroine to present a realistic assessment of the times. As Smith observes:

> Her sensibility was not the exotic production of those forced and un-natural descriptions of tenderness, that are exhibited by the *imaginary heroine of impossible adventures;* it was the consequence of *right and genuine feelings* . . . that intuitive sense, by which she knew how to put herself, in imagination, in the place of another, and to feel for all who were unhappy, made her active in doing all the good that her age and situation admitted. (3:38; emphasis added)

Almost all of the fourth volume is taken up with Medora's heroinish adventures (the second volume belonged to her mother). Again Smith is at pains to disprove the "Pamela" escapades assumed to belong to the heroine—any female masked "in a fine romantic disguise, and fancying herself like Pamela" (3:313)—and portray the true, crip-pling effect of such unrealistic behavior.

The "young philosopher's tale," George Delmont's, is quickly sub-sumed by the more pressing and demanding needs of the woman and her imaginative story. Delmont and his adventures merely provide the mask that allows Smith to explore the interior woman.

\* \* \*

It is interesting to note the changes that occurred from Barker's Galesia to Smith's Mrs. Denzil and Miss Ludford. Autobiography and romance mix, to be sure, but in the earlier works in a state that was unpredictable. Smith writes with a degree of sophistication that was unavailable to Barker or Davys. Smith does not disguise the plight of the woman (nor did Barker, Davys, Haywood, and others), nor does she shrink from outlining the pitfalls of being a novelist. She examines the romance from unabashedly and uses it in a high-handed fashion that both explores and exploits it. The examination of Smith's work has caused this study to come full circle. Both the disguise and the romance have been uncovered and anatomized.

What direction does the feminine fiction of the late eighteenth century take next?

Chapter 12
# Elizabeth Inchbald and Jane West

By the end of the century, the masquerading romances had a decidedly different look from those of the earlier years. The adventures of the heroine still made up the mainstay of the romance plot, and the writers continued their feminist bias by depicting the abduction, disguises, rapes, attempted rapes, and escapes of their female protagonists, with little to relieve the intensity of the attacks. Much like Aubin's novels, though with a far greater degree of sophistication, and, therefore, more insidiousness, these heroines lead far from ideal lives. What makes the later novels even more grim is not just the continued harassment of the heroines but the author's rational, outspoken critique of this tortured, romance form. (The nonfiction tracts of the period support this increased outspokenness, though there had been little amelioration of the feminine situation.)[1]

The rhetorical structure also indicates an increased awareness of the feminine plight. Rather than Haywood's technique of euphoric plot subversion and distortion, the later writers such as Fielding, Lennox, and Smith maintain the happily-ever-after ending, but precede it with so many "adventures" that the reader can hardly believe the heroine will survive. These "adventures" are patterned on the real-life exploits of the authors themselves who clearly define and state their positions in their numerous prefaces. It is impossible to mistake the feminist attitude—in real life, as in fiction, women are harassed, exploited, and subjugated. Fielding, Lennox, and Smith speak directly to these conditions. Elizabeth Inchbald and Jane West, however, exploit the romance rhetoric completely by thoroughly inverting the form itself.

\* \* \*

Elizabeth Inchbald's (1753–1821) *A Simple Story* (1791)[2] appears as the most stylized of these late eighteenth-century romances. It becomes literally "a romance's romance," though such esoteric labels did not hinder its popularity, which required a second printing just three months after its initial publication. Maria Edgeworth writes to Inchbald that the realistic elements in the novel were unsurpassed: "I never read a novel that . . . so completely possessed me with the belief in the real existence of all the people it represents."[3] Such believable detail can be used because realism had already been introduced by Fielding, Lennox, and Smith, but Inchbald's Miss Milner is a far cry from Pamela. She is full of faults; she is vain, willful, a tease. She despises men and yet manages to catch one of the most important bachelors of the town. Unlike the qualified euphoric tone of the midcentury novelist, Inchbald presents characters who lead tragic lives. She cannot draw delightful young women with minor faults who are educated by the men. Forthright and outspoken, her women, Miss Milner and Agnes Primrose especially, can only be punished by the controlling male ideology for the position they adopt. The following year Mary Wollstonecraft would publish *A Vindication of the Rights of Woman*, making explicit the demands and judgments that Inchbald was able to present only fictionally.

Occupying much the same place of importance as Fielding's *The Cry* (1754), with its outspoken analysis and critique of the romance genre, so *A Simple Story* also exploits and explodes the romance convention. Inchbald achieves these results this time not by analytically dissecting the genre but instead by actually creating, first, the romance itself with a seventeen-year lapse in the story (between the two volumes) and, second, the tragic fate of the heroine.

Inchbald begins *A Simple Story* demurely enough by borrowing Charlotte Smith's unmasking technique and writing about herself in the preface:

> It has been the destiny of the writer of this Story, to be occupied throughout her life, in what has the least suited either her inclination or capacity—with an invincible impediment in her speech, it was her lot for thirteen years to gain a subsistence by public speaking—and, with the utmost detestation to the fatigue of inventing, a constitution suffering under a sedentary life, and an education confined to the narrow boundaries prescribed to her sex, it has been her fate to devote a tedious seven years to the unremitting labour of literary productions. (1)

After an extensive career in the theater,[4] Inchbald turns her attention to the novel, most specifically to investigate educational issues. She is quite candid as she remarks about the type of education she herself had, and it is just this concern that provides the main plot of *A Simple Story,* for here Inchbald provides another treatment of the ubiquitous "young woman's entrance into the world" narrative. Like her volatile predecessors, Inchbald wants to uncover the shocking naïveté of her female readers and educate them out of their complacency. Like Miss Milner, they must enter the world fully cognizant of their needing to deal with unscrupulous men. If nothing else, *A Simple Story* presents stark realism.

Miss Milner is introduced by a well-seasoned slightly jaundiced narrative voice, who observes: "Yet let not our over-scrupulous readers be misled, and extend their idea of her virtue so as to magnify it beyond that which frail mortals commonly possess; nor must they cavil, if, on a nearer view, they find it less" (14). Miss Milner is human, and, initially, controlled only by vanity. Early on, she learns to put on a good face to the outside world. Because she is so young, decisions are left to her guardian.

> How much do different circumstances not only alter the manners, but even the persons of some people! Miss Milner in the drawing room at Lord Elmwood's surrounded by listeners, by admirers (for even her enemies beheld her with admiration), and warm with their approbation and applause—and Miss Milner, with no giddy observer to give a false eclat to her actions, left destitute of all but her own understanding, (which severely condemns her), and upon the point of receiving the censure of her guardian and friend, are two different beings.—Though still beautiful beyond description, she does not look even in person the same.—In the last mentioned situation, she was shorter in stature than in the former—she was paler—she was thinner—and a very different contour presided over her whole air, and all her features. (50)

Miss Milner is not really disguising; it is only the priest, Sandford, friend of Dorriforth, who thinks Miss Milner is other than she appears, and he spends most of his time trying to trap her in a plot that will reveal what he thinks is her true nature. No other level exists in Miss Milner, however, that cannot be discovered and excused because of her age. Dorriforth favors an alliance with Sir Edward Ashton; Miss Milner appears to favor Lord Frederick Lawnley. The object of her affection is immaterial; power and control are at issue here. Initially, Dorriforth "was charmed to find her disposition so little untractable" (33) and thinks this bodes well for "the future prosperity of his guardianship" (33). Yet he is only seeing a masked Miss Milner. It is Miss Woodley (another woman) who is able to unmask her and who discovers an extraordinary mature and sophisticated woman underneath the ingenue who boldly, unabashedly asserts (concerning her relationship with Dorriforth): "I love him with all the passion of a mistress, and with all the tenderness of a wife" (72). She has uncovered the heart of the woman.

When Miss Milner, at last, confronts Dorriforth alone, she casts all disguises off:

In his presence, unsupported by . . . a third person, every grace she had practised, every look she had borrowed, to set off her charms were annihilated, and she became a native beauty, with the artless arguments of reason, only for her aid.—Awed thus, by his power, from everything but what she really was, she never was perhaps half so bewitching as in those timid, respectful, and embarrassed moments she passed alone with him. (82)

Miss Milner is able to "read" this scene correctly; Dorrisforth is not. She is aware that the issue is one of power and control. And she wants to have it.

She continues to not express her affection for Dorriforth, but resorts to more and more subterfuge to mask her true feelings and test her power over him. She baits him; she determines to go to the masquerade though strictly forbidden. She constantly forces Dorriforth/Elmwood to take a position vis-à-vis her femininity.

Both Woodley and Dorriforth force Miss Milner to mask; like the controlling feminine ideologies, they must keep the woman in her place and that means she must be disguised. Dorriforth can only comprehend her if she is the pupil and he the instructor. When he learns of Miss Milner's love for him, *he* discards *her* mask of powerlessness and replaces it with one of romantic though still male-controlled love:

Within a few days, in the house of Lord Elmwood, every thing and every person wore a new face.—His Lordship was the profest lover of Miss Milner—she, the happiest of human beings—Miss Woodley partaking in her joy—while Mr. Sandford was lamenting with the deepest concern, that Miss Fenton had been supplanted. (136)

With this declaration, power and control shift. Now Miss Milner masks herself:

Perfectly secure of the affections of the man she loved, her declining health no longer threatened her; her declining spirits returned as before; and the suspicions of her guardian being now changed to the liberal confidence of a doating lover, she now again professed all her former follies, all her fashionable levities, and indulged them with less restraint than she had ever done. . . . she, who as his ward, had been ever gentle, and (when he strenuously opposed) always obedient; he now found as a mistress, sometimes haughty; and to opposition, always insolent. (139)

Inchbald presents a story of iconographic masquerade in this late-century tale, which culminates in the first volume with the masked ball given by the fashionable Mrs. G——. Miss Milner had never attended a masquerade and was anxious to go; Lord Elmwood forbids her attendance." 'I am sure your lordship,' continued she, 'with all your saintliness, can have no objection to my being present at the masquerade, provided I go as a Nun. . . . that is a habit . . . which covers a multitude of faults'" (152). When he refuses to attend, saying he will not "play the buffoon at a masquerade" (153), Miss Milner resolves that nothing will stop her from attending short of being physically locked into Lord Elmwood's house. Instead of the nun disguise, she decides to go as Diana, but Miss Woodley "was astonished at her venturing on such a character—for although it was the representative of the goddess of Chastity, yet from the buskins, and the petticoat made to festoon far above the ankle, it had, on the first glance, the appearance of a female much less virtuous" (155).

Such behavior tests Dorriforth to the limit, and Miss Milner finally forces his hand; it is a power struggle to the end. When he writes and severs their engagement and almost the entire relationship, "her tones sunk into the flattest dejection.—Not only her colour, but her features became changed; her eyes lost their brilliancy, her lips seemed to hang without the power of motion, her head drooped, and her dress was wholly neglected" (179). Strangely enough, the denouement of this volume finds Dorriforth/Elmwood marrying Miss Milner, with a slight hint of doom to follow, since in the haste of the ceremony, the only ring that he had to give her was a mourning ring. In other words, the wedding did nothing to explain or consolidate the issue of power.

The second volume begins after a seventeen-year hiatus, with Lady Elmwood on her deathbed; her virtuous life has been thrown away on a life of dissipation that has lead to her early death. The plot focuses on the fate of Dorriforth and Miss Milner's daughter, Lady Matilda. Supervised by an older Miss Woodley, Miss Matilda practices deception from the first because she is secretly loved by Dorriforth's ward, Lord Rushbrook. Unlike her mother, Matilda is forced physically to hide her person when either Dorriforth/Elmwood is living in the country house or when Rushbrook comes for a visit. She willingly accepts the situation that puts her in male control; in fact, she seems to welcome it. Because she indulges in disguise, Miss Matilda is also subject to the romance heroine's mask, and, predictably, she is abducted by Lord Margrave's henchmen in an effort to make her submit to his offers. But the seduction is too informal, too predictable; Miss Matilda remains too calm. It is as if she is a character playing a part.

In the second portion of the story, Inchbald has given the reader an allegorization of the first part. It is the working out of Miss Milner's history in the disguise of her daughter that brings the reader to the necessary sense of denouement that fiction demands, to a sense of closure. The honesty of the daughter more than makes up for the disguise and guile of the mother. Inchbald's moralizing is obvious: in terms of the male ideology, Miss Milner is an example of what not to be; she cannot be controlled. Her daughter provides the man with a heroine, the one who willingly accepts domination. Part One exhibits the negative effects of masquerade, while Part Two strips away the disguise and shows the true worth of the heroine according to male law. Part One tries to present the feminine text, while Part Two is the man's story. Because of the highly contrived and artificial seventeen-year hiatus that occurs between the sections, Inchbald consciously presents a "made artifact" to the reader. The archetypal suspension of disbelief is called into question as the reader watches her conscious creation of a story that unmasks the masquerade and the romance to reveal the bare bones of the romance genre. A Simple Story is a deceptively simple fable.

\*   \*   \*

Inchbald's Nature and Art (1795) continues this deceptive presentation, again turning large issues of revolution and the treatment of women into almost allegorically stylized, simplistic fare. Nature and Art, perhaps patterned on Thomas Day's Sandford and Merton, is the story of two brothers, William and Henry, and the account of their adolescence and mature lives together, with a more detailed story of the lives of their sons, cousins William and Henry. The elder, Henry, is an accomplished violinist; William attends the university and becomes a clergyman. Henry marries a singer; William becomes even more snobbish and finally marries a woman of consequence, the Lady Clementina. The brothers drift apart. Henry's wife dies within a year, and William's Lady Clementina becomes more and more vain and haughty. After his wife's death, Henry goes to Africa with his infant son; eleven years later, Little Henry is sent to London to be taken care of by his uncle and aunt because of serious uprisings in Africa. The major portion of the book, then, focuses on the different educations of the two cousins. The two characters speak a different language: William, like his father, thinks of only himself; Henry, however, considers others. As Inchbald notes, Henry "would call compliments, lies—reserve he would call pride—stateliness, affection—and for the words war and battle, he constantly substituted the word massacre" (27:246; emphasis added). This difference in the characters' rhetoric extends, naturally, to their life philosophies as well. When they reach their twentieth year, the men fall in love: Henry with Rebecca, the fourth daughter of the curate of the parish; William with Agnes, the daughter of a poor cottager in the village. William aims only at seduction and triumph; Henry, virtuous devotion. Henry finds a chaste, sublime mate in Rebecca, whereas William disguises, seduces, and abandons poor Agnes Primrose.

Inchbald gives us a moral allegory here about the use and abuse of disguise and power. Her presentation is stylized; her preference is clear, as she writes when William and Henry return to their summer estate:

> While Henry flew to Mr. Rymer's house with a *conscience* clear, and a *face enlightened* with gladness; while he met Rebecca with open-hearted friendship and frankness, which charmed her soul to peaceful happiness; William *skulked around* the cottage of Agnes, *dreading detection;* and when towards midnight he found the means to obtain the company of the sad inhabitant, he grew impatient at her tears and sobs, at the delicacy with which she withheld her caresses, that he burst into bitter upbraidings at her coyness; and at length . . . abruptly left her. (27:286–87; emphasis added)

Agnes "felt herself debased by a ruffian—yet still, having loved him when she thought him a far different character, the blackest proof of the deception could not erase a sentiment formed whilst she was deceived" (27:287). Inchbald, however, writes so the reader will not be "deceived." She exposes the romantic expectations of her reader claiming that "Rebecca Rymer and Agnes Primrose are its heroines" (27:270) and tells the reader to read on for more moral instruction than romantic escapism.

Further, she writes to expose the intense cruelty of men and their legal system. In the recounting of Agnes's tale of seduction (the story of the rake and the wanton), all the blame is attached to the man. Agnes is seduced by William, abandons her baby, is made to appear first before the dean (the grandfather of the child), reclaims the child but is forced to leave the village and leads a life ultimately ending in a brothel, only at the last to appear before Judge William, who sentences her to death. Faced with this barrage of male authority and power, Agnes "was still more disconcerted; said, and unsaid; confessed herself the mother . . . declared she did not know, then owned she *did* know, the name of the man who had undone her, but would never utter it" (27:318–19). As William delivers his verdict, "she shrunk, and seemed to stagger with the deadly blow; writhed under the weight of *his* minute justice (27:350). Her deathbed confession (27:352ff.) is a further indictment of the male system, for she still shoulders the blame and accepts the responsibility. Inchbald, however, is not done with her castigation of the male for she has even the virtuous Rebecca judged by the male (the Dean and William), browbeaten, and punished.

This surely is not a romance world that Inchbald presents. Like *A Simple Story,* she has pared down the romance rhetoric so one is faced with the skeleton structure, the stark confrontation between a man and woman. Inchbald does not disguise the romance tale; with no fanfare, she unmasks it and offers no panacea to her female readers. Unlike the midcentury Pamela, no happy-ever-after ending occurs for the heroine of the 1790s. All the Inchbald heroine can do is survive. Inchbald satirizes the sentimental, romantic midcentury romance. Jane West also teaches realism rather than romance; her heroines, choosing virtue rather than immorality, introduce tragic notes into the supposedly euphoric text.

\* \* \*

Jane West (1758–1852) writing in the preface to *The Advantages of Education; or, The History of Maria Williams* (1793)[6] echoes Inchbald's sentiments as she addresses her readers:

> Writing professedly for the inexperienced part of her own sex, she thought it more advisable *to describe life as they are likely to find it, than to adorn it with those gaudy and romantic colours in which it is commonly depicted.* She wishes to convince them, that it is *but seldom* that they will be called forth *to perform high acts of heroic excellence,* but that they will be daily required *to exert those humble duties* and social virtues, wherein the chief part of our merit and happiness consists. (preface; emphasis added)

She writes, West continues, to "counteract the evils incident to the romantic conclusions which youth are apt to form" (preface). She thoroughly unmasks the romance genre. Her narrator, whose voice is so close to her own that it is impossible to distinguish one from the other, remarks in the first chapter, that

> it is my intention to explode those notions which novel reading in general produces by delineating human life in false colours, expectations are formed which can never be realized; the consequence of which is, that life is begun in error, and ended in disappointment. (1:3)

Rather than following the usual romance scenario that moves the heroine from severe trials to ultimate wealth and felicity (1:3), Prudentia Homespun says she will present an unvarnished tale that teaches innocent virgins about unreclaimed rakes, that preaches marriage is not the happy ending always to be expected.

> I do not chuse to hold up *matrimony* as the *great desideratium of our sex;* I wish them to look to the general esteem of worthy people, and the

approbation of their own hearts, for the recompense of their merit, rather than to the particular addresses of a lover. (1 : 3–4; emphasis added)

Her friend chastizes her saying that these "honest, realistic" intentions "are as romantic as those which you design to eradicate" (1 : 4). But the narrator/recorder claims "all the veracity of a faithful historian" (1 : 5) and goes on with her realistic tale, thus unmasking the romance genre so that it is the narrator as well as Maria Williams who becomes the protagonist of the tale.

The narrator almost destroys the illusion that a novel exists, for she continually interrupts as if the true, main story is really her own. She writes of Kitty Spier and Lady Bab Lardoan, of her niece Elizabeth, and the reader is aware that these are real people. No longer need the writer hide behind the ambiguous masks of heroines and romances.

Yet West does use some of the major romance symbols as a way to uncover the form. Specifically, one of the first major lessons of reality versus romance occurs when Charlotte Raby offers Maria tickets to attend the masquerade. Her mother wisely cautions that Maria cannot afford to indulge in such diversions and so, she questions, can Maria "after having once experienced the wild throb of tumultuary transport" (1 : 50), forgo a repetition and return happily to her peaceful pleasures? Maria assures her mother that masquerades are not to her taste and turns instead to the history of Regulus: "she reads of his invincible fortitude with increasing complacency, and fancying herself a heroine of ancient times, resolved with all the firmness of a Portia or a Lucretia, to smile in misery and triumph in suffering" (1 : 54–55). As it turns out, by Charlotte's account, the masquerade was less than successful.

This masquerade event is only a prelude to the main disguising and learning event of the novel—the unmasking of the unreformed rake. West's Maria is as far distant from Richardson's Pamela as can be imagined. West, much like Fielding did in *The Cry,* translates the typical seduction as it should be read:

> He then avowed his love in similar terms to what my readers must have met with in at least an hundred of my predecessors *in the novel line;* the terms being invariable, *and reduced to plain language,* are, "I love you, and if you don't pity me, I shall die."
> But as all the Carolina's, Sophia's and Henrietta's do not give exactly the same answer as Maria did, it may not be unnecessary to say, that with a great deal of timidity, she confusedly replied, "that she did not think herself authorized to answer an address, which had not received the approbation of her mother." (1 : 157; emphasis added)

Although Maria claims not to be a heroine, West gives her a heroine's qualities. After she begins to see the artificiality and falsity of Mr. Stanley/Sir Charles Neville and to learn of his dastardly deeds, Maria gets sick and has a high fever. Even here, however, West introduces a note of realism, for the fever is a prelude to unheroine-like measles.

West further criticizes romances by openly anatomizing them, declaring that "There is unfortunately a flatness in love scenes, which the most skilful artists can scarcely avoid. For this reason, I shall pass over this . . . as cursorily as possible" (1:215). She further translates the romance rhetoric should any of her readers be the last bit in doubt as to the realism she hopes to instill: "Whenever a lover assumes an unusual degree of tenderness in his looks and expressions, I would advise my fair readers to be guarded. A kneeling posture, with the words, angel, idol of my fond heart, queen of my soul, and a variety of similar expressions, have often far worse consequences than all the imprecations and coarse epithets of Billingsgate" (1:21).

West, however, though she will parody the romance and criticize the masquerade, still, to conclude her tale, must resort to some sort of happily-ever-after ending. Mr. Stanley is discovered to be Henry Neville, dishonest baronet. Maria is rewarded with honest Mr. Herbert, and the tale ends euphorically not without, however, a final word from the narrator who observes: "There are now neither dragons, enchanters nor giants, for these zealous knight-errants to combat. The evils most dangerous to the damsels of the present age, lurk in the bosoms of their pretended champions" (2:204).

*    *    *

West continues to attack the romantic sensibility in *A Gossip's Story* (1797)[7] with Mrs. Prudentia Homespun, who observes in the introduction that

> She was not romantic enough to imagine, that a little novel issuing from a general repository, unsupported by puff, unpatronised by friends, and even unacknowledged by its author, could rise into celebrity . . . besides. . . . It had no splendour of language, no local description, nothing of the marvelous, or the enigmatical, no sudden elevation, and no astonishing depression. It merely spoke of human life as it is, and so simple was the story, that at the outset an attentive reader must have forboded the catastrophe. . . . not ambitious of dazzling the imagination, and of inflaming the passions, it uniformly pursued its aim of meliorating the temper and the affections. (xi–xii)

Homespun continues this "realistic approach" by creating what in today's jargon would be known as a women's networking group, as she tells us of the "many single ladies, like myself, [who] . . . have established a very agreeable society" (1:2) that exhibits "their" prudence to the world. In a word, they are gossips. "A Gossip's Story" is recorded merely as a way to entertain themselves. Mrs. Homespun records that she keeps a journal; from its entries she gets the raw material for her fiction. She observes:

> The vents which really happen in a small neighbourhood, are not sufficient to furnish the supplies conversation eternally requires, without the aid of fiction. I have often, though encumbered with my umbrella and patterns, carried a piece of intelligence round the town in the morning, which in the evening I was again forced to step out and contradict. (1:35)

A conscious intention, then, to misread the facts to get a more plausible, entertaining, and romantic story occurs.

In fact, Homespun consciously instructs her readers that she is creating romance in order to show them the falseness of the form. "I wish to ask the fair enthusiasts of heroick generosity, romantick love, and exuberant friendship, whether they really suppose it possible to improve upon the model which Christianity . . . presents for our imitation . . . these romantick notions indeed generally leave us on our Journey; but what is the consequence? Repeated disappointments" (1:48–51). We rail at Providence for giving us a life that is not like the happily-ever-after fictionalized romance. West writes to dispel this romantic delusion. Through the instruction of the garrulous Mrs. Homespun, like Fielding in *The Cry*, West anatomizes the romance. She does so through the two sisters, Marianne and Louisa Dudley. (*Sense and Sensibility* is patterned on West's novel.) Marianne has read too many adventures and romances and, as West writes, now presents a "portrait of an amiable and ingenuous mind, solicitous to excel, and desirous to be happy . . . forming to itself a romantick standard, to which nothing human ever attained; sinking under fancied evils; destroy its own peace by the very means which it takes to secure it" (I, 47). Marianne Dudley is the culmination of all the Placentias, Pamelas, Arabellas, and so on that the century produced. Marianne *will* turn the world and reality into a romance novel. Louisa Dudley, conversely, is all common sense and realism.

The entire novel conspires against the romantic vision that Marianne adheres to and unmasks the romantic apparatus. In fact, *A Gossip's Story* almost becomes a manual in how not to be romantically deceived. With chapter titles like "Humbly dedicated to the improvement of all fair Quixotes in heroism," West/Homespun strips away all romantic paraphernalia. For example, Mr. Dudley presents a realistic picture of marriage, remarking that "The romantick part of love quickly evaporates, and the soonest with him who has been the most visionary in his expectations. Think yourself happy if the kneeling slave does not change into the tyrant" (1:96). Further, the narrator deflates reader expectation à la romantic description and describes Marianne's wedding by remarking that "the whole proceedings appeared nothing but a chain of improprieties, and I therefore think it better to omit a description which could only excite the painful duty of unfavourable criticism" (2:37). If this comment were not enough to destroy reader expectations thoroughly, West even has the "hero," Clermont, describe the change in his vision and "his romantick enthusiasm [which] had raised the mortal nymph into a goddess" now "magnified her errors into indelible offences" (2:166).

The final word in this total destruction of the romance and the romantic vision is presented by the arch feminist, Miss Milton, who "spends her time in writing satires against perjured swains, and elegies upon deceived nymphs" (2:211).

Miss Milton's closing remarks together with the entire frame story of the single women's coterie emphasize the romance unmasking West so adequately presents in *A Gossip's Story*.

*   *   *

West continues to instruct through a satiric unmasking of the romance conventions in *A Tale of the Times* (1799).[8] The tone of the work is different from her earlier pieces. Although Prudentia Homespun claims to be the narrator, the easy, jocular familiarity of the earlier character is now replaced with a more sterile, cynical tone.

Initially, *A Tale of the Times* begins fashionably enough with Lady Powerscourt compared to "some fair damsel in romance, whom a terrible Saracen is carrying away to his enchanted castle" (1:62–63). The story also begins with Geraldine having too active an imagination, which creates portraits of her beloved Monteith that are unreal, and with Monteith the hero, storming the castle and freeing the lady (see 1:133). Yet, in comparison with the earlier pieces, the descriptions lack life and are flat. The problem, the narrator muses, is in the age itself. The only appropriate tone is satiric. Glancing at Addison, Goldsmith, and Fielding, the narrator sees the shallowness of the age, remarking that "I in vain endeavour to be amused with ghosts and dungeons, incident without character, or character without effect" (2:164). In an effort to produce a more truthful picture of the times, the narrator cannot "shrink with reluctance from the disgusting task of describing systematic villainy mining the outworks with decorum and religion have placed around female virtue, while the unsuspecting heart becomes entangled by satanic guile and inbred vanity" (2:6). The notes change to tragic as the narrator records the sorrowful downfall of Geraldine Monteith. "While I prosecute my arduous task, I rely on the lenity of those who sincerely regret the alarming relaxation of principle that too surely discriminates a declining age" (2:80). Everything is in decline, and it is not the age of romance as Lady Arabella quickly discovers; "the swains who flourished in the close of the eighteenth century were of a very different order of beings" (2:83).

West is careful here to address the "young female reader, whose notions of nuptial felicity are drawn from the delusive pages of a circulating library" (2:24–25) and much of the novel is taken up exposing and disproving the romance rhetoric that proliferated in those circulating-library romances. This unmasking includes the destruction of the heroine, her marriage, and so forth by an unreformed rake.

West ultimately concludes[9] that it is the age itself that is responsible for this weakening of the romance form, and the generally deplorable morals and manners practiced by the romantic characters.

The final notes, then, are satiric and can be so only because a realistic picture has been drawn. In the post-1740s romances, the rakes remain unreformed, the heroines are harassed and die, and the narrative voice takes on an increasingly more important role. So important, in fact, that the thinly disguised author-narrator really becomes the chief protagonist of the piece, and the later-century novels become more critical examinations of the entire form than those before 1740. The controlling male ideologies have been examined and found wanting. Women will no longer remain powerless and unhappy.

Chapter 13

# Conclusion

Numerous "histories of the novel" usually concentrate on the five male "greats"—Defoe, Richardson, Fielding, Smollett, and Sterne. Another history of the eighteenth-century novel exists, however: the history of female fiction, the story of the "romance," and woman's search for self through its pages and conventions. The romance novel is an important vehicle for the articulation of women's concerns and fosters the growth of this same woman's voice. It is important to hear this voice.

A recent surge in eighteenth-century feminine studies by Spacks, Rogers, Spencer, Spender, and others has occurred; each has contributed valuable information to the picture that is emerging concerning eighteenth-century feminism. My own study has focused on the masquerading romance, the most popular form of the novel scene.

This masquerading romance was the most predominate and articulate form of the early years of the novel. Typically, the first or male story concerned a heroine, who, in her quest for love, her mate, and inclusion into society (all the benefits society offered) had to go about the world disguised. Ostensibly, the disguise was worn as a protective device, yet its "protection" is paradoxical. On the one level, it protected her from the vicious male world that would torment and harass her were her true identity to be known. Yet, conversely, the disguise allowed her to turn the tables on this controlling male and his imprisoning ideologies, and, instead of remaining passive and powerless, by becoming an "other" permitted her to demonstrate her own strength, power, and control. The romance provides a "bildung" setting as the writer and characters use the form as a way to investigate selfhood. Thus, the romance story moves the female from a position of asexuality and lack of development to a position of knowledge of self and power. Such a movement, however, cannot always be told in a straightforward fashion, and the operative topos here is one of disguise and of masquerade.

The major female writers of this period adopt the masquerading romance for their own purposes. Elizabeth Boyd's early work, *The*

*Happy Unfortunate,* for example, sets an upbeat note for the early part of the century; on closer examination, however, one finds the unhappiness and uneasiness that is always close to the surface even in her "happy" romance. Boyd's title indicates the ironic, paradoxical relationship that woman have toward the masquerade topos in their works of fiction: they could be happy in the momentary freedom that the masquerade gave them, but the final outcome was unfortunate, for it merely made them aware of the misery and unhappiness, the exploitation and harassment that they are subject to outside the pages of the romance. The masquerade supports the ideology of female powerlessness even when such a prolific writer as Haywood demonstrates, with her many novels, that the woman need not be entirely powerless.

So Boyd paints a pretty picture and romances the form that allows disguise to be viewed as a positive force in the eighteenth century; at the opposite extreme, Penelope Aubin uses the ubiquitous disguise topos to illustrate the totally powerless and exploited state of the eighteenth-century woman. Unable to disguise themselves to pursue a beloved, heroines are forced to cover up their real selves so that they can just continue to live. Disguise becomes a matter of survival in the black, chaotic world that Aubin portrays.

Eliza Haywood, conversely, unwilling and unable to kowtow to such unabated misery, employs the popular topos to see if she can help alleviate the horrid situation in which the eighteenth-century woman finds herself. Haywood attempts to redefine the popular ideologies that dominate the eighteenth century's notion of womanhood. She dispels the notion of female powerlessness by disguising soft, malleable women in the guise of the Gigantillas and Baroness de Tortillees of the age. She combats the ideology of romantic love by writing romance endings that conclude with death or exile. Like Aubin, hers is not a pretty world for the eighteenth-century woman; hers is not a world that positively romanticizes and glamorizes the masquerade.

Boyd, Haywood, and Aubin have demonstrated the discrepancies in the popular eighteenth-century ideologies concerning women. Women need not be powerless, nor must they be made dependent on the romantic notion of perfect love and happy marriage. No fulfillment exists for the woman in either ideology, just as the eighteenth-century woman cannot live without a disguise.

The use of the masquerade topos did not dramatically stop in the 1740s with the new direction of the romance genre. The grandiose masquerade charades in the later feminine novels, however, no longer exist. Part of this change in sensibility can be attributed to the great success of Richardson's *Pamela: or, Virtue Rewarded.* (It should be

noted that the second volume of *Pamela II* features a masquerade
scene that is pivotal for the denouement of the novel.) Suddenly, it
seems less important to disguise one's true self and, instead, the
importance of the real person comes to the fore. Disguise was still
used but in a much less prominent position. Instead, attention was
turned to the romance. Following Lennox's lead with *The Female
Quixote* (in fact, several good pieces appeared much earlier), the novel
vogue now focused on the masquerading romance, the love story that
hides under cover of its love story, a true description of the life and
times of the eighteenth-century woman.

Specifically, such early figures as Jane Barker and Mary Davys were
already adept at using the masked romance to critique the early-
century woman and her discontent. Under the cover of the romance,
Barker especially was able to examine her own life; much later in the
century, Charlotte Smith would attempt the same as she cast herself,
together with her foibles and adventures, as the heroine. Smith's
honesty is brutal at times; she almost totally discards the mask, and so
her vision is stark and horrific. Sarah Fielding and Charlotte Lennox
also present a scathing portrait of the feminine age; they examine the
genre and plainly point out the foibles inherent in the form. Paradoxically enough though, both writers also are able to write extraordinarily effective romances even as they criticize the form.

Part Two, "Masquerading the Romance," examines the romance
genre as the feminine writers of the later century use the form as a
cover, much as the early novelists had masked their intentions in the
disguising of characters to examine the romance form. Just as the
masquerade topos allowed them to explore the inner female self under
the cover of the disguise, so using the romance form permitted a
thorough examination of the life of the eighteenth-century woman as
lived in the pages of the romance. By the last decade, especially with
Charlotte Smith's novels the two topoi have blended together to
present Smith's unique pastiches of disguise, romance, and autobiography.

The unmasking of the romance and its heroine, like the uncovering
of the masquerade and the masquerader, reveals the woman as a
different person from that presented in the popular ideologies. Looking underneath, one discovers that the heroine is neither helpless and
submissive, nor is she enthralled with the capitulation and condescen-
sion of the romance story. Romance novelists are savvy and understand how to disguise themselves and their characters to win as many
readers as possible.

The culmination of this masquerading romance in terms of the
female novelist comes in the early years of the nineteenth century with

the work of Jane Austen. The female quixote becomes her central character and is representative of all humankind, with her self-deceiving mind and clouded vision. Like Jane Barker's Dorinda, her ancestor of one hundred years earlier, the Austen heroine also thinks that footman are princes in disguise. Her delusion is momentary, however. Austen has read the earlier female novelists and is well aware of the masked faces; instead, she creates unmasked minds.

# Notes

## Chapter 1. The Masquerading Romance

1. William Park, "What Was New about the 'New Species of Writing'?" *Studies in the Novel* 2(1970): 112–30.

2. Carol Thurston, *The Romance Revolution: Erotic Novels for Women and the Quest for a New Sexual Identity* (Urbana: University of Illinois Press, 1987), 10.

3. Ibid., 43.

4. Janice A. Radway, *Reading the Romance: Women, Patriarchy, and Popular Literature* (Chapel Hill: The University of North Carolina Press, 1984), 151, and Janice Radway, "Women Read the Romance: The Interaction of Text and Context," *Feminist Studies* 9 (Spring 1983): 53–78.

5. See Ernest Baker, *The History of the English Novel*, 3 vols. (London: H. F., and G. Witherby, 1929); Sheridan Baker, "The Idea of Romance in the Eighteenth-Century Novel," *Publications of the Michigan Academy of Arts, Sciences and Letters* 49(1964): 507–22; Helen Sard Hughes, "Translations of the *Vie de Marianne* and their Relation to Contemporary English Fiction," *Modern Philology* 15 (1917): 491–512; Henry Knight Miller, "Augustan Prose Fiction and the Romance Tradition," *Studies in the Eighteenth Century*, ed. R. F. Brenenden and F. L. Eade (University of Toronto Press, 1976); Dieter Schultz, 'Novel,' 'Romance,' and Popular Fiction in the First Half of the Eighteenth Century," *Studies in Philology* 70 (1973): 77–91; Harrison R. Steeves, *Before Jane Austen* (London: George Allen and Unwin, 1965).

6. Leslie W. Rabine, *Reading the Romantic Heroine: Text, History, Ideology* (Ann Arbor: University of Michigan Press, 1985), 2.

7. Ian Watt, *The Rise of the Novel: Studies in Defoe, Richardson and Fielding* (Berkeley: University of California Press, 1957).

8. Clara Reeve, *The Progress of Romance* (New York: Facsimile Text Society, 1930), 66.

9. Hazel Mews, *Frail Vessels: Woman's Role in Women's Novels from Fanny Burney to George Eliot* (London: The Athlone Press, 1969), 9. See also W. L. Blease, *The Emancipation of Women* (London: Constable & Company, 1910); Alice Clark, *Working Life of Women in the Seventeenth Century* (New York: Harcourt, Brace and Howe, 1920); Eva Figes, *Patriarchal Attitudes* (New York: Stein and Day, 1970); Paul Fritz and Richard Morton, eds., *Women in the 18th Century and Other Essays* (Toronto: Hakkert and Co., 1976); Dorothy M. George, *London Life in the Eighteenth Century* (New York: Harper & Row, 1964); Josephine Kamm, *Hope Deferred: Girl's Education in English History* (London: Methuen & Co., 1965); I. B. O'Malley, *Women in Subjection: A Study of the Lives of English Women before 1832* (London: Duckworth, 1933); Susan Staves, "British Seduced Maidens," *Eighteenth-Century Studies* 14 (1981): 109–34; and Lawrence Stone, *The Family, Sex and Marriage in England. 1500–1800* (New York: Harper and Row, 1977).

10. Mary Astell, *A Serious Proposal to the Ladies for the Advancement of Their True and Greatest Interest* (1701; reprint, New York: Source Book Press, 1970), 6–7.

11. Ibid., p 14.

12. Ibid., p 17.

13. Daniel Defoe, *The Early Life and the Chief Earlier Works of Daniel Defoe,* ed. Henry Morley (London: George Routledge and Sons, 1889).

14. Joseph Addison and Richard Steele, *The Spectator,* ed. Gregory Smith, 4 vols. (London: J. M. Dent and Sons, 1945).

15. Ibid., no. 66.

16. See Judith Lowder Newton, *Women, Power, and Subversion: Social Strategies in British Fiction, 1778–1860* (Athens: University of Georgia Press, 1981); John Dollard, *Frustration and Aggression* (New Haven: Yale University Press, 1939), 1, 2, 10; Claudeen Cline-Naffziger, "Women's Lives and Frustration, Aggression, and Anger: Some Alternatives," *Journal of Counseling Psychology* 21 (1974): 54.

17. Ernest Baker, *The History of the English Novel,* 3 vols. (London: H., F., and G. Witherby, 1929): 26–27.

18. Ibid., 28.

19. Radway, *Reading the Romance,* 138.

20. Ibid., 20.

21. Newton, *Women, Power, and Subversion,* 9.

22. Eliza Haywood, *The Female Spectator,* 179.

23. Barbara Bellow Watson, "On Power and the Literary Text," *Signs* 1 (1975–76): 113.

24. Patricia Meyer Spacks, *Imagining a Self: Autobiogrpahy and Novel in Eighteenth-century England* (Cambridge: Harvard University Press, 1976); Elaine Showalter, *A Literature of Their Own: British Women Novelists from Brontë to Lessing* (Princeton: Princeton University Press, 1977); and Sandra M. Gilbert and Susan Gubar, *The Madwomen in the Attic: The Woman Writer and the Nineteenth-Century Literary Imagination* (New Haven: Yale University Press, 1979) are aware of the private-public dichotomy of the female writer. Terry Castle extends this discussion in her *PMLA* article about masquerade to explore the "otherness" that is the raison d'être of the topos. No critical study, to date, exists that explores the necessary and ubiquitous use (in eighteenth-century feminine fiction) of the two topoi. Although Castle's book *Masquerade and Civilization: The Carnivalesque in Eighteenth-Century English Culture and Fiction* (California: Stanford University Press, 1986) investigates the masquerade novel, she does so primarily with masculine texts; Castle does not discuss the difference in the female text of the masquerade novel.

25. Terry Castle, "Eros and Liberty at the English Masquerade, 1710–90," *Eighteenth-Century Studies,* 17 (Winter 1983–84): 156–76; Aileen Ribeiro, *The Dress Worn at Masquerades in England, 1730–1790, and Its Relation to Fancy Dress in Portraiture* (New York: Garland Publishing, 1984); Aileen Ribeiro, "The Exotic Diversion," *The Connoisseur* 197 (1978): 3–13.

26. Castle, "Eros and Liberty," 160.

27. Mikhail Bakhtin, *Rabelais and His World,* trans. Helen Iswolsky (Cambridge: Massachusetts Institute of Technology Press, 1965); Terry Castle, "The Carnivalization of Eighteenth-Century English Narrative," *PMLA* 99 (October 1984): 903–16; and Maximillian E. Novak, ed., *English Literature in the Age of Disguise* (Berkeley: University of California Press, 1977).

28. Novak, *English Literature,* 4.

29. Castle, "Eros and Liberty", 160.

30. Ibid., 159.

31. Ibid., 159.

32. Ibid., 164.

33. Castle, *Masquerade and Civilization,* 122.

34. Rachel Blau DuPlessis, *Writing Beyond the Ending: Narrative Strategies of Twentieth-Century Women Writers* (Bloomington: Indiana University Press, 1985), 3.

35. Ibid., 5.

36. Ibid., 6.

37. Nancy K. Miller, *The Heroine's Text: Readings in the French and English Novel, 1722–1782* (New York: Columbia University Press, 1980).

38. Rabine, *Reading the Romantic Heroine*, 7–8.

39. Radway, *Reading the Romance*, 134.

40. *Masquerades, or What You Will*, 2:12.

## Chapter 2. Elizabeth Boyd

1. Elizabeth Boyd, *The Happy Unfortunate, or the Female Page* (1732: reprint, New York: Garland Publishing Company, 1972). Reissued in 1737 as *The Female Page*. Subsequent citations are noted parenthetically in the text.

2. A long interlude in part 2 recounts the story of Luvania, who was the dupe of Carlo; she believed his professions of undying love and found herself pregnant. Luvania is abandoned by him shortly after this discovery. She has cheated on her husband, but, fortunately, he dies while the child is still young, and the baby does become his heir. Luvania then enters the convent only to have Carlo return and wreck the convent and rape her again. Carlo remains the blackest of villains. When he grows tired of her this time, he devises a scheme to get her shipped off to Venice. In reality, however, he sold her into slavery in Persia. When she learns her fate, Luvania is ill, partly as a reaction to this news and partly because she is pregnant again. At this point, she is befriended by Osorio, who arranged to have her sold privately to the Vizier; Osorio then returns to Naples. Five years pass, and Osorio goes in search of Luvania. During this time, the Vizier has died, and a revolution has taken place.

> This Revolution made for the Advantage of *Osorio*, who, in the tumultuous Palace was undistinguished; he mask'd as a black Eunuch, got Admission, and boldly ventur'd his Life to free *Luvania* whom he, by strategem, convey'd safely on board a Vessel that waited for her by his Orders, where the noble Youth, with honest Vows of real Friendship soon prevail'd on *Luvania* to pardon him, and consent to be his Fellow-Voyager to *Paris*. (pt. 2, p. 184)

Finally, Osorio is able to convince her of his love, and they marry. When he asks her about her past, "the pensive, thoughtful Beauty made herself known to her new-wedded Husband for the Fair Vestal, and Dizanga's Dutchess" (pt. 2, p. 192). They live happily ever after.

## Chapter 3. Penelope Aubin

1. Penelope Aubin, *A Collection of Entertaining Histories and Novels, Designed to Promote the Cause of Virtue and Honour*, 3 vols. (London: D. Midwinter, A. Bettesworth, and C. Hitch 1739). Emphasis added. Subsequent citations are noted parenthetically in the text.

2. Penelope Aubin, *The Strange Adventures of the Count de Vinevil and His Family* (1721; reprint, New York: Garland Publishing, 1973). Subsequent citations are noted parenthetically in the text.

3. Penelope Aubin, *The Noble Slaves: or, The Lives and Adventures of Two Lords and Two Ladies, A Collection of Entertaining Histories and Novels, Designed to Promote the Cause of Virtue and Honour* (London: D. Midwinter, A. Bettesworth et al., 1739), vol. 1. Subsequent citations are noted parenthetically in the text.

4. Aubin, *The Amorous Adventures of Lucinda, an English Lady,* in *Entertaining Histories and Novels*. vol. 1. Subsequent citations are noted parenthetically in the text.

5. My only consolation was, that they had not discovered my sex, being more willing to undergo any Slavery they should enjoin me as a Man, than be force to submit my self as a Woman to their libidinous desires. (1:231)

6. Aubin's *The Life of Charlotta DuPont, an English Lady* (London: A Bettesworth, 1723) is by far her longest but certainly not the most complex work. In fact, it is a pastiche of tales buried within other tales. Each of the "histories" mirrors the main story that is Charlotta's own. Subsequent citations are noted parenthetically in the text.

7. Penelope Aubin, *The Life and Adventures of the Lady Lucy* (1726; reprint, New York: Garland Publishing, 1973). Subsequent citations are noted parenthetically in the text.

# Chapter 4. Eliza Haywood

1. Eliza Haywood, *The Masqueraders; or, Fatal Curiosity, Being the Secret History of a Late Amour,* 2 pts. (London: J. Roberts, 1724, 1725). Subsequent citations are noted parenthetically in the text.

2. Eliza Haywood, *Fantomina: or, Love in a Maze,* in *Secret Histories, Novels, and Poems,* 2d ed. (London: Brown and Chapman, 1725), vol. 3. Subsequent citations are noted parenthetically in the text.

3. Eliza Haywood, *Philidore and Placentia: or, L'Amour trop Delicate,* in *Four Before Richardson,* ed. William H. McBurney (Lincoln: University of Nebraska Press, 1963). Subsequent citations are noted parenthetically in the text.

4. Philidore has these imaginative thoughts about Placentia:

The truth is, he saw not that she loved him because he wished not she should do so. With so pure and disinterested a zeal did he worship his goddess of his Soul that he desired not to inspire her with a passion which, as their circumstances were, could not but be uneasy to her. The height of his ambition was to remain always in her presence, to be blessed with her commands, and in fine to be regarded by her as he seemed to be at present. (169)

5. Eliza Haywood, *The Unequal Conflict; or, Nature Triumphant* (London: J. Walthoe and J. Crokatt, 1725). Subsequent citations are noted parenthetically in the text.

6. Antonia concocts this "romantic" scheme to get the lovers together: "the house is to be this night broken open by robbers, but I will pass my word that all they shall take away, shall be Philenia.—In short, your love, accompanied by his two servants, all disguis'd and mask'd, are to enter forcibly . . . under the pretence of rifling the house" (22).

7. Eliza Haywood, *The Injur'd Husband: or, The Mistaken Resentment* in *Secret Histories, Novels, and Poems,* 3d ed. (London: Bettesworth, Hitch, Browne, Astley, and Green, 1732), vol. 2. Subsequent citations are noted parenthetically in the text.

8. See Paula R. Backscheider, "Woman's Influence," *Studies in the Novel* 11 (Spring 1979): 3–22, and Susan Staves, "British Seduced Maidens," *Eighteenth-Century Studies* 14 (1981): 109–34.

9. Eliza Haywood, *The Perplex'd Dutchess; or, Treachery Rewarded,* 2d ed. (London: J. Roberts, 1728). Subsequent citations are noted parenthetically in the text.

10. Eliza Haywood, *Idalia: or, The Unfortunate Mistress, in Secret Histories, Novels, and Poems,* 2d ed. (London: Browne and Chapman, 1725), vol. 3. Subsequent citations are noted parenthetically in the text.

## Chapter 5. Jane Barker

1. Jane Barker, *The Lining of the Patch-Work Screen; Design'd for the Further Entertainment of the Ladies* (London: A Bettesworth, 1726). Subsequent citations are noted parenthetically in the text.
2. Jane Spencer, "Creating the Woman Writer: The Autobiographical Works of Jane Barker," *Tulsa Studies in Women's Literature* 2 (Fall 1983): 165–82.
3. Jane Barker, *Love Intrigues: or, The History of the Amours of Bosvil and Galesia, as Related to Lucasia, in St. Germain's Garden* (1713; reprint, New York: Garland Publishing, 1973). Subsequent citations are noted parenthetically in the text.
4. Jane Barker, *Exilius: or, The Banished Roman: Written after the Manner of Telemachus* (1715; reprint, New York: Garland Publishing, 1973). Subsequent citations are noted parenthetically in the text.
5. Jane Barker, *A Patch-Work Screen for the Ladies: or Love and Virtue Recommended* (1723; reprint, New York: Garland Publishing, 1973). Subsequent citations are noted parenthetically in the text.
6. Jane Spencer, *The Rise of the Woman Novelist* (Oxford: Basil Blackwell, 1987), 69.

## Chapter 6. Mary Davys

1. Mary Davys, *The Works of Mrs. Mary Davys: Consisting of Plays, Novels, Poems, and Familiar Letters* (London: H. Woodfall, 1725), "Preface."
2. Davys, *The Fugitive,* in *Works,* "Preface."
3. Mary Davys, *The Reform'd Coquet* (1720; reprint, New York: Garland Publishing, 1975), x.
4. Davys, *The Accomplish'd Rake: or, Modern Fine Gentleman,* in *Four Before Richardson,* ed. William H. McBurney (Lincoln: University of Nebraska Press, 1963), 235. Subsequent citations are noted parenthetically in the text.
5. Davys, "Preface," in *Works,* 2:vi.
6. Ibid.
7. Davys, "Preface," *Reform'd Conquet,* ix–x.
8. William H. McBurney, "Mrs. Davys: Forerunner to Fielding," *PMLA* 74 (1959): 355.
9. Davys, *The Lady's Tale,* in *Works,* 2:121–204. Subsequent citations are noted parenthetically in the text.
10. Davys, *The Merry Wanderer,* in *Works,* 1:162–272.
11. Another edition of *The Reform'd Coquet* is found in vol. 2 of *Works.*
12. Davys, *The Familiar Letters Betwixt a Gentleman and a Lady,* in *Works,* 2:265 to end. Subsequent citations are noted parenthetically in the text.
13. Josephine Grieder, "Introduction," *The Reform'd Coquet and the Familiar Letters Betwixt a Gentleman and a Lady* (1718, 1720: reprint, New York: Garland Publishing, 1975.

## Chapter 7. Mary Collyer

1. Samuel Johnson, *Rambler,* 3 vols. (London: Thomas Tegg, 1826), 1:16–17.
2. Jerry C. Beasley, "English Fiction in the 1740s: Some Glances at the Major and Minor Novels," *Studies in the Novel* 5 (Summer 1973): 155–76.

3. Dale Spender, *Mothers of the Novel: 100 Good Women Writers before Jane Austen* (London: Pandora, 1986), 162.

4. Ibid., 162.

5. Mary Collyer, *Letters from Felicia to Charlotte* 2 vols. (1744; reprint, New York: Garland Publishing, 1974). Subsequent citations are noted parenthetically in the text.

## Chapter 8. The Later Haywood

1. Eliza Haywood, *The History of Miss Betsy Thoughtless,* 4 vols. (1751; reprint, New York: Garland Publishing, 1974). Subsequent citations are noted parenthetically in the text.

2. Jane Spencer, *The Rise of the Women Novelist* (Oxford: Basil Blackwell, 1987), chap. 5, passim.

3. Eliza Haywood, *The Female Spectator,* 7th ed., 4 vols. (London: H. Gardner). Subsequent citations are noted parenthetically in the text.

## Chapter 9. Sarah Fielding

1. Dale Spender, *Mothers of the Novel: 100 Good Women Writers before Jane Austen* (London: Pandora, 1986).

2. Sarah Fielding, *The Adventures of David Simple,* 3 vols. (1744; reprint, in one volume, New York: Oxford University Press, 1973). Subsequent citations are noted parenthetically in the text.

3. Sarah Fielding, *The Governess, or Little Female Academy* (1749; reprint, London: Oxford University Press, 1968). Subsequent citations are noted parenthetically in the text.

4. Sarah Fielding, *The Cry: A New Dramatic Fable,* 3 vols. (London: R. and J. Dodsley, 1754). Subsequent citations are noted parenthetically in the text.

5. Sarah Fielding, *The Lives of Cleopatra and Octavia* (1757; reprint, n.p. The Scholars Press, 1928). Subsequent citations are noted parenthetically in the text.

6. Sarah Fielding, *The History of the Countess of Dellwyn,* 2 vols. (1759; reprint, New York: Garland Publishing, 1974). Subsequent citations are noted parenthetically in the text.

7. Sarah Fielding, *The History of Ophelia,* 2 vols. (1760; reprint, New York: Garland Publishing, 1974). Subsequent citations are noted parenthetically in the text.

## Chapter 10. Charlotte Lennox

1. For accounts of her life see Philippe Séjourne, *The Mystery of Charlotte Lennox* (Aix-en-Provence: 1967), and Miriam Rossiter Small, *Charlotte Ramsey Lennox: An Eighteenth Century Lady of Letters* (New Yaven: Yale University Press, 1935).

2. Charlotte Lennox, *The Life of Harriet Stuart,* 2 vols. (London: J. Payne and J. Bouquet, 1750). Subsequent citations are noted parenthetically in the text.

3. Charlotte Lennox, *The Female Quixote: or, The Adventures of Arabella,* 2 vols. (1752; reprint in one volume London: Pandora, 1986). Subsequent citations are noted parenthetically in the text.

4. Laurie Langbauer, "Romance Revised: Charlotte Lennox's *The Female Quixote,*" *Novel* 18 (Fall 1984): 40.

5. The History of Sir George is cast in romantic style. He turns his first love affair with the farmer's daughter into a romance with a goddess, but when she throws him over for the lover her father has chosen for her, Sir George turns to valor and war deeds to vent his frustration. Disguised as the knight in black armor, he proves

valorous during the Battle of ————. When he falls in love with Sydimiris, the daughter of his enemy, he resorts to yet another disguise and an apartment in a hidden part of town to be near her. When he is recaptured and tortured, Sydimiris, in order to spare his life, agrees to marry a man she detests. Sir George, in total despair, is freed and goes to live in the country; there after ten month's time, again he becomes the hero as he saves Philonice from ravishment and death.

Time passes, however, and he is unable to find Philonice. Sir George gives up, so to speak, and transfers his affections to Arabella. That lady is shocked at that behavior; she declares him "Ungrateful" and "unjust" (116); he should be ranked only among "the falsest of men" (116). In her final judgment she says: "be assured . . . that Heaven will never restore you the Crown of your Ancestors, and place you upon the Throne to which you pretend, while you make yourself unworthy of its Protection, by so shameful an Inconstancy" (117). Even with his romantic air, Sir George loses.

6. Charlotte Lennox, *Henrietta,* in *The Novelist's Magazine* (1758; reprint, London: Harrison & Co., 1788). Subsequent citations are noted parenthetically in the text.

7. Charlotte Lennox, *Sophia,* 2 vols. (London: T. Cadell and J. Evans, 1762). Subsequent citations are noted parenthetically in the text.

8. Charlotte Lennox, *Euphemia,* 4 vols. (London: T. Cadell and J. Evans, 1790). Subsequent citations are noted parenthetically in the text.

9. Miriam Rossiter Small suggests in *Charlotte Ramsey Lennox,* 145, that it is a "book of reminiscences" based on Lennox's early years in the colonies.

## Chapter 11. Charlotte Smith

1. Charlotte Smith, *The Young Philosopher,* 4 vols. (1798; reprint, New York: Garland Publishing, 1974). Subsequent citations are noted parenthetically in the text.

2. See Florence Hilbish, *Charlotte Smith, Poet and Novelist* (Philadelphia: University of Pennsylvania, 1941), and Dale Spender, *Mothers of the Novel: 100 Good Women Writers before Jane Austen* (London: Pandora, 1986) for autobiographical details.

3. Charlotte Smith, *Emmeline: or, the Orphan of the Castle,* 5 vols. (1788; reprint in one volume, London: Oxford University Press, 1971), with an introduction by Anne Ehrenpreis. Subsequent citations are noted parenthetically in the text.

4. See Jane Austen's "Catherine, or the Bower" (August 1792) for a delightful, tongue-in-cheek critique of the length of a Smith novel.

5. Charlotte Smith, *Ethelinde, or The Recluse of the Lake,* 5 vols. (London: T. Cadell, 1789). Subsequent citations are noted parenthetically in the text.

6. Charlotte Smith, *Desmond: A Novel,* 3 vols. (1792; reprint, New York: Garland Publishing, 1974). Subsequent citations are noted parenthetically in the text.

7. Charlotte Smith, *The Old Manor House,* 4 vols. (1793; reprint, New York: Garland Publishing, 1974). Subsequent citations are noted parenthetically in the text.

8. Walter Allen, *The English Novel: A Short Critical History* (New York: E. P. Dutton & Co., 1954), for example, raves about *The Old Manor House.*

9. His father claims that Orlando is only in love because of his romance reading:

> An angel! every idle boy that reads ballads or writes them, every scribbler that sends his rhymes to a magazine, calls the nymph who inspires him an angel; and such an angel is this Monimia of yours! and from such sort of reading you have learned to fancy yourself in love with her. (3:49–50)

10. Charlotte Smith, *The Banished Man: A Novel,* 4 vols. (London: T. Cadell, Jr., and W. Davies, 1794). Subsequent citations are noted parenthetically in the text.

11. The Insults I have indured, the inconveniences I have been exposed to, are not to be described—but let it not be a matter of surprise or blame, if the impression made by them on my mind affects my writings. . . . I will make no other defence than that which is lent me by a sister art:—The History Painter gives to his figures the cast of countenance he is accustomed to see around him—the Landscape Painter derives his predominant ideas from the country in which he has been accustomed to study—a Novelist, from the same causes, makes his drawing to resemble the characters he has had occasion to meet with. . . . I have "fallen among thieves," and I have occasionally made sketches of them—and . . . . it is very probable that I may yet be under the necessity of giving the portraits at full length, and of writing under those portraits the names of weazles, wolves, and vultures, they are meant to describe. (1 : vii–xi)

12. Author: Alas! my dear Sir! if you had yourself even seen much of that part of the critical world who descant on novels, you would be aware of the extreme difficulty of the task that a Novelist has to execute:—besides that the number of strange situations under which the heroes and heroines have been represented, are so numerous as to leave hardly any new means of bewildering them in difficulties, that are such objections continually made to some part or other of our fabricated stories. . . . I have been assaulted with remonstrances on the evil tendency of having too much love—too much of violent attachments in my novels; and as I thought in the present instance, the situation of my hero was of itself interesting enough to enable me to carry him on for some time without making him violently in love, I was determined to try the experiment. (2 : vii–viii)

13. I know that resentment will deprive us of our candour, and that it is difficult to be angry and just. But when I see my children deprived of their patrimony, deprived of education, deprived of all but what I have been able to do for them, with an heart sickening from long years of calamity; when I am condemned to unceasing toil, only that the basest and most infamous of mankind may be enriched with my children's property—when I look at these children, who seem to me to merit a fate so different, I lose my temper with my hopes of redress. (3 : 183)

14. Charlotte Smith, *Montalbert: A Novel,* 3 vols. (London: S. Low for E. Booker, 1795). Subsequent citations are noted parenthetically in the text.

15. Charlotte Smith, *Marchmont: A Novel,* 4 vols. (London: Sampson Low, 1796). Subsequent citations are noted parenthetically in the text.

# Chapter 12. Elizabeth Inchbald and Jane West

1. See Katherine Rogers, *Feminism in Eighteenth-Century England* (Urbana: University of Illinois Press, 1982).

2. Elizabeth Inchbald, *A Simple Story,* 4 vols., (1791; reprint in one volume, London: Oxford University Press, 1967). Subsequent citations are noted parenthetically in the text.

3. Ibid., p. vii.

4. See Dale Spender, *Mothers of the Novel: 100 Good Women Writers before Jane Austen* (London: Pandora, 1986) for an excellent discussion of Inchbald's stage career.

5. Elizabeth Inchbald, *Nature and Art,* in *The British Novelists.* ed. Mrs. Barbauld (1794; reprinted, London: Rivington, et al. 1820), vol. 27.

6. Jane West, *The Advantages of Education: or The History of Maria Williams* (1793; reprint, New York: Garland Publishing, 1974). Subsequent citations are noted parenthetically in the text.

7. Jane West, *A Gossip's Story* (1797; reprint, New York: Garland Publishing, 1974). Subsequent citations are noted parenthetically in the text.

8. Jane West, *A Tale of the Times* (1799; reprint, New York: Garland Publishing, 1794). Subsequent citations are noted parenthetically in the text.

9. The classical embellishments of the heroic ages gave infinite advantages to descriptive narrations, to which the cold copyist of modern manners can never aspire. How animating is the personification of winged loves, and choral graces, white-armed nymphs strewing flowers, and sportive fawns chanting an epithalamium, Juno on her radiant car, and Hymen in his saffron mantle! What can the brightest imagination do with such uncouth figures as lawyers in tie wigs, with their green bags and parchments, or even a little painted French milliner with her bandbox? The British like the Grecian bride offers sacrifices, but not to the deities of Complacence and nuptial Harmony—Her devoirs are too frequently directed to the shrines of Fashion and Vanity; and the merits of the villa, the townhouse, the jewels, and the nuptial paraphernalia are discussed with all imaginable scrupulosity, while the lover's character is overlooked. He on the other hand is too busy in balancing the chances of the lady's fortune against her father's demand of settlement, and the possibility of *privately* clearing off his most pressing incumbrances, to consider his destined wife in any other light than as a necessary appendage, which entitles him to take possession.

# Bibliography

## Primary Sources

Aubin, Penelope. *A Collection of Entertaining Histories and Novels, Designed to Promote the Cause of Virtue and Honour.* 3 vols. London: D. Midwinter, A. Bettesworth, 1739. Vol. 1: *The Noble Slaves; The Life and Amorous Adventures of Lucinda; The Strange Adventures of the Count de Vinevil.* Vol. 2: *The Life and Adventures of the Lady Lucy; The Life and Adventures of Young Count Albertus.* Vol. 3: *The Life of Charlotta Du Pont; The Life of Madam de Beaumont.*

———. *The Life and Adventures of the Lady Lucy.* 1726. Reprint. New York: Garland Publishing, 1973.

———. *The Life of Charlotta DuPont, English Lady.* London: A. Bettesworth, 1723.

———. *The Strange Adventures of the Count de Vinevil and His Family.* 1721. Reprint. New York: Garland Publishing, 1973.

Barker, Jane. *Exilius: or, the Banished Roman.* 1715. Reprint. New York: Garland Publishing, 1973.

———. *The Lining of the Patch-Work Screen: Design'd for the Further Entertainment of the Ladies.* London: A. Bettesworth, 1726.

———. *Love Intrigues: or, The History of the Amours of Bosvil and Galesia.* 1713. Reprint. New York: Garland Publishing, 1973.

———. *A Patch-Work Screen for the Ladies: or, Love and Virtue Recommended.* 1723. Reprint New York: Garland Publishing 1973.

Boyd, Elizabeth. *The Happy Unfortunate, or Female Page.* 1732. Reprint. New York: Garland Publishing Company, 1972.

Collyer, Mary. *Letters from Felicia to Charlotte.* 1744. Reprint. New York: Garland Publishing, 1974.

Davys, Mary. *The Accomplish'd Rake: or, Modern Fine Gentleman,* in *Four Before Richardson.* Edited by William H. McBurney. Lincoln: University of Nebraska Press, 1963.

———. *The Familiar Letters Betwixt a Gentleman and a Lady.* 1718. Reprint New York: Garland Publishing, 1975.

———. *The Reform'd Coquet.* 1720. Reprint. New York: Garland Publishing, 1975.

———. *The Works of Mrs. Mary Davys: Consisting of Plays, Novels, Poems and Familiar Letters.* London: H. Woodfall, 1725.

Fielding, Sarah. *The Adventures of David Simple.* 1744. Reprint. New York: Oxford University Press, 1973.

———. *The Cry: A New Dramatic Fable,* 3 vols. London: R. and J. Dodsley, 1754.

———. *The Governess, or Little Female Academy.* 1749. Reprint. London: Oxford University Press, 1968.

———. *The History of Ophelia*. 1760. Reprint. New York: Garland Publishing, 1974.

———. *The History of the Countess of Dellwyn*. 1759. Reprint. New York: Garland Publishing, 1974.

———. *The Lives of Cleopatra and Octavia*. 1757. Reprint. n.p.: The Scholars Press, 1928.

Haywood, Eliza. *Fantomina: or, Love in a Maze*, in *Secret Histories, Novels, and Poems*. 2d ed. London: Brown and Chapman, 1725.

———. *The History of Miss Betsy Thoughtless*. 1751. Reprint. New York: Garland Publishing, 1974.

———. *Idalia: or, The Unfortunate Mistress*, in *Secret Histories, Novels, and Poems*. 2d ed. London: Browne and Chapman, 1725.

———. *The Injur'd Husband: or, The Mistaken Resentment* in *Secret Histories, Novels, and Poems*, 3d ed. London: Bettesworth, Hitch, Browne, Astley, and Green, 1732.

———. *The Masquerades: or, Fatal Curiosity, Being the Secret History of a Late Amour*, 2 vols. London: J. Roberts, 1724, 1725.

———. *The Perplex'd Dutchess: or, Treachery Rewarded*. 2d ed. London: J. Roberts, 1728.

———. *Philidore and Placentia: or, L'Amour trop Delicat*, in *Four before Richardson*. Edited by William H. McBurney (Lincoln: University of Nebraska Press, 1963).

———. *The Unequal Conflict: or, Nature Triumphant*. London: J. Walthoe and J. Crokatt, 1725.

———. *The Works of Mrs. Eliza Haywood*. 4 vols. London: Dan Browne and Sam Chapman, 1724. Vol. 1: *Love in Excess*. Vol. 2: *The British Recluse; The Injur'd Husband; The Fair Captive: A Tragedy*. Vol. 3: *Idalia; Letters from a Lady of Quality*. Vol. 4: *Lasselia; The Rash Resolve; A Wife to be Lett; Poems*.

Inchbald, Elizabeth. *Nature and Art*, vol. 27 in *The British Novelists*. Edited by Mrs. Barbauld. London: Rivington, et al. 1820.

———. *A Simple Story*. Edited by J. M. S. Tompkins. 1791. Reprint. London: Oxford University Press, 1967.

Lennox, Charlotte. *Euphemia*. 4 vols. London: T. Cadell and J. Evans, 1790.

———. *The Female Quixote, or The Adventures of Arabella*. 1752. Reprint. London: Pandora, 1986.

———. *Henrietta*. In *The Novelist's Magazine*. London: Harrison & Co., 1788.

———. *The Life of Harriet Stuart*. London: J. Payne and J. Bouquet, 1750.

———. *Sophia*. London: T. Cadell and J. Evans, 1762.

Smith, Charlotte. *The Banished Man: A Novel*. London: T. Cadell, Jr., and W. Davies, 1794.

———. *Desmond: A Novel*. 1792. Reprint. New York: Garland Publishing, 1974.

———. *Emmeline: or, the Orphan of the Castle*. 1788. Reprint. London: Oxford University Press, 1971.

———. *Ethelinde, or The Recluse of the Lake*. London: T. Cadell, 1789.

———. *Marchmont: A Novel*. London: Sampson Low, 1796.

———. *Montalbert: A Novel*. London: S. Low for E. Booker, 1795.

———. *The Old Manor House*. 1793. Reprint. New York: Garland Publishing, 1974.

———. *The Young Philosopher*. 1798. Reprint. New York: Garland Publishing, 1974.

West, Jane. *The Advantages of Education: or, The History of Maria Williams* 1793. Reprint. New York: Garland Publishing, 1974.

———. *A Gossip's Story*. 1797. Reprint. New York Garland Publishing, 1974.

———. *A Tale of the Times*. 1799. Reprint. New York Garland Publishing, 1974.

## Secondary Sources

Adams, Martin Ray. *Studies in the Literary Background of English Radicalism*. Franklin & Marshall College Studies no. 5 (Lancaster, Pa., 1947).

Adburgham, Alison. *Women in Print: Writing Women and Women's Magazines from the Restoration to the Accession of Victoria*. London: George Allen & Unwin, 1972.

Addison, Joseph, and Richard Steele. *The Spectator*. Edited by Gregory Smith. 4 vols. London: J. M. Dent & Sons, 1945.

Allen, Walter. *The English Novel: A Short Critical History*. New York: E. P. Dutton & Co., 1954.

Astell, Mary. "An Essay in Defense of the Female Sex." 1696.

———. "A Farther Essay Relating to the Female Sex." 1696.

———. *A Serious Proposal to the Ladies for the Advancement of Their True and Greatest Interest*. 1701. Reprint. New York: Source Book Press, 1970.

———. "Some Reflections upon Marriage." 1703.

Auerbach, Nina. *Communities of Women: An Idea in Fiction*. Cambridge: Harvard University Press, 1978.

Backscheider, Paula, Felicity Nussbaum, and Philip Anderson. *An Annotated Bibliography of Twentieth-Century Critical Studies of Women and Literature, 1660–1800*. New York: Garland Publishing, 1977.

Backsheider, Paula R. "Woman's Influence." *Studies in the Novel* 11 (Spring 1979): 3–22.

Baker, Ernest A. *The History of the English Novel*. 3 vols. London: H., F., & G. Witherby, 1929.

Baker, Sheridan. "The Idea of Romance in the Eighteenth-Century Novel." *Publications of Michigan Academy of Arts, Sciences, and Letters* 49 (1964): 507–22.

Bakhtin, Mikhail. *Rabelais and His World*. Translated by Helene Iswolsky. Cambridge: Massachusetts Institute of Technology Press, 1965.

Ballou, Patricia K. *Women: A Bibliography of Bibliographies*. Boston: G. K. Hall and Co., 1980.

Barrett, Michele, ed. *Virginia Woolf: Women and Writing*. New York: Harcourt Brace Jovanovich, 1980.

Bate, W. Jackson. *The Burden of the Past and the English Poet*. New York: W. W. Norton and Co., Inc., 1970.

Beard, Mary R. *Woman as Force in History: A Study in Traditions and Realities*. New York: The MacMillan Company, 1946.

Beasley, Jerry C. *English Fiction 1660–1800: A Guide to Information Sources*. Detroit: Gale Research Co., 1978.

———. "English Fiction in the 1740s: Some Glances at the Major and Minor Novels," *Studies in the Novel* 5 (Summer 1973): 155–76.

———. *Novels of the 1740s*. Athens: The University of Georgia Press, 1982.

———. "Romance and the 'New' Novels of Richardson, Fielding, and Smollett." *Studies in English Literature* 16 (1976): 437–50.

Birkhead, Edith. "Sentiment and Sensibility in the Eighteenth-Century Novel." In *Essays and Studies by Members of the English Association,* edited by Oliver Elton, vol. 11. Oxford: Clarendon Press, 1925.

Black, Sidney J. "Eighteenth-Century 'Histories' as a Fictional Mode." *Boston University Studies in English* 1 (1955): 38–44.

Blanchard, Rae. "Richard Steele and the Status of Women." *Studies in Philology* 26 (1929): 325–55.

Blease, W. L. *The Emancipation of English Women.* London: Constable and Company, 1910.

Bleich, David. *Subjective Criticism.* Baltimore: Johns Hopkins University Press, 1978.

Bloom, Harold. *The Anxiety of Influence: A Theory of Poetry.* Oxford: Oxford University Press, 1973.

Blum, Harold P., ed. *Female Psychology: Contemporary Psychoanalytic Views.* New York: International Universities Press,, 1977.

Boaden, James, ed. *Memoirs of Mrs. Inchbald.* 2 vols. London: Richard Bentley, 1853.

Bodkin, Maud. *Archtypal Patterns in Poetry: Psychological Studies of Imagination.* London: Oxford University Press, 1934.

Boyce, Benjamin. "The Effect of the Restoration on Prose Fiction." *Tennessee Studies in Literature* 6 (1961): 77–83.

Bradbrook, Frank W. *Jane Austen and Her Predecessors.* Cambridge: Cambridge University Press, 1966.

Braudy, Leo. "The Form of the Sentimental Novel." *Novel* 7 (1973): 5–13.

Brisssenden, R. F. *Virtue in Distress: Studies in the Novel of Sentiment from Richardson to Sade.* New York: Barnes and Noble, 1974.

Brownmiller, Susan. *Against Our Will: Men, Women and Rape.* New York: Bantam Books 1975.

Brownstein, Rachel M. *Becoming a Heroine: Reading about Women in Novels.* New York: Viking Press, 1982.

Buck, Anne. *Dress in 18th Century England.* New York: Holmes & Meier Publishers, n. d.

Butt, John. *The Augustan Age.* London: Hutchinson House, 1950.

Byrd, Max. "The Madhouse, the Whorehouse, and the Convent." *Partisan Review* 44 (1977): 268–78.

Castle, Terry. "The Carnivalization of Eighteenth-Century English Narrative," *PMLA* 99 (October 1984): 903–16.

———. *Masquerade and Civilization: The Carnivalesque in Eighteenth-Century English Culture and Fiction.* Stanford: Stanford University Press, 1986.

———. *Clarissa's Cipher: Meaning and Disruption in Richardson's Clarissa.* Ithaca: Cornell University Press, 1982.

———. "Eros and Liberty at the English Masquerade, 1710–90." *Eighteenth-Century Studies* 17 (Winter 1983-84): 156–76.

*Catalogue of a Collection of Engravings, Etchings and Lithographs by Women.* New York: The Grolier Club, 1901.

Chester, Phyllis. *Women and Madness.* New York: Doubleday and Company, 1972.

Christ, Carol P. *Diving Deep and Surfacing*. Boston: Beacon Press, 1980.

Clark, Alice. *Working Life of Women in the Seventeenth Century*. New York: Harcourt, Brace and Howe, 1920.

Cline-Naffziger, Claudeen. "Women's Lives and Frustration, Aggression and Anger: Some Alternatives." *Journal of Counseling Psychology* 21 (1974): 51–6.

Colby, Vineta. *The Singular Anomaly: Women Novelists of the Nineteenth Century*. New York: New York University Press, 1970.

———. *Yesterday's Women: Domestic Realism in the English Novel*. Princeton: Princeton University Press, 1974.

Collins, G. S. "The Growth of the Reading Public During the Eighteenth Century." *Review of English Studies* 2 (1926): 284–94; 428–38.

Congreve, William. *Incognita and The Way of the World*. Edited by A. Norman Jerrares. Columbia: University of South Carolina Press, 1966.

Cornillon, Susan Koppelman, ed. *The Fiction of Fiction: Images of Women in Fiction: Feminist Perspectives*. Bowling Green, Ohio: Bowling Green University Popular Press, 1972.

Craigie, W. A. "The Abbe Prevost and the English Novel." *PMLA* 42 (1927): 443–64.

Cummings, Dorothea. "Prostitution as Shown in Eighteenth Century Periodicals." *Ball State University Forum* 12 (1971): 44–49.

Day, Robert Adams. *Told in Letters: Epistolary Fiction Before Richardson*. Ann Arbor: The University of Michigan Press, 1966.

Defoe, Daniel. *The Earlier Life and the Chief Earlier Works of Daniel Defoe*. Edited by Henry Morley. London: George Routledge and Sons, 1889.

Diamond, Arlyn, and Lee R. Edwards. *The Authority of Experience: Essays in Feminist Criticism*. Amherst: University of Massachusetts Press, 1977.

Dinnerstein, Dorothy. *The Mermaid and the Minotaur: Sexual Arrangements and Human Malaise*. New York: Harper and Row, 1963.

Dollard, John. *Frustration and Aggression*. New Haven: Yale University Press, 1939.

Doody, Margaret Anne. "Deserts, Ruins and Troubled Waters: Female Dreams in Fiction and the Development of the Gothic Novel." *Genre* 10 (1977): 529–72.

Duncan, Jeffrey L. "The Rural Ideal in Eighteenth-Century Fiction." *Studies in English Literature* 8 (1968): 517–35.

Du Plessis, Rachel Blau. *Writing Beyond the Ending: Narrative Strategies of Twentieth-Century Women Writers*. Bloomington: Indiana University Press, 1985.

Ehrenreich, Barbara, and Deirdre English. *For Her Own Good: 150 Years of the Experts Advice to Women*. Garden City, N.J.: Anchor Press, 1978.

Eisenstein, Hester. *Contemporary Feminist Thought*. Boston: G. K. Hall and Co., 1983.

Ek, Grete. "The Glory, Jest, and Riddle: The Masque of Tom Jones in London." *English Studies* 60 (1979): 148–58.

Ellis, Havelock. *Studies in the Psychology of Sex*. Philadelphia, Pa.: F. A. Davis Co., 1928.

Ellmann, Mary. *Thinking about Women*. New York: Harcourt, Brace, and World, 1968.

Figes, Eva. *Patriarchal Attitudes*. New York: Stein and Day, 1970.

Folkenflik, Robert, "Tom Jones, the Gypsies, and the Masquerade." *University of Toronto Quarterly* 44 (1974–75): 224–37.

Friedman, Arthur. *Aspects of Sentimentalism in Eighteenth-Century Literature: The Augustan Milieu.* Edited by H. R. Miller, Eric Rothstein, and M. S. Rousseau. Oxford: Clarendon Press, 1970.

Fritz, Paul, and David Williams, eds. *City and Society in the 18th Century.* Toronto: Hakkert and Co., 1973.

Fritz, Paul, and Richard Morton, eds. *Woman in the 18th Century and Other Essays.* Toronto: Hakkert and Co., 1976.

Frye, Northrop. *Anatomy of Criticism.* 1957. Reprint. New York: Atheneum, 1969.

———. *The Secular Scripture: A Study of the Structure of Romance.* Cambridge: Harvard University Press, 1976.

Fussell, Paul. *The Rhetorical World of Augustan Humanism: Ethics and Imagery from Swift to Burke.* London: Oxford University Press.

George, M. Dorothy. *London Life in the Eighteenth Century.* New York: Harper and Row, 1964.

Gilbert, Sandra M., and Susan Gubar. *The Madwoman in the Attic: The Woman Writer and the Nineteenth-Century Literary Imagination.* New Haven: Yale University Press, 1979.

Girard, Rene. *Deceit, Desire and the Novel: Self and Other in Literary Structure.* Baltimore: Johns Hopkins Press, 1965.

Gisborne, Thomas. *An Enquiry into the Duties of the Female Sex.* 1797. Reprint. New York: Garland Publishing, 1974.

de Goncourt, Edmond and Jules. *The Woman of the Eighteenth Century.* New York: Morton, Balek and Co., 1927.

Graham, John. "Character Description and Meaning in the Romantic Novel." *Studies in Romanticism* 5 (1966): 208–18.

Green, Andre. "Aggression, Femininity, Paranoia and Reality." *International Journal of Pscyho-Analysis* 53 (1972): 205–11.

Greenberg, Janelle. "The Legal Status of the English Woman in Early Eighteenth-Century Common Law and Equity." *Studies in 18th-Century Culture* 4 (1974): 171–82.

Greene, Donald. *The Age of Exuberance: Backgrounds to Eighteenth-Century Literature.* New York: Random House, 1970.

Greer, Germaine. *The Obstacle Race: The Fortunes of Women Painters and Their Work.* New York: Farrar, Straus, and Giroux, 1979.

Gregory, John. *A Father's Legacy to his Daughters.* 1774. Reprint. New York: Garland Publishing, 1974.

Halsband, Robert, ed. *The Complete Letters of Lady Mary Wortley Montague.* 3 vols. Oxford: Clarendon Press, 1965.

Hampsten, Elizabeth. "Petticoat Authors: 1660–1720." *Women's Studies* 7 (1980): 21–38.

Harth, Phillip, ed. *New Approaches to Eighteenth-Century Literature: Selected Papers from the English Institute.* New York: Columbia University Press, 1974.

Haviland, Thomas P. "The Serpent in Milady's Library." *University of Penn Library Chronicle* 4 (1936): 57–61.

Hays, H. R. *The Dangerous Sex: The Myth of Feminine Evil.* New York: Simon and Schuster, 1966.

Hazen, Helen. *Endless Rapture: Rape, Romance, and the Female Imagination.* New York: Charles Scribner's Sons, 1983.

Hedges, Elaine, and Ingrid Wendt. *In Her Own Image: Women Working in the Arts.* New York: The Feminist Press, 1980.

Heilbrun, Carolyn G, and Margaret Higonnet, eds. *The Representation of Women in Fiction:* Selected Papers from the English Institute. Baltimore: Johns Hopkins University Press, 1981.

Hill, Christopher. *The Century of Revolution, 1603–1714.* Edinburgh: Thomas Nelson and Sons, 1961.

———. "Clarissa Harlowe and Her Times." In *Richardson: Twentieth-Century Views,* edited by John Carroll. Englwood Cliffs, N.J.: Prentice Hall, 1969.

Hillard, Raymond F. "Desire and the Structure of Eighteenth-Century Fiction." In *Studies in Eighteenth-Century Culture,* edited by Rosann Runte, vol. 9. University of Wisconsin Press, 1979.

Horner, Joyce. "The English Women Novelists and Their Connection with Feminist Movement." *Smith College Studies in Modern Languages* 11 (1929–30).

Hughes, Helen Sard. "The Middle-Class Reader and the English Novel." *Journal of English and Germanic Philology* 25 (1926): 362–78.

———. "Translations of the *Vie de Marianne* and Their Relation to Contemporary English Fiction." Modern Philology 15 (1917): 491–512.

Humphreys, A. R. "The 'Rights of Woman' in the Age of Reason." *Modern Language Review* 14 (1946): 256–69.

Hunter, Jean. "The Eighteenth-Century Englishwoman: According to the Gentleman's Magazine." In *Woman in the Eighteenth Century and Other Essays,* edited by Paul Fritz and Richard Morton. Toronto: Hakkert and Co., 1976.

Iser, Wolfgang. *The Act of Reading: A Theory of Aesthetic Response.* Baltimore: Johns Hopkins University Press, 1978.

———. *The Implied Reader: Patterns of Communication in Prose Fiction from Bunyan to Beckett.* Baltimore: Johns Hopkins University Press, 1974.

Kamm, Josephine. *Hope Deferred: Girls' Education in English History.* London: Methuen and Co., 1965.

Kelly, Gary. *The English Jacobin Novel, 1780–1805* Oxford: Clarendon Press, 1976.

Kelly-Gadol, Joan. "The Social Relation of the Sexes: Methodological Implications of Women's History." *Signs: A Journal of Women in Culture and Society* 1 (Summer 1976): 809–23.

Keohane, Nannerl O., Michelle Z. Rosaldo, and Barbara C. Gelpi, eds. *Feminist Theory: A Critique of Ideology.* Chicago: University of Chicago Press, 1981.

Kessler-Harris, Alice. *Women Have Always Worked: A Historical Overview.* Old Westbury, N.Y.: The Feminist Press, 1981.

Koon, Helene. "Eliza Haywood and the *Female Spectator.*" *Huntington Library Quarterly* (1980): 43–55.

Langbauer, Laurie. "Romance Revised: Charlotte Lennox's *The Female Quixote.*" *Novel* 18 (Fall 1984): 29–49.

Laslett, Peter, ed. *Bastardy and its Comparative History.* Cambridge: Harvard University Press, 1980.

Leavis, Q. *Fiction and the Reading Public.* London: Chatto and Windus, 1932.

Le Gates, Marlene. "The Cult of Womanhood in Eighteenth-Century Thought." *Eighteenth-Century Studies* 10 (1976–77): 21–40.

Leranbaum, Miriam. "Mistresses of Orthodoxy: Education in the Lives and Writing of Late Eighteenth-Century English Woman Writers." *Proceedings of the American Philosophical Society* 121 (1977): 281–301.

Lieberman, Marcia R. "Sexism and the Double Standard in Literature." In *Images of Women in Fiction: Feminist Perspectives,* edited by Susan Koppelman Cornillon. Bowling Green, Ohio: Bowling Green University Popular Press, 1972.

Lund, Roger D. *Restoration and Early Eighteenth-Century English Literature, 1660–1740: A Selected Bibliography of Resource Materials.* New York: The Modern Language Association of America, 1980.

MacFarlane, Alan. *Illegitimacy and Illegitimates in English History: Bastardy and Its Comparative History.* Edited by Peter Laslett. Cambridge: Harvard University Press, 1980.

Major, John Campbell. *The Role of Personal Memoirs in English Biography and Novel.* Philadelphia: n.p., 1935.

Mayo, Robert D. *The English Novel in Magazines, 1740–1815.* Evanston, Ill.: Northwestern University Press, 1962.

McBurney, William H. "Edmund Curll, Mrs. Jane Barker, and the English Novel." *Philological Quarterly* 37 (1958): 385–99.

McGrath, Kathleen Conway. "Popular Literature as Social Reinforcement: The Case of Charlotte Temple." *Images of Women in Fiction. Feminist Perspectives.* ed. Susan Koppelman Cornillon. Bowling Green, Ohio: Bowling Green University Popular Press, 1972.

McKillop, Alan D. *English Literature from Dryden to Burns.* New York: Appleton-Century-Crofts, 1948.

———. *The Early Masters of English Fiction.* Lawrence: The University Press of Kansas, 1956.

McKee, William. *Elizabeth Inchbald, Novelist.* Washington, DC: The Catholic University of America Press, 1935.

Mews, Hazel. *Frail Vessels: Woman's Role in Women's Novels from Fanny Burney to George Eliot.* London: The Athlone Press, 1969.

Miller, Henry Knight. "Augustan Prose Fiction and the Romance Tradition." In *Studies in the Eighteenth Century,* edited by R. F. Brenenden and F. L. Eade. Toronto: University of Toronto Press, 1976.

Miller, Jean Baker, ed. *Psychoanalysis and Women. Contributions to New Theory and Therapy.* New York: Brunner/Nagel Publishers, 1973.

Miller, Nancy K. "Emphasis Added: Plots and Plausibilities in Women's Fiction." *PMLA* 96 (January 1981): 36–47.

———. "The Exquisite Cadavers: Women in Eighteenth-Century Fiction." *Diacritics* 5 (1975): 37–43.

———. *The Heroine's Text: Readings in the French and English Novel. 1722–1782.* New York: Columbia University Press, 1980.

———. "Novels of Innocence: Fictions of Loss." *Eighteenth-Century Studies* 11 (1978): 325–39.

Miller, P. J. "Women's Education, 'Self Improvement' and Social Mobility—A Late Eighteenth Century Debate." *British Journal of Educational Studies* 20 (1972): 302–14.

Mish, Charles C. "English Short Fiction in the Seventeenth Century." *Studies in Short Fiction* 6 1968–69): 233–330.

———. *Restoration Prose Fiction—1666–1700: An Anthology of Representative Pieces.* Lincoln: University of Nebraska Press, 1970.

Mitchell, Juliet. *Psychoanalysis and Feminism.* New York: Random House, 1974.

———. *Woman's Estate.* New York: Random House, 1973.

Modleski, Tania. *Loving with a Vengeance: Man-Produced Fantasies for Women.* Hamden, Conn. Anchor Books, 1982.

Moers, Ellen. *Literary Women.* New York: Doubleday and Company, 1976.

Moler, Kenneth L. *Jane Austen's Art of Allusion.* Lincoln: University of Nebraska Press, 1968.

More, Hannah. *Essays on Various Subjects, Principally Designed for Young Ladies.* 1791.

———. *Strictures on the Modern System of Female Education.* 1802.

Morgetson, Stella. *Leisure and Pleasure in the Eighteenth Century.* London: Carsell, 1970.

Morgan, Charlotte E. *The Rise of the Novel of Manners: A Study of English Prose Fiction between 1600 and 1740.* New York: The Columbia University Press, 1911.

Munsterberg, Hugo. *A History of Women Artists.* New York: Clarkson N. Potter, 1975.

Myers, Mitzi. "Reform or Ruin: 'A Revolution in Female Manners.'" In *Studies in Eighteenth-Century Culture,* edited by Nancy C. Payne. Madison: University of Wisconsin Press, 1982.

Newton, Judith Lowder. *Women, Power, and Subversion: Social Strategies in British Fiction, 1778–1860.* Athens: University of Georgia Press, 1981.

Novak, Maximillian E., ed. *English Literature in the Age of Disguise.* Berkeley: University of California Press, 1977.

Okin, Susan Moller. "Patriarchy and Married Women's Property in England: Questions of Some Current Views." *Eighteenth-Century Studies* 17 (Winter 1983–84): 121–38.

O'Malley, I. B. *Women in Subjection: A Study of the Lives of English Women before 1832.* London: Duckworth, 1933.

Owen, Joan Hildreth. "Philosophy in the Kitchen; or Problems in Eighteenth-Century Culinary Aesthetics." *Eighteenth-Century Life* 3 (March 1977): 77–79.

Park, William. "Fielding and Richardson." *PMLA* 81 (1966): 381–88.

———. "What was New about the 'New Species of Writing'?" *Studies in the Novel* 2 (1970): 112–30.

Perry, Ruth. *Women, Letters, and the Novel.* New York: AMS Press, 1980.

Pierce, Robert B. "Moral Education in the Novel of the 1750's." *Philological Quarterly* 44 (1965): 73–87.

Plumb, J. H. *The Commercialization of Leisure in Eighteenth-Century England.* Reading: University of Reading, 1973.

Pratt, Annis. *Archetypal Patterns in Women's Fiction.* Bloomington: Indiana University Press, 1981.

Preston, John. *The Created Self: The Reader's Role in Eighteenth-Century Fiction.* London: Heinemann, 1970.

Price, Martin. *To The Place of Wisdom: Studies in Order and Energy from Dryden to Blake.* Carbondale: Southern Illinois Press, 1964.

Rabine, Leslie W. *Reading the Romantic Heroine: Text, History, Ideology.* Ann Arbor: University of Michigan Press, 1985.

Rabinowitz, Peter J. "Assertion and Assumption: Fictional Patterns and the External World." *PMLA* 96 (May 1981): 408–20.

Radway, Janice A. *Reading the Romance: Women, Patriarchy, and Popular Literature.* Chapel Hill: University of North Carolina Press, 1984.

———. "Women Read the Romance: The Interaction of Text and Context." *Feminist Studies* 9 (Spring 1983): 53–79.

Reeve, Clara. *The Progress of Romance.* New York: Facsimile Text Society, 1930.

Reynolds, Myra. *The Learned Lady in England, 1650–1760.* Boston: Houghton Mifflin, 1920.

Ribeiro, Aileen. *The Dress Worn at Masquerades in England, 1730–1970, and Its Relation to Fancy Dress in Portraiture.* New York: Garland Publishing, 1984.

———. "The Exotic Diversion." *The Connoisseur* 197 (1978): 3–13.

Richetti, John J. *Popular Fiction Before Richardson: Narrative Patterns, 1700–1739.* Oxford: Clarendon Press, 1969.

———. "The Portrayal of Women in Restoration and Eighteenth-Century English Literature." in *What Manner of Woman*, edited by Marlene Springer. New York: New York University Press, 1977.

Rivers, Isabel, ed. *Books and Their Readers in Eighteenth Century England.* Leicester: Leicester University Press, 1982.

Rodgers, Betsy. *Cloak of Charity: Studies in Eighteenth-Century Philanthropy.* London: Methuen and Co., 1949.

Rogal, Samuel J. "The Selling of Sex Mandeville's Modest Defence of Publick Stews." In *Studies in Eighteenth-Century Culture*, edited by Ronald C. Rosbottom. Madison: University of Wisconsin Press, 1976.

Rogers, Katherine M., ed. *Before Their Time: Six Women Writers of the Eighteenth Century.* New York: Frederick Ungar, 1979.

———. *Feminism in Eighteenth-Century England.* Urbana: University of Illinois Press, 1982.

———. "Inhibitions in Eighteenth-Century Women Novelists: Elizabeth Inchbald and Charlotte Smith." *Eighteenth-Century Studies* 11 (1977–78): 63–78.

———. *The Troublesome Helpmate: A History of Misogyny in Literature.* Seattle: University of Washington Press, 1966.

Rogers, Pat. *The Augustan Vision.* London: Methuen and Co., 1974.

Roussel, Roy. *The Conversation of the Sexes: Seduction and Equality in Selected 17th and 18th Century Texts.* New York: Oxford University Press, 1986.

Rowbotham, Sheila. *Women, Resistance and Revolution: A History of Women and Revolution in the Modern World.* New York: Random House, 1972.

Ruitenbeck, Hendrik M., ed. *Psychoanalysis and Female Sexuality.* New Haven: Yale University Press, 1966.

Sale, William M., Jr. "From 'Pamela' to 'Clarissa,'." In *Samuel Richardson*, edited by John Carroll, Englewood Cliffs, N.J.: Prentice Hall, 1969.

Saville, Sir George. "The Lady's New Year's Gift: or, Advice to a Daughter." In *The Life and Letters of Sir George Saville*, edited by H. C. Foxcroft, London: Longman, Green and Co., 1898.

Scheuermann, Mona. *Social Protest in the Eighteenth Century English Novel.* Columbus: Ohio State University Press, 1985.

Schietz, Dieter. "The Coquette's Progress from Satire to Sentimental Novel." *Literature in Wissenshaft und Unterricht* 6 (1973): 77–89.

Schleiner, Winfried. "Rank and Marriage: A Study of the Motif of 'Woman Willfully Tested'." *Comparative Literature Studies* 9 (1972): 365–75.

Schnoerenberg, Barbara Brandon. "Toward a Bibliography of Eighteenth-Century Women." *Eighteenth-Century Life* 1 (1975): 50–52.

Schultz, Dieter. "Novel,' 'Romance,' and Popular Fiction in the First Half of the Eighteenth Century." *Studies in Philology* 70 (1973): 77–91.

Sedgwick, Eve Kosofsky. "The Character in the Veil: Images of the Surface in the Gothic Novel." *PMLA* 961 (March 1981): 255–71.

Sennett, Richard. *The Fall of Public Man.* New York: Alfred A. Knopf, 1977.

Sharma, O. P. "Emergence of Feminist Impulse as Aesthetic Vision in the English Novel." *Punjab University Research Bulletin* 2 (1971): 1–28.

Showalter, Elaine. *A Literature of Their Own: British Women Novelists from Brontë to Lessing.* Princeton: Princeton University Press, 1977.

Shugrue, Michael F. "The Sincerest Form of Flattery: Imitation in the Early Eighteenth-Century Novel." *South Atlantic Quarterly* 70 (1971): 248–55.

Small, Miriam Rossiter. *Charlotte Ramsey Lennox.* New Haven: Yale University Press, 1935.

———. "Early Fiction and the Frightened Male." *Novel: A Forum on Fiction* 8 (1974–75): 5–15.

———. "Ev'ry Woman's at Heart a Rake." *Eighteenth-Century Studies* 8 (1974–75), 27–46.

———. *The Female Imagination.* New York: Alfred A Knopf, 1975,

———. *Imagining a Self: Autobiography and Novel in Eighteenth-Century England.* Cambridge: Harvard University Press, 1976.

———. "Reflecting Women." *Yale Review*, n.s. 63 (1973–74): 26–46.

Sparrow, Walter Shaw, ed. *Women Painters of the World From the Time of Caterina Vigori, 1413–1463, to Rosa Bonheur and the Present Day.* New York: Hacher Art Books, 1976.

Spencer, Jane. "Creating the Woman Writer: The Autobiographical Works of Jane Barker." *Tulsa Studies in Women's Literature* 2 (Fall 1983): 165–82.

———. *The Rise of the Woman Novelist.* Oxford: Basil Blackwell, 1987.

Spender, Dale. *Mothers of the Novel: 100 Good Women Writers before Jane Austen.* London: Pandora, 1986.

Springer, Marlene ed. *What Manner of Woman.* New York: New York University Press, 1977.

Staves, Susan. "British Seduced Maidens." *Eighteenth-Century Studies* 14 (1981): 109–34.

Steele, Richard. *The Tatler.* Edited by Lewis Gibbs. London: J. M. Dent and Sons, 1953.

Steeves, Edna L. "Pre-feminism in Some Eighteenth-Century Novels." *Texas Quarterly* 16 (1973): 48–57.

Steeves, Harrison R. *Before Jane Austen: The Shaping of the English Novel in the Eighteenth Century.* London: George Allen and Unwin, 1965.

Stenton, Doris Mary. *The English Woman in History.* London: George Allen and Unwin, 1957.

Stone, Lawrence. *The Family, Sex and Marriage in England, 1500–1800.* New York: Harper and Row, 1977.

Suleiman, Susan R, and Inge Crossman, eds. *The Reader in the Text: Essays on Audience and Interpretation*. Princeton: Princeton University Press, 1980.

Thurston, Carol. *The Romantic Revolution: Erotic Novels for Women and the Quest for a New Sexual Identity*. Urbana: University of Illinois Press, 1987.

Tieje, Arthur J. "A Peculiar Phase of the Theory of Realism in Pre-Richardsonian Fiction." *PMLA* 28 (1913): 213–52.

Tompkins, Jane P. *Reader-Response Criticism from Formalism to Post-Structuralism*. Baltimore: Johns Hopkins University Press, 1980.

Tompkins, J. M. S. *The Popular Novel in England*. Lincoln: University of Nebraska Press, 1961.

Tufts, Eleanor. *Our Hidden Heritage: Five Centuries of Women Artists*. London: Paddington Press, 1974.

Turner, Victor. *The Ritual Process: Structure and Anti-Structure*. Ithaca, N.Y.: Cornell University Press, 1969.

Wakefield, Priscilla. *Reflections on the Present Condition of the Female Sex*. New York: Garland Publishing, 1974.

Wallas, Ada. *Before the Bluestockings*. New York: Macmillan, 1930.

Warren, Leland E. "Of the Conversation of Women: The Female Quixote and the Dream of Perfection." In *Studies in Eighteenth-Century Culture*, edited by Harry C. Payne. University of Wisconsin Press, 1982.

Watson, Barbara Bellow. "On Power and the Literary Text." *Signs* 1 (1975–76): 111–18.

Watt, Ian. *The Rise of the Novel: Studies in Defoe, Richardson and Fielding*. Berkeley: University of California Press, 1957.

Weinstein, Arnold. *Fictions of the Self: 1550–1800*. Princeton: Princeton University Press.

Williams, Jean, ed. *Novel and Romance, 1700–1800: A Documentary Record*. London: Routledge and Kegan Paul, 1970.

Williams, Kathleen. *Backgrounds to Eighteenth-Century Literature*. Scranton, N. J.: Chandler Publishing Co., 1971.

Williams, Murial Butlain. *Marriage: Fielding's Mirror of Morality*. University: University of Alabama Press, 1973.

Wilson, W. Daniel. "Readers in Texts." *PMLA* 96 (October 1981): 848–63.

Wolff, Cynthia Griffin. "A Mirror for Men: Stereotypes of Women in Literature." *The Massachusetts Review* 13 (1972): 205–18.

Wolowitz, Howard M. "Hysterical Character and Feminine Identity." In *Readings on the Psychology of Women*, edited by Judith M. Bardwich. New York: Harper and Row, 1972.

Wood, Gordon S. "Conspiracy and the Paranoid Style: Casuality and Deceit in the Eighteenth Century." *William and Mary Quarterly* (1982): 401–41.

Woolf, Virginia. "Women and Fiction." In *Granite and Rainbow. Essays by Virginia Woolf*. New York: Harcourt, Brace and World, 1958.

Zeman, Anthea. *Presumptious Girls: Women and their World in the Serious Woman's Novel*. London: Weidenfeld and Nicolson, 1974.

# Index